VOICES in the CLASSROOM

BY PETER SCHRAG

Voices in the Classroom: Public Schools and Public Attitudes

Village School Downtown:
Politics and Education — A Boston Report

VOICES *in the* CLASSROOM

Public Schools
and
Public Attitudes

by Peter Schrag

Beacon Press   Boston

Acknowledgments

THIS BOOK could not have been written without the assistance and cooperation of the superintendents of schools and the school boards of the communities visited. Although I disagree with some of them I respect them all. I am also indebted to many individuals who provided information, advice and, frequently, hospitality: Mr. and Mrs. R. Lanier Anderson III in Macon, Ga.; Dean Ernest A. Becker of California State College at Fullerton, Mr. and Mrs. Harry M. Caudill in Whitesburg, Ky.; Dr. and Mrs. Philip S. Holzman in Topeka, Kan.; the Rev. and Mrs. C. Leon Hopper in Denver; Dean and Mrs. Richard Wasserstrom at Tuskegee Institute, Ala.; Mr. and Mrs. Lawrence M. Watts in Denver; and to many others—teachers, administrators, lawyers, newspapermen, politicians, housewives—who were so generous with their time. Their interest and dedication make it clear why American education—despite its problems and shortcomings—is such a great and exciting enterprise.

I am also grateful to many friends and colleagues at Amherst and elsewhere who read portions of the manuscript and offered suggestions; and to President Calvin H. Plimpton and the Trustees of Amherst College, and to Horace W. Hewlett, Secretary of the College, for their willingness to grant me a leave of absence to undertake the research.

Finally I want to emphasize that the opinions and assumptions of this book are strictly my own and not necessarily those of Amherst, that I was operating as a writer, not a college administrator, and that—insofar as errors are concerned—the buck stops here.

P. S.

For Mitzi and Erin

Contents

VOICES in the CLASSROOM

Introduction

There are 42,800,000 children in the public elementary and secondary schools of America.

They attend classes in 110,000 buildings operated by 25,000 districts and staffed by 1,600,000 teachers, two-thirds of them women.

Their education costs about $20 billion a year, of which roughly 60 per cent is raised through local taxes.

They have many things in common. But in many more they are as different as suburbia and Appalachia, Nob Hill and Harlem, poverty and wealth, ambition and apathy.

The schools they attend are as different as they are, and as different as the communities that created those schools and operate them.

There is no American school system, only a multitude of different systems, each with its own concerns, its own problems, its own needs and its own internal kind of perfection. Each is affected by a complex interaction of national and local attitudes and pressures, community conditions, university scholarship, and legislative requirements. Many of them are similar, and a few may be almost interchangeable, but each of them is in some respect unique.

The schools have always been subject to criticisms and pressures—local and national—and to a range of obligations peculiar to American society. "No other people," said Henry Steele Commager, "ever demanded so much of its schools and of education. . . . None other was ever so well served by its schools and its educators.

"From the very beginning of our national existence, education has had very special tasks to perform in America. Democracy could not work without an enlightened electorate. The states and sections could not achieve unity without a sentiment of nationalism. The nation could not absorb tens of millions of immigrants from all parts of the globe without rapid and effective Americanization. Economic and social distinctions and privileges, severe enough to corrode democracy itself, had to be overcome. To schools went the momentous responsibility of doing these tasks—of inculcating democracy, nationalism and equalitarianism."

Some of these tasks are still unfinished, others have been added, and now the demands are greater than ever before. The problems òf modern technology, the increasing mobility of the population, the social, moral and cultural consequences of affluence, concentrated power and depersonalization of community relations—all these factors are making their impact on American education. At the same time the schools are being asked to win the Cold War, stop tooth decay, restore the national moral fiber, prevent Communist brainwashing, warn about the evils of alcohol and tobacco, close the missile gap, entertain the community, open the college gates, teach "spiritual values," save the cities and promulgate cleanliness. When the Russians beat the United States into space with Sputnik the schools were blamed; when the Chinese Communists brainwashed prisoners in Korea the schools were blamed; and when someone detects a shortage of doctors or dentists or engineers, the schools are blamed for that, too. It's a great old American tradition: the first Massachusetts School Law (1647) was written to combat a public menace known as "ye oulde deluder, Satan."

Every school, no matter where located, is now educating children who will live somewhere else, and who will share a common culture. All of them will be exposed to the complexity and the moral and social ambiguities of a civilization that denies simple answers, ridicules schoolboy maxims and destroys those who have not learned efficient methods of dealing with its technological and social machinery. This is, in great measure, one world, and children who are educated only for life on a Mississippi cotton farm or a mountain hollow are, in a sense, not educated at all. The products of inadequate education are going to live in *this* world. Chicago is full of school children—and adults—who started the trail of inadequacy in West Virginia or Arkansas; and Alabama is full of angry white men who are frustrated by their failure to understand the political and social background of the forces now marching through their streets. Thus the schools must take children from different backgrounds—black, white, Chinese, Mexican-American, poor, rich, urban and suburban—and with different abilities and attitudes, and prepare them for a common culture and common difficulties. It must educate them for incredibly complex social and political situations, and it must do so at a time when the informal agencies of education—the church, the community, the shop and the farm—are losing their educational effectiveness. It has always been one of the functions of the schools to generate unity out of social and economic diversity, but never before have the stakes been so high. There are few places left for uneducated men.

And with the new demands and the new problems have come new courses and new pedagogical techniques: the new math and the new biology, and the audio-lingual method of teaching French or German or Spanish; school architecture has changed and the textbook has begun slowly to give way to the paperback, the collections of source materials and the use of inductive teaching—generally known as "the discovery method." At the same time special programs are being introduced for special groups: the culturally deprived, the advanced student, the mentally retarded and the emotionally disturbed, the deaf and the blind. Most important, perhaps, is the revolutionary increase in educational awareness. The launching of Sputnik, pressure for college admission, the civil rights movement and the explosive accumulation of knowledge have shaken the schools from their comfortable lethargy. School budgets, teachers' salaries, the quality of buildings and materials have all improved, and although the academic time-servers and the incompetents are still with us, there is, even in the most unlikely places, a new sense of professional confidence and competence. Every suburban mother is now an academic critic and in the slums Negro leaders know to the penny how much is allocated for school library books. The newspapers are devoting columns not only to battles at the school board, but also to descriptions of the forty-letter alphabet, the rationale for the new mathematics courses and the intricacies of team teaching. Formulas are being issued for the ideal school program: a good high school requires a minimum of one hundred students per class to maintain an effective academic program; no student can be considered educated unless he knows at least one foreign language; twenty-five students per classroom is an optimum "learning situation"; there should be at least one guidance counselor for every three hundred students (or is it five hundred?).

And yet—

While the schools are often responsive to national demands and attitudes, and while they are affected by state laws specifying who may or may not teach, by regional accrediting associations, professional organizations, and by legislative curriculum requirements, they are also the creatures of local conditions and local demands. The new programs and ideas, the formulas, the new books are wares in a vast new educational supermarket from which particular schools can make choices, but there is no model school, no model system applicable to all situations. The ideas and policies which affect a particular classroom are as dependent on the garage mechanics, the businessmen and the lawyers who govern the school board, on parent-teacher organizations, citizens' committees, and other local forces, as they are on teachers' colleges, university scholars or national organizations of educational reformers. There are thousands of different local situations, poor towns and rich towns, motivated parents and recalcitrant ones. Some communities spend $200 per year in the education of each child; others spend close to $1000. Some are predominantly Negro, others uniformly white. Some are trying to educate the children of mountaineers who have little education themselves, and others are trying to keep up with a Parent Teachers Association in which half the male membership is addressed as "Doctor." To be a high school teacher in a New York suburb is a totally different enterprise from being a high school teacher in Leatherwood, Kentucky, or even in Harlem, and the man or woman who is successful in one place might well be a dismal failure somewhere else.

To understand what happens in a classroom, and to control and improve it—these things require not only assessment or reform of teacher training techniques, not only new funds and new methods and courses. They also demand an understanding of national and local attitudes and conditions. The Cold War, the Negro revolution, the various national pressure groups have all had an effect on the classroom, but what has the effect been, and how has it, in turn, influenced particular decisions and policies? In what way do regional conditions and limitations determine what is actually being taught? What does a community in a depressed Kentucky coal region expect of its schools? What kind of education is relevant for children who have never seen a department store, a movie, or even a community where most people hold regular jobs? What is the impact of racial intolerance and religious fundamentalism on a southern classroom? What does an Alabama cotton town want taught? And what does it want to exclude? How do you make the middle-class world comprehensible to children who know only life in a slum? What impact do college-ambitious parents have on schools they consider primarily devices to get their children into Yale or Princeton or Stanford? Do the parents of children who learn social dancing in school consider that activity a frill? Who's paying attention to the constitutional prohibitions against classroom Bible reading? And who isn't? And how do you replace the moral and cultural certainties of another age in a world where everything seems committed to change and where all existence seems to be relative?

Professional educators—educationists to those who don't like them—have justly been charged with some of the major inadequacies of American schools. Too frequently they have been followers rather than leaders, have thought small when they should have thought big, have been more interested in preserving their bureaucracy and administrative convenience than in stimulating the minds and curiosity of children. But is it also possible that most of them have been doing just what the dominant community elements expected, and that their accusers have succeeded in drawing attention to only one element in the complex of the local school situation? Only rarely have the critics looked at what the community has demanded, what it has sought to include in a school program, and what it wanted to leave out. Too rarely have they considered the entire system and its internal harmony: the system of ideas and materials, books and teachers, pay scales and budgets, and of community problems and regional beliefs and goals. What is going on in the classroom, and why? Is the tired textbook, for example, merely an archaic device sustained by pedants, or is it also an effective instrument protecting the community from the teacher's incompetence and the teacher from the community's prejudices—a warranty of acceptable ideological practice? Are all those ludicrous education methods courses just capricious inventions of teachers' colleges, or have they also served a genuine need in training the kind of people who were attracted to a profession traditionally low in pay and prestige? How do the various elements of school system and community fit together? Who makes the decisions in the school and where do the ideas come from? What kind of teachers are wanted? What kind of books are considered acceptable, and why? What effect do social and economic conditions have on the possibilities of academic success? What, finally, does the community want, and to whom does the school respond?

This book is a journalist's attempt—not a scholar's—to examine a variety of American schools and communities, rich, poor, large, small, each with its own social and regional characteristics, and to answer some of these questions. The material is based on a three months' trip around the United States in the fall of 1964 and—with the exception of the chapter on Newton, Massachusetts, which was written early in 1964 and then revised—represents conditions as they existed at that time. The material is based on interviews with teachers, students, administrators, school board members, parents, leaders of community organizations, clergymen, journalists, and on twelve weeks in classrooms as far apart as Hazard, Kentucky, the South side of Chicago and the suburbs of Los Angeles. It also draws on the mounting bibliography of educational commentary, newspaper and magazine articles, on the literature of the Commission on Professional Rights and Responsibilities—and other divisions—of the National Education Association, on the publications of certain state education associations, state departments of education, the United States Office of Education, the Southern Education Reporting Service, and on many specialized studies and reports dealing with particular aspects of American education.

The public schools are so varied as to defy broad generalizations about their quality. But in examining them as social and cultural systems, in studying the questions raised above, it may be possible to determine some of the reasons schools are "good" or "bad," how they can become more relevant and effective, and how American education can meet the awesome responsibilities with which it is now charged.

1

Mid-America Fair

I

This land is your land,
This land is my land,
From California to the New York Island
From the redwood forest to the Gulf Stream water
This land was made for you and me.

As I went walking
That ribbon of highway
I saw above me that endless skyway,
I saw below me that golden valley,
This land was made for you and me.

You HEAR IT SUNG by Japanese-Americans and white Americans and Negroes at the Cleveland School in Oakland, California, by the children of West Virginia mountaineers at the Goudy School on Winthrop Avenue in Chicago, and here in Kansas by Negroes, Mexican-Americans and old-stock white children in the auditorium of the East Topeka Junior High School. Probably, without searching long, one could hear it in a thousand other assemblies and classrooms in a thousand other American towns: hear it sung by children with an almost incomprehensible diversity of backgrounds, abilities and aspirations, many of whom have never seen the things they are singing about, and some of whom have never been more than a few blocks from home. In certain areas they come to school without shoes, in made-over shirts and dresses handed down from older brothers and sisters; elsewhere they appear in silk stockings, bouffant hairdos and Norwegian sweaters. Some have never worn a pair of new shoes or a new coat, have never ridden an elevator or even a bus, and many think that theater and opera are two-dimensional presentations like television. A few have never seen a cow or a horse, have rarely heard a complete English sentence and have never seen anyone outside school reading a book. Others have never left the suburbs, and have never seen a slum or a Negro. They attend classes in build-ings resembling warehouses and prisons, new electronics plants and ranch houses, where they get lunch free, or buy it, or eat no lunch because they have no money. They live in the same coun-try, but they come from different worlds, must deal with the same complexity but must approach it with different kinds of training, and sometimes without training.

"This land is your land, this land is my land . . ." But what kind of land is it? The diversity is so vast, the contrasts so over-whelming, the paradoxes so great that the song itself is left with-out adequate words. It is a land of suburbs and rural hamlets, of missile plants and grain elevators, of slums and cottages at the beach, of hot rods and Sunday schools, of an incredible variety of styles, and sometimes of no style at all. But its central fact is change—change from moral simplicity to ambiguity, from direct answers to qualifications, from belief to doubt, from substance to process. No single place is entirely typical, no idea universal, no technique comprehensive. At the same time every community is affected by the tension between what seems, in retrospect, a clear-ly defined world and the pressures and anxieties of a world not yet fully made. Probably it has always been this way, and has seemed this way to every age, but that provides little solace and only the beginning of an approach to the tensions of the present or the problems of the future.

Topeka is one of those places—and there are undoubtedly many others—which seem roughly representative of contempo-rary American experience, of the stress between an older and a newer America, between the familiar, apparently well-ordered life, and the universe of fission, missiles, newspeak and double-think. Equidistant from California and the New York island, Topeka is the home of Alf Landon and modern psychiatry; of teen-agers resembling Henry Aldrich, the All-American adoles-cent of the old radio days, and the college-ambitious high school senior of the suburbs; of small-city conservatism and Du Pont cellophane; of American Gothic, Norman Rockwell figures and split-level ranchhouses, and of regimented by-the-book classes and modern mathematics. This is a kind of American microcosm, a piece of evidence for Max Lerner's argument that "if Middle America is unattractive or undigestible to anyone experiencing or studying it, then he had better conclude that this is true of America as a whole."

Topeka is not so much symbolic of the Midwest, new and old, as it is of America as a whole. A one-time crossroad of the old Santa Fe and Oregon trails, it was incorporated a century ago by settlers who came during the days of bleeding Kansas when Black Republican Yankees fought southern defenders of slavery to determine the allegiance of the state. Then came the railroads and the grain markets, Washburn University—founded by Yankees on the pattern of the New England college—and the state government, and later, the Menninger Foundation and the Air Force. Now, although Topeka is gradually falling into the commercial orbit of Kansas City, seventy-five miles to the east, the city is a slowly growing regional center of about 125,000 people. It has an excellent public library, a lively concert and art program, and the grounds of the annual Mid-America Fair, now used to display new automobiles and appliances as well as pickles and jellies. Because of the Menninger Foundation with its modern psychiatric and psychological research, Topeka is something other than a "typical" small city; and yet in its mixture of traditional sense, community pride, and urbane modernism, the city is not unrepresentative of America as a whole, a small amalgam of thinkfactory modernism, rural fundamentalism, city and suburb, old and new. Many of Topeka's 10,000 Negroes, some of them descendants of early families, still live in ghettos in North Topeka and on the city's East Side, along with the Mexicans who were brought in a half century ago to work in the railroad shops of the Santa Fe; on the west and southwest are the new suburbs, the new schools and the new people. Seven miles to the south is Forbes Air Force base, newly converted from a post for the Strategic Air Command to a home for transportation squadrons, and at the center is the state Capitol, erected a half century ago in typical American statehouse neoclassicism, complete with a tower which resembles nothing so much as a railroad lantern.

The state Capitol, the gothic structure of the Topeka High School three blocks away, and the modern office of the Kansas

State Teachers Association, located across Tenth Street from Topeka High, form a symbolic triangle reflecting at least some, if
not all, of the pressures that confront American education. The
legislature, which traditionally represented acres rather than people, is still reluctant to provide an adequate foundation program
(e.g. state support) for the schools; the KSTA, directed for many
years by an old and able professional named C. O. Wright, is
bringing pressure to get it, and the high school across the street
is caught in the crosscurrent between the old apathy and conservatism and the demands for modern methods and high-quality
education. In Topeka, that conflict is apparent everywhere. Oscar Stauffer, the publisher of the city's two daily newspapers,
wonders, on behalf of the taxpayers, "if we are not proceeding
too fast with our building program" while the highly educated
professionals, often led by psychiatrists and psychologists from
the Menninger Foundation, feel that changes and improvements
are coming too slowly; the Topeka chapter of the NAACP is demanding a broader program of compensatory education for the
culturally deprived, better schools for Negro children and less
de facto segregation, while the old business interests—the utili-
ties, the banks, and the realtors—are trying to hold the line.
"The power structure is dominated by the Chamber of Commerce," said C. O. Wright, who is a Dewey Progressive in education, and who is very much in the tradition of Kansas Populism
in his politics. "It's dominated by the First National Bank,
Kansas Power and Light, and Capitol Federal Savings. They feel
it's all right to support the schools as long as the burden falls on
the poor people. We've been slow in Kansas in getting the newer
forms of school support. . . . A lot of these people have not been
interested in schools, just in commercial values. Forgive these
mossbacks, for they know not what they do." As in many other
communities, apathy and lack of understanding reinforce native
conservatism. "It's not enough to put pressure on the school administrators," said a friendly critic of the schools. "The bad guys
may not be all bad; they may not realize how they are opposing
their own ends. The Chamber of Commerce, if they realized that
better schools would result in more purchasing power for more
people, would be in the front line, firing away for better education."

Despite this conservatism, Topeka and Kansas are changing their attitudes—and so, indeed, is the whole Midwest. There are still citizens who are suspicious of modern schools where, according to one Kansan, "infiltration and riots are most likely to happen." When schools are consolidated, he said, students become too sophisticated, Communist ideas begin to filter in, local citizens lose control, and education becomes centralized. Nevertheless, Kansas is slowly consolidating its school districts, it is beginning to talk about more state support, and it has embarked on a program to foster the development of regional vocational schools. A few years ago Topeka declined federal money through the National Defense Education Act and the school lunch program; now it is taking it, and even Stauffer says that he sees no evidence of federal control. During the same period Topeka fired a superintendent named Wendell R. Godwin, probably for offenses that included too much of a commitment to modernism, but its present superintendent, Merle R. Bolton, now speaks hopefully of new programs, of a new area vocational-technical school, to be supported largely by federal funds, of educational television, and of compensatory education. Bolton, caught in the crosscurrent between modernism and tradition, is trying to adapt new ideas and methods in an area which, he believes, "is committed to old American values, to pride in the home town and the community, and to the more traditional kinds of things." (He said, however, that "we do have good community acceptance of sound educational programs.") That tradition is still apparent in the school board, whose members include an exterminator, an insurance man, an optometrist and a telephone executive. It is apparent in the pedagogical approaches of many of its teachers, especially at the older schools, and in the attitudes of the older administrators. "If those teachers would learn to be a little thrifty, and not buy everything at once," one of them said, "they could live within their salaries."

But running against the traditions, and literally thriving side-by-side with them, is the newer current of modernism. Topeka is still conservative-Republican, but at Topeka West High School a teacher named Richard Barrett is sponsoring a flourishing model United Nations. And although the city is still somewhat suspicious of fancy new things, it has gone in heavily for the new mathematics and . . . on a more limited scale, for programs of independent study and ungraded elementary schools. Pressed by civil rights groups, by the socially conscious people affiliated with Menninger's and by some of its own teachers, it has started a small program of compensatory education called Project Assurance for East Topeka Negroes and other culturally disadvantaged children; it sponsors an exchange of students with Mexican schools; and it has started to experiment with a number of other departures.

This somewhat uncomfortable mixture of the old and new appears almost everywhere; inside the Topeka High School, where traditional learning by the book is being challenged by some new courses, at East Topeka Junior High where a magnificent principal named Otto Bodenhausen is trying to overcome public apathy about the education of underprivileged kids, and even at meetings of the school board itself. In each instance it is obvious that changes are coming, that rote learning and old books and old methods are slowly giving way; but it is almost equally obvious, as one critic said, that "the administration is still thinking small," that it still has a tendency to respond rather than lead, that it thinks of going to the federal government for $20,000 for a special project when nothing less than $250,000 will do, and that Topeka, this somewhat imperfect microcosm of American education, still tolerates inequities between schools that it should be fighting desperately to combat.

II

Topeka High, which won the Bellamy Award a few years ago as one of the state's outstanding secondary institutions, is the most socially heterogeneous of the city's three high schools, but it is now considered by some socially ambitious Topekans as a poor cousin to the newer, glassier, Topeka West. "Scholastically and socially," said a Topeka High senior, "this school is on the way down. It's past its peak." There are other students—and their parents—who would agree, and there is even an unfounded rumor that there are people in the Topeka High district who pay tuition so that their children may go West.

Both schools, nevertheless, have their share of competent teachers, their exciting classes and their dull ones. Topeka High has the older faculty and administration, the older building, and the more established ways. Topeka West, located in the middle of a suburban development, is organized on a house plan, locally called "schools within a school," in which each house has its own counseling staff, a group of assigned teachers, and a student complement of between 300 and 400 boys and girls. Its 1500 students are assigned to one house for their three years in school and take most of their classes in that house, thus breaking down the anonymity of the larger unit. Unlike Topeka High, Topeka West is almost entirely white, Protestant, and middle class, its students are college oriented—seniors are sometimes invited to fraternity parties at the University of Kansas in Lawrence, twenty-five miles away, so that they can be looked over by the rushing committees —and its tensions and anxieties are rooted more in parental ambitions and status seeking than in cultural deprivation and potential racial friction. (In Kansas, fraternity and sorority membership is still a matter of importance; when pledge delegations are announced the Topeka papers devote columns to the lists of new members.) Being new, Topeka West tends to be somewhat more venturesome, modern and, in most respects, to resemble the better schools in any of the nation's more affluent suburbs. It has a program of "social science seminars" in which students hear outside speakers on contemporary issues, it is experimenting with team teaching on a small scale, it encourages the annual model United Nations, and it has a small but flourishing program of independent study where students, under the direction of a teacher, can do research and write papers on a topic of their choice. (Recent papers have dealt with the Punic Wars, abstract algebra systems, and the behavior of animals.) Many of the school's innovations, excepting the house plan itself, still tend to be peripheral; most classroom dialogue is of the kind that has taken place in American schools for a half century: "Next we have Fletcher versus Peck . . . Now the politicians embarked on the era of good feelings, but in our country it is impossible to have one party in which all the people can join; therefore, we can expect the Republican Party to split . . . in 1828 the Party split. The conservative side became the National Republicans and the liberal side became the Democrats . . ." As the teacher speaks, the students listen with their textbooks open in front of them, and when a question is asked you can hear the pages rustling. Nevertheless, Topeka West, directed by an energetic principal named Owen Henson, is very much committed to the implementation of a vital academic program, and Henson is willing to provide the freedom required to do it. In English and history, teachers are collaborating on an interdisciplinary team teaching program, and when students invited the president of the local chapter of the NAACP to speak to the social science seminar, even while the school board was being picketed by the organization, the administration was willing to let him appear, despite protests from the community. Henson meets with the various departments to do "brainstorming," he encourages curricular innovations and he takes delight in every success. "Innovation," he said, "always takes place on a broken front."

"*Our* biggest problem," said Glenn E. Burnette, the Topeka High principal, "is the lack of student concern with education. A lot are just idling away their lives; they take no books home and bring nothing back." But his description, he said, applies only to about one third of the students. Most of the rest are working hard, are interested in getting an education and, usually, are planning to go on to college, almost always at institutions in the state of Kansas. Burnette is proud that "athletics do not run this school," of the little art gallery in one of the wings, of the school's record of interscholastic debating, and of its music and drama. (The latter usually runs to musicals and light comedy with the hells and damns and drinking expurgated.) He is pleased that the Menninger Foundation sends two of its psychiatric interns twice a week to help out in the counseling program, and he is encouraged by the school's high attendance record. He knows what goes on at Topeka High, knows its strengths and weaknesses, and his pleasures and frustrations seem to reflect those of a large cross-section of American high school principals. He is, in many respects, a typical—and competent—school administrator.

And Topeka High is, in some measure, a typical American school. Its 2100 students would show up well in a composite photograph; there are all shades of skin, all modes of dress, all levels of maturity. At the same time, the group photo would not show that the Negroes tend to be socially isolated, that they are rarely elected to posts of leadership in school organizations—and that the graduates of certain junior high schools dominate the affairs of the institution. Nor would the photo reveal the degree of competence of the teaching staff, the sameness of the classrooms, and the social and disciplinary order the school imposes.

> It is necessary [says the manual of regulations for teachers] that all rooms must be supervised. All teachers are asked to enter the rest room on their floor at intervals during the school day. A check during the free period is needed. Some misuse may occur while classes are in session. This should be corrected by irregular checks. We are particularly concerned that there be no smoking. Adequate supervision will also reduce damage to fixtures. Please make it a habit to supervise the rest room on your floor.

Like many comprehensive high schools, Topeka High embodies two cultures, one composed of predominantly white, middle class, college-oriented students who usually live by the rule book (there are some notable exceptions) and according to the wishes of the teachers, the other made up of a generally darker-skinned, somewhat isolated, and often ignored minority. Some administrators say that the Negroes don't really try to succeed, a self-reinforcing observation that sometimes leads socially conscious souls in East Topeka to extremes of frustration. Some Negro students are accepted by their white classmates, a student said, "but if they start going around with white students they seem to lose standing with their Negro friends." As in most other high schools, status goes to the college prep kids. They are the ones that cooperate, that teachers are most interested in, and that are consciously or unconsciously blessed with social acceptance. At the same time the marginal students soon learn where they stand. Although no one has ever organized a program for doing so, the American high school is one of the most effective social mechanisms for selecting people *out*. No one has described this process better than Edgar Z. Friedenberg in *The Vanishing Adolescent:*

> The high school still reflects and transmits faithfully the esteem or disparagement in which the community holds its students and their families. *All* aspects of a youngster's life in high school

—not just his social life outside the classroom—are strongly influenced by his family's social status. Lower-status youngsters, in turn, come to perceive the school as exclusively concerned with socioeconomic status; unless they want to use it to get ahead, they have no interest in it and expect it to have none in them. In the United States, education, as distinct from earning a secure place for oneself, is a highly controversial matter in which the school tries not to get too involved.

There is another kind of impact, too, and it is one of which many administrators seem to be unaware: in a Topeka High English class—as in thousands of other classes across the country —students are reading a national school magazine called *Practical English,* a publication devoted to articles about literature and the arts, to various tests and puzzles designed to improve reading, and to advertisements for General Electric transistor radios ("Take Rock, Rhythm and Pop Wherever You Go"), soft drinks and "the new flavor lipstick, Forbidden Fruits, by Cutex":

> Four new ways to taste as delicious as when you wore Caramel Kiss and Peppermint Kiss—the original "Forbidden Fruits."
>
> Put on Kola, taste cola! Put on pineapple, taste pineapple!
>
> As for grape, yum, yum!
>
> But be prepared! One kiss and he wants TWO, THREE, FOUR MMMMORE!

Television and radio and other magazines would carry the message, even if *Practical English* did not, but the advertisement indicates that someone is staking good money on a different kind of educational program, and on a well-defined idea of what high school students are really interested in. Many teachers consider television and popular literature a threat to formal academic learning, but in the choices teachers and schools make, that culture is ubiquitously present.

The era [Friedenberg said] when a youngster would be likely to be seriously snubbed or mocked for coming to school in odd clothes, or with a lunchbox packed with queer foreign foods, is largely past; the TV has already shown him and his parents what may acceptably be worn or eaten, and the school will prob-

ably have taken a rather strong line about accepting the interesting customs of our friendly Latin or whatever neighbors. But
it is more firmly convinced than ever that its job is to teach
youngsters to respond to other people's expectations. While it
emphasizes the expression of personality, it conveys to the student that personality should be built on certain standard plans,
superficially varied according to taste, and that expression
should consist of a fairly continuously emitted code signal by
which other persons can recognize what they want when they
see it. If they don't want it, there must be something wrong
with either the personality or the signal, and it must be changed.

Topeka High has made few concessions to the ultramod-
ern; many of its teachers follow conventional textbooks, impart
information when they can, ask direct questions that can be answered by finding the right page or the right set of notes, and
conduct laboratories by the recipe method. One of the most popular teachers says he runs his science classes by "giving them instructions. They have to listen. If they make mistakes they come
back after school. I tell them that if they don't like the grades I
give them on a lab exercise they can come back and do some more
work." His cosmos leaves little room for originality, and the
grade is—as they say in the trade—negative reinforcement imposed according to the number of errors the student makes in
mixing up the recipe.

The style is familiar to almost every adult who has ever been
through an American high school (and its effects are therefore,
not fatal) and it can be witnessed in many, if not most, of the
classes.

On the blackboard of a drab brown and green room on the
second floor, the teacher has written a standard outline summa-
rizing politics in the Jacksonian period: there are references to
Whigs and Democrats, to Federalists and Jeffersonians. The
walls are decorated with some aging brown photographs of San
Marco's in Venice, Notre Dame, Chartres, and the British Houses
of Parliament, and with a roll-up map which the teacher has just
pulled down. The students—this is an average-ability junior
class in history—shuffle in and wait for something to happen. As
they are settling down the teacher shows the visitor the textbook,
saying, "I don't like it. It makes you do too much of the work if

you want them to learn anything." Then she turns to the class.

"Who were the two fellows who debated in the movie Friday?" she asks.

"Lincoln and Douglas," a boy answers.

"Lincoln and Douglas," she confirms. "Tell me what the gag rule was." There is no response so she says "What's a gag?" asking simpler and simpler questions until, in effect, she has given the class the answer.

"Which side were the Whigs on—Federal or anti-Federal?"

"Federal."

"What about the Democrats?" she asks.

"Anti-federal."

"Who was the vice-president in Jackson's time?" a student asks, without explaining the reason for the question.

"I don't think we said," she replies. "You can look it up in your book . . . I want you to memorize page 286—not word for word, but the main ideas." The class has already heard about Hamilton and Jefferson, and about the struggle between the sections, about how the cotton gin made slavery profitable, about how Jackson was a man of the West, and Webster a man of the North, and about Calhoun and Clay. It is now learning about squatter sovereignty and bleeding Kansas, and soon it will read about "The War Between the Sections," and then about Grant and corruption, about carpetbaggers and scalawags, Teddy Roosevelt and the Yellow Press, and ultimately, if the teacher has timed it right, even about Lindbergh and prohibition. On and on it goes—the aimless repetition of social studies, one teacher called it, even as he was doing it. It has already been done once in the fifth grade, and then again in the eighth, covering the same material, asking the same questions and using books that cover essentially the same material in the same way. There is really only one American history text, a critic once said, but you can get it in thirty different covers.

To some degree the teacher is trapped, he is a prisoner of the system and of the materials the system provides. More exciting techniques—and better books, films and tapes—are being developed, but many school systems are just beginning to try them, and some refuse to do even that. In the meantime, the old clichés, copied, repeated, and repackaged, march on. The film in the government class, appropriately populated by men in double-breasted suits and women with skirts below their knees, depicts in a series of stilted episodes how a town chooses its form of government. Narrated by a condescending male voice, it includes such dialogue as:

> "Good morning, Miss Anderson."
> "Good morning, Mr. Mayor."
> "Anything new today?"
> "There have been many calls from people who want to know what you're going to do about the streets in . . ."

At the same time the textbooks—even the best ones—continue to present colorless narratives of history, irrelevant accounts of the machinery of government, uninteresting descriptions of geography and, almost inevitably, carefully balanced evasions of controversial questions. They *tell* the students, requiring mastery of what Jerome S. Bruner, the Harvard psychologist, calls a "middle language," a textbook language. Since this language is almost inevitably confused with the thing itself (e.g. history *is* what is in the book) and since there is only one source which tells all, the texts are written in such a way as to avoid offense to any party, sect, belief, or prejudice. The history text used at Topeka High and at Topeka West, *The Adventure of the American People* by John A. Krout and Henry F. Graff, is considered one of the most modern and most outspoken, but even it continues to straddle issues that might be considered offensive by some groups or regions. After quoting from Justice Warren's opinion in its discussion of the Supreme Court school segregation cases of 1954—one of which originated in Topeka—the book goes on to say: "By 1958 desegregation had proceeded in Kentucky, Maryland, Missouri, North Carolina, Oklahoma, Tennessee, Texas and West Virginia." There is no mention of Little Rock, of pupil placement laws, or of other forms of official evasion. The book's description of Senator McCarthy, probably the most liberal in any text, follows a brief reference to the Alger Hiss trial and states:

> Into this picture stepped an ambitious, self-assured young politician, the junior Senator from Wisconsin, Joseph R. Mc-

Carthy. He boldly claimed that he had a list of 205—later reduced to 57—names of people he asserted were Communists
who were shaping policy in the Department of State. A Senate
Committee was not able to verify the charge, but McCarthy,
undeterred, went from one accusation to another, inflaming the
public.

McCarthy was skillfully exploiting a public inclination to
believe that wicked conspirators here at home had brought us
our troubles in international affairs. His accusations of disloyal-
ty intimidated many Americans in public and private life in the
years 1950 to 1954.

Among the Senator's critics, the expression "McCarthyism"
became familiar all over the land—and abroad, too—as a syno-
nym for reckless name calling. McCarthyism divided Americans
badly at a moment when they should have been united to face
the threat from abroad.

This description—to repeat—is the most critical of the textbook accounts; most books simply say that "some Americans believed" one thing while "other Americans" believed something
else. But even here there is no mention of blacklisting, of Eisen-
hower's conduct in the George C. Marshall affair, of Cohn and
Schine, no reference to the ruined careers and reputations, to the
state and congressional investigating committees, no indication
that civil rights and human decency were officially violated before an audience of millions; just the limp statement that Mc-
Carthyism (some sort of semantic abstraction) "divided Americans badly at a moment when they should have been united to
face the threat from abroad."

Many of Topeka's teachers, recognizing the limitations of
the textbook, have gone to supplementary materials—paperbacks, pamphlets, magazines, newspapers, and a number of other
sources—recognizing the boredom of students subjected to
learning "one damn thing after another." But, like all teachers,
they have rarely had the time or the resources (or the training)
to break away completely, to abandon the idea of "coverage" and
to start entirely fresh. To do that, they must wait until national
curricular experiments in the social sciences and the humanities
catch up with the natural sciences, with the programs of the
School Mathematics Study Group (SMSG), the Physical Science

Study Committee (PSSE), and with the many other courses in "new" science and mathematics.

The most significant break with the common style of teaching at Topeka High—and perhaps in all of Topeka—is in mathematics and, most dramatically, in the advanced classes of Marjorie French who, a few years ago, was justifiably chosen as the nation's "teacher of the year." Marjorie French looks and talks like the all-American school teacher; what makes her in any way special is not new material but her own understanding that memorization of facts and formulas is a dull and unproductive process. Despite her gray hair and the glasses which hang on a band around her neck, she combines youthful energy with a display of efficient confidence. Never flashy, never cute, and always orderly, she would make an ideal model for the *NEA Journal* or the *Nation's Schools*. Which, of course, is what she is.

"What is a group?" she asks the class of advanced seniors—twenty-eight boys and four girls.

"It is a set of elements with an operation," one of them says.

"What characteristics must be true?"

"It must have closure."

"It must have an identity element."

"And inverses."

They are using two books, one of them an elegantly written text by C. B. Allendoerfer and C. O. Oakley called *Principles of Mathematics,* which begins with the elements of logic, and then goes on to sets, number systems, groups, fields, and Boolean algebra, trigonometric, algebraic and logarithmic functions, analytic geometry, limits, the calculus and statistics and probability. It lucidly explains the logical foundations of mathematics, making it clear that any mathematical or logical system necessarily begins with certain undefined terms and axioms, that, for example, a wholly new geometry has been constructed by assuming the "truth" of the axiom: "the sum of the interior angles of a triangle exceeds 180 degrees." (The class will not cover all of the book, but they will—after studying other topics—spend four weeks on analytic geometry and eight weeks on the calculus, the equivalent of at least half a normal year's introductory college course.) The book explains that groups—the topic now under study—are applicable to a number of mathematical theories, and it goes on to specify one example of why it is ever necessary to learn anything or to organize any set of facts or experiences:

> In each of these theories we naturally desire to find a set of significant theorems and to learn how to calculate within each theory. If we do this for each theory separately, we shall have a large body of information to remember. We can save ourselves work by proving the theorems just once for the absolute system called a "group." The results thus proved can then be applied to each concrete case without serious mental labor. The advantage, then, is that we have one inclusive theory to remember instead of a large number of separate ones.

"Do we have to have commutativity?" Mrs. French asks. A student answers in the negative and then says, "Can you give us an example of a noncommutative group?" Commutativity, they already know, is the mathematical definition for a situation in which the order of the elements has no effect on the result of an operation—as for example in addition of integers (e.g. 1 plus 2 is equal to 2 plus 1). They also know that the associative law in algebra deals with the grouping of elements in an operation and states that if $a, b,$ and c are elements of Group G, then:

$$(a \circ b) \circ c = a \circ (b \circ c)$$

where $\circ$ represents the same operation. Subtraction, Marjorie French points out, is not associative.

Having proceeded so far on the definition, Marjorie French now asks students to work and explain some of the exercises in the text.

"Form the addition table for the integers modulo 4," the problem says. A girl goes to the board and writes:

+	0	1	2	3
0	0	1	2	3
1	1	2	3	0
2	2	3	0	1
3	3	0	1	2

The book explains that ordinary clocks are based on this type of addition (modulo 12 in this instance). In the case of a clock with a dial divided into four hours, three o'clock plus two hours would be one o'clock, just as, on an ordinary clock, nine o'clock plus four hours would be one o'clock.

There are more questions: "Verify the associative law when $a=1$, $b=2$, $c=3$ ... Is there an identity? What is it? What are the inverses 0′, 1′, 2′, 3′? Verify the commutative law when $a=2$, $b=3$; is this a group?" All of them discussed with a calm professionalism, with no sign of anxiety, and with a great deal of mutual respect and order.

What the students are doing here is not "new" math, for this is a transitional class of kids who have never had School Mathematics Study Group (SMSG) or any of the other new programs which Topeka, like many systems, is now beginning to institute. Their course is similar to advanced courses in other high schools. But as Marjorie French teaches it, it demands the same kind of mathematical understanding that the newer courses require, and it is taught with the same attitude. "These are kids you don't regiment," Marjorie French says. "You can put a good deal of the responsibility on them."

As supervisor for mathematics for the Topeka secondary schools, Marjorie French has become a traveling saleswoman explaining what she calls "modern mathematics"—not "new" math—to parents, teachers and principals. The history of her involvement began in simple dissatisfaction with old methods and materials, continued with summer study at Kansas University under Max Beberman, who headed the Illinois Mathematics Program, and subsequently developed into a full-time occupation. Part of her job is to help orient teachers—for "you don't move until your teachers move," and part is simply to overcome the awe, the doubt and, at times, the resistance of the parents and the community. She neither looks nor talks nor thinks like a revolutionary, but the message she conveys and the attitudes she represents extend far beyond the significance, however great, of just a new approach to mathematics. When she talks of "emphasis on deductive reasoning, use of guided discovery, emphasis on structure and emphasis on unifying ideas," she is speaking of exciting teaching in any field, and when she refers to the fact that the old techniques are "somewhat barren of the fascinating, interesting phases of mathematics," she is describing some part of almost every school in the United States. If there is such a thing

s an Establishment in American public education, Marjorie
rench is very much part of it. But her part, while conservative,
1ows as much willingness to change as any establishment and to
o it with at least as much grace.

By giving up legal segregation before the unanimous opin-
on in *Brown* v. *Board of Education of Topeka,* the schools of the
ity became one of the last systems in the United States to deseg-
egate on a genuinely voluntary basis. After May 1954, despite
1e language of voluntarism and gradualism, every system that
1tegrated was doing so under threat of ultimate legal pressure—
ven if there happened to be no direct court order, no federal
oops and no hysterical women—and every system that did not
as violating the Constitution of the United States. But Topeka,
ke other cities, retained its share of de facto segregation, its
1equities, and its cultural deprivation. "We're at the stage of dis-
rimination with a smile," said Homer C. Floyd, the young Ne-
ro who directs the city's Human Relations Commission. The
arious Topeka eating and drinking clubs (established partly to
et around the Kansas blue laws, which prohibit service by the
rink) are racially segregated, Negroes and Mexicans are ex-
luded from barbershops, there are no members of racial minor-
ies in the union apprenticeship programs (although most of
1e unions deny the existence of racial barriers), and most of the
ity's better housing is restricted. "Discrimination in housing,"
1id a Human Relations Commission report published in 1964,
has been generally sanctioned by the entire community. We ob-
erve a preponderance of Negroes and Mexican Americans re-
ding in East and North Topeka, and in traditional areas in and
round the central city." As in many other cities, that discrimi-
ation has been reflected in the racial composition of the schools,
1 the courses they offer and, until recently, in how the teachers
ere assigned.

East Topeka, just a few blocks from the state Capitol on
ighth Street, is a grid of rutted streets, some of them unpaved, of
nall houses with rusty automobiles in front and rotting wrecks
ehind, of poor Negroes and Mexican-Americans, and some
nglos, too, of little corner stores and "problem" schools. It is a
eighborhood of ADC (Aid to Dependent Children), of impetigo

and ringworm and, occasionally, of simple malnutrition. At th
new Lafayette School, the principal, Walter V. Cormack, collect
overshoes, gloves, socks and sweaters for his needy pupils—"
mooch it," he says—and he makes almost daily visits to the home
of some of his 600-odd pupils. His well-known red Falcon indi
cates to suspicious mothers, aunts, grandmothers and uncles tha
he is not a bill collector, a cop, or a welfare moralist, and thus h
gains entry to the houses where many of his academic problem
originate. Some of his pupils start kindergarten almost totall
mute; they don't know their last names or their addresses; the
have never been read to, have never seen a book, and sometime
don't get more than one adequate meal per day. In Joyce Paul'
kindergarten class (her 26 pupils have a total of 77 siblings) a bo
named Ralph complains of being tired, and when she offers hin
a can of soup, he devours it. He has a pale blond face with larg
blue eyes—eyes that seem to plead without begging—and now
after a few months in kindergarten, he speaks well enough so tha
he may be able to start first grade next year. By then he will b
almost eight years old.

"What do you like to eat?" Mrs. Paul asks a robust Mexican
American boy who is sitting next to Ralph.

"I like chicken," he answers.

"What did you have for lunch, Ralph?" Mrs. Paul asks.

"Chicken," he replies vaguely, looking at the Mexican boy

Lafayette School, like several others in the city, participate
in Project Assurance, a program to reduce class size (at Lafayette
the average class used to be 37; the Project classes are down t
25) and to employ additional reading specialists, social worker
and other resources in an effort to bring disadvantaged kids u
to grade level. So far, however, Project Assurance is underfi
nanced—it received $52,000 in 1964–65 out of a total budget o
over $12 million—and its effect remains only marginal. Thus th
prime burden for the culturally deprived still falls on individua
teachers and administrators working on their own, and on sucl
community support as they can generate or, as Cormack say:
mooch. It falls on people like Cormack himself, and on Joyc
Paul, trying to convert tired, and sometimes hungry childre
who can hardly speak, into first graders, and on people like Ott
Bodenhausen, the principal at East Topeka Junior High, wh

is one of the many unrecognized great men in American schools.

Bodenhausen presides over a yellow brick building on East Eighth Street which houses three grades with a total of about 550 students, two thirds of them Negroes and Mexican-Americans, many of them poor and already far behind in their reading levels. But what Bodenhausen runs is not so much an academic course, as it is an Americanization project, a program in which 'you try to give them something to make them proud to be Topekans, Kansans and Americans," and where attempts are made to bring the school and the community closer together, to relate one to the other, and to give students some sense of the relevance of learning, and of middle-class attitudes in general. When some of them come in tardy, he says, "it's a major victory. You're glad they're in school at all." Bodenhausen has established relationships with the Boys Club, the YMCA and other youth organizations, he helped start a "shared story program" in which older people from the community come after school to read to slow-learning junior high school students, and he is deeply involved with East Topeka community leaders—social workers, clergymen, and others—in trying to develop additional collaborative programs, and in exchanging information about kids who are, or are likely to be, in trouble.

Under Bodenhausen's direction, East Topeka Junior High divides its students into many tracks and ability groups; there is a special "core" program for slow learners from stable families— they are assigned to one teacher for three hours per day of social studies, English, and reading; there are tracks for the "more able," for the "average" and for slow learners, which the school has in a ratio of about double the national average; there is a special homeroom program in which teachers are encouraged to counsel students, and there are many assemblies and other activities to give them some sense of self respect, of who they are, and of concern for others.

It is all done on a shoestring; there are no big foundation grants, no special consultants (other than some part-time assistance from a Menninger psychiatrist), no cadre of experts, no project directors, no special equipment. When Bodenhausen, by winning a commercially sponsored contest, obtained some overhead classroom projectors, most of the teachers had to be taught to use them; only a few of them had even seen one before. Now Bodenhausen wonders where he can get the funds to buy more of the transparent overlay materials on which teachers can draw or write information to be projected. The material provided with the machines is almost exhausted and—for the moment— the school has no budget for more.

On the west side of the building, Orene Carroll Edmonds, the wife of a Topeka attorney, teaches a seventh grade "core" class (English, social studies and reading) composed of three Mexican-Americans, four Anglo-Americans and seven Negroes. The map of the United States which hangs on the wall, she says, "doesn't mean much to them." Most of the kids in her class have never been anywhere, know nothing of the life of Dick and Jane in the pleasant suburb, and are not particularly interested in why Alexander Hamilton wanted to establish a national bank. Like most teachers of slow learners and of kids living on the edge of middle-class society, she is never satisfied with the old materials, and she has begun, strictly on her own, to try some new things.

The booklet they are reading was written by a New York teacher named Richard H. Turner and is called *The Town You Live In*. Orene Edmonds learned of it not through some elaborate training program or from any careful school survey, but because the publisher's salesman told her about it. Today's lesson is called "Big Mistake":

> One night the following week, Joey's sister Clara came home late from work. She was employed as a packer in a factory that manufactured candy. She'd had to go to work two years ago when her husband, Ralph, died suddenly. The factory had hired her for the packing job, even though she hadn't had any experience.
>
> All during supper Joey noticed that Clara was unusually quiet. He waited until his nephew Alec had left the table and then asked her what was bothering her. "I lost my job today," Clara said. "That's why I was late getting home. The foreman stopped me after work and told me not to come in tomorrow."
>
> "Why?" Joey wanted to know.
>
> "Because business is slow," Clara replied. "I guess people

aren't eating as much candy as they used to." She tried to smile, but she couldn't. She was feeling too worried.

"I can help out," Joey said. "I've saved the money I earned as a messenger boy."

"Thanks, Joey," Clara said, "but I don't need it right now. I might have to borrow some from you later on if I can't find another job. But meanwhile, I can start collecting money for unemployment. Tomorrow I'll go to the unemployment office and register.

"My big mistake," Clara told Joey, as she poured herself a cup of tea, "was not to have finished high school before I got married. I always wanted to be a nurse. But I thought that after I was married, I'd never have to work. Then Ralph died, and I found out differently. I did have to work, and I wasn't trained to do anything." She gave a deep sigh. "Now it's too late to be trained for a really good job."

The episode is followed by a series of exercises on word definitions, true or false questions, and questions requiring short-answer sentences, but for the time being Orene Edmonds is concentrating on class discussion.

Q. What happened to Clara?
A. She got fired.
Q. Why did she lose her job?
A. People stopped buying as much candy.
Q. Why couldn't she get another job?
A. She didn't know how to do anything.
A. She didn't finish high school. [Mrs. Edmonds tells a boy to turn around in his seat and, when she is no longer looking, he makes an obscene gesture in her direction.]
Q. What is training?
A. You go to college.
Q. Do you have to go to college?
A. You can go to school.
Q. What kind of school?
A. Night school.
Q. What's the foreman?
A. Sort of like the boss.
Q. What did Clara do after she lost her job?
A. She got another job?

Q. Did she?

A. She went to an employment office.

A. They lend her money.

Q. Was she right when she said it was too late to be trained?

A. No, she could go to night school.

A. She could go to a school that teaches people how to do things.

Toward the end of class, Orene Edmonds opens a couple of huge paper sacks, one filled with cans of Chinese chow mein noodles, the other containing fortune cookies, and she passes them out. She tells the class about the fortune cookies, about where the noodles came from, and how they are eaten. Some of the kids are amused and one or two appear to be totally hostile, but they all eat, and show each other the little fortune slips. A Negro boy has received one that says "You will attract cultured and artistic people to your home," and he asks his teacher what the words mean. In the back of the room sits the fourteen-year-old mother of an illegitimate child. Her fortune says, "You will be showered with good luck."

Despite the efforts of people like Bodenhausen, Walter Cormack, Orene Edmonds, and many other East Topeka citizens, the children of the area remain the victims of educational inequities which only the city can correct, of unintended discrimination, and of a vast heritage of injustice which is only now coming to public attention. Children on the more affluent west side pay two to three cents for milk under the federal lunch program, but at East Topeka, which has no cafeteria and no lunch provisions, the students must obtain their milk from vending machines for a nickel, and must either bring their lunch, or buy it from one of the neighboring stores. Since the school system does not furnish school buses or other transportation, East Topeka teachers find it hard to take their students on field trips which, with their limited experience, they desperately need. (Bodenhausen, master moocher, sometimes gets a bus from the YMCA, of which he happens to be a director.) But the most obvious sign of educational inadequacy lies in the simple fact that Negro and Mexican American children begin school with general reading and ability levels below those of middle-class whites, and that they never catch up. In a study conducted for the Topeka Human Relations Commission—and done simply to demonstrate what some Topekans felt was already obvious—Dr. Philip S. Holzman, a Menninger psychologist, concluded that "children from middle class neighborhoods absorb the skills taught in elementary school more effectively than do childen from lower class neighborhoods. Within schools in lower-class neighborhoods, Negroes and Americans of Mexican descent are more handicapped than are white children in acquiring the intellectual skills taught at those schools." Dr. Holzman's findings demonstrated that underprivileged children in East Topeka are no different from their counterparts in East Harlem, South Chicago or any other lower class environment:

> The results of the survey showed unequivocally [Dr. Holzman said in his report] that the parents of Negro children in the lower socioeconomic areas had only hazy knowledge about the subjects their children were taking in school. The survey showed that children from low socioeconomic areas tend to stay close to the home, rarely engage in projects with their families, tend to do little or no reading except that required for their school work, and the parents tend to have few magazines, books, or newspapers in the home. These Negro children, then, enter school and continue their education under the handicap of deficient verbal interaction in the home and a lack of intellectually-stimulating experiences attributable to the poor verbal skills of the parents. These parents had very little hope for their children to become anything more than unskilled or semi-skilled laborers. An occasional Negro parent expressed the hope that her child could become an athletic coach. The children themselves seemed disillusioned about their futures. A representative answer is that of a 14½ year old tenth grade Negro boy attending Highland Park High School. He said that he wanted to be an engineer or an architect; but he hoped to be a truck driver, at least. This kind of answer contrasted with that of white children in the same area, or Negro children in the middle-class area, where more ambitious goals were set by the parents for the children and by the children themselves.

People like Dr. Holzman, Dr. Edward Greenwood, and Dr. Harry Levinson—all of them affiliated with the Menninger

Foundation—represent what is undoubtedly the most progressive force in Topeka. The Foundation provides free psychiatric counseling to any school child referred to it, while individual staff members are active in a whole range of educational and community activities: they provided expert testimony in the Brown case, and helped establish the city's recently created Human Relations Commission—and are now active on its various committees. Collaborating with others, they have pressed the school board to expand its special programs for culturally deprived children and to raise its educational standards generally, and have worked quietly to combat discrimination in jobs and housing and professional organizations. It was Harry Levinson who spearheaded a Citizens Committee for Better Schools, organized after a school bond issue was defeated in 1960, and which helped line up enough support from local industrial organizations to get a succeeding bond proposal passed. It was also Levinson who organized a so-called "Mayor's Breakfast" to collect on Mayor Hal Gerlach's campaign promise that a Human Relations Commission would be established, and it was the League of Women Voters, heavy with Menninger wives, which helped get Gerlach to make the promise in the first place. It was also the league which helped convince the school administration a few years ago that it needed more than one remedial reading teacher, and it was Holzman (against the background of a threatened boycott by the NAACP) who told the school administration that federal funds were available to support programs for culturally deprived children, and that the school board should start thinking big.

The community interests of members of the Menninger staff, their wives and, occasionally of faculty members at Washburn College, represent an unusual combination of urbane intelligence and criticism with small town activism, a mixture bringing cosmopolitan worldliness into the discussion of local affairs. With the exception of such organizations as the NAACP, which is tuned to the news of civil rights developments in major cities, and excepting those teachers and school administrators who are in touch with the curricular and pedagogical changes through summer institutes, especially at the University of Kansas, the Menninger people represent probably the single most ef-

fective pipeline from the outside world. Karl and William Menninger, affectionately headlined in the local papers as "Doctor
Karl" and "Doctor Will," are native Topekans, thoroughly established and highly respected; most members of the professional
Menninger staff are outsiders, natives of the east and middle
west, but all of them, native or not, are in contact with the literature and attitudes of New York and Cambridge and Berkeley,
not to mention Paris, London, and Zurich; at the same time most
of them have absorbed something of Topeka, and although they
are sometimes amused by it, and sometimes excluded from its
more restrictive and parochial social circles, they are rarely con-
temptuous. Rather than isolating themselves from what they consider local atrocities, many of them have gone to work to abolish
them, knowing that often they are still considered outsiders, even
after ten or fifteen years in the city, but aware also that "in Topeka psychiatry is a major industry" and that local suspicion of
"headshrinkers" has declined dramatically in the past two decades. The Menningers helped bring a Veterans Administration
Hospital to Topeka, they were major forces in convincing the
state legislature of the importance of good mental health facilities and in eliminating local suspicion of the state hospital. Kansans have always respected the importance of education but they
have sometimes been slow to admit that what was good enough
for grandpa isn't good enough now. Topeka's departure from this
attitude is at least partly a result of the Menninger presence.

Some other forces have also been at work. Although he recently joined the Menninger staff, Dr. Robert Harder, formerly
pastor of the East Topeka Methodist Church and one of the few
liberal Democrats in the state legislature, has long been active
in fostering the interests of his underprivileged area. Collaborating with people like Bodenhausen, with younger leaders of the
Mexican-American community (which is slowly becoming civil
rights conscious), with representatives of youth organizations,
with Menninger psychiatrists and with welfare workers, Harder
has constantly pressed for better educational facilities, and is now
trying to work up a community-wide plan to attract funds under
the federal poverty program. Every month Harder, Bodenhausen
and other East Topekans get together as the East Topeka Professional Association to discuss their plans, and to talk of par-

ticular youths who are in trouble, to hear reports from the director of the Boys Club or from the county probation officers, and to exchange general information. What Harder now wants most is to be able to make effective use of the federal funds which have recently become available, to expand the Child Day Care Center now operating in East Topeka, to find additional resources for all of the area's schools, and to give East Topeka the general social attention it needs.

Harder's interests are shared at least in part by the NAACP which, like its counterparts everywhere, has been agitating for an end to de facto segregation, for revision of school attendance boundary lines, for a better guidance program, and for more relevant textbooks, especially in history. Until recently, said Samuel C. Jackson, the local NAACP president, teachers discouraged Negro students from taking retail sales and cooperative education courses on the ground that downtown stores were reluctant to take them on, acting, said Jackson "as if the businesses were doing the schools a favor." Negro pressure, including full-dress protests at school board meetings, has also generated a review of employment practices (from 1945 until 1963, Jackson said, the schools discriminated against Negro teachers and janitors) and has produced some shift in the attendance boundary lines. Now Jackson wants to use federal poverty funds to bolster vocational education, to set up work-study projects and to encourage the establishment of something similar to the New York Higher Horizons Program, the city-wide project designed to provide extra educational services for culturally deprived children in an effort to improve their skills and motivation.

Because of people like Harder and Holzman and Harry Levinson, and organizations like the NAACP, and partly because of Superintendent Bolton himself, the schools are undergoing a slow process of change. Three years ago Topeka's teacher salaries were just below the state average; in 1963–64 the average had risen to $5908, almost $500 above the state level; during the same period the schools were able to reduce the average class size, to begin a nongraded program known as the Continuous Progress Plan, to initiate modern mathematics, conduct an expanding exchange of students with Canada and Mexico, and to begin planning an area technical-vocational school. Bolton, considered a liberal by Topeka standards, straddles the old and the new, and must be responsive to both. "The Board must have made a mistake when they hired him," said a sardonic admirer. "He's enough of a liberal so that he may not be long for this world." Bolton's own instincts are undoubtedly sympathetic to a continuing upgrading of educational standards, but he must also deal with ingrained attitudes in the community, with apathy, with tax-minded businessmen, with conservative Americanism and with the inertia that is common to any large organization. Bolton is aware of these problems, but he also feels that attitudes have begun to change all through the Midwest, that "all School Boards are more receptive to new ideas than they used to be." When the Supreme Court declared classroom Bible reading and prayers unconstitutional the few Topeka teachers who were still conducting devotional exercises simply dropped them—and there was no protest; neither is there any serious protest against the social science seminars at Topeka West, even though they often venture into politically controversial issues. Topeka high school students use an economics textbook that contains statements like "liberal socialism retains political democracy" and "ours is a mixed, or welfare, capitalism"; they are exposed to all the paraphernalia of internationalism, from the UN and French travel posters to foreign exchange students and courses in Russian (at Topeka West), and are encouraged to read books like *Fail-Safe* and *Grapes of Wrath,* works that have elicited vociferous protests elsewhere. At the same time, the Midwest's traditional resistance to federal subsidies has weakened ($300,000 in federal money, Bolton points out, is worth three mills on the local property tax rate, and that is a powerful argument for anybody); its passion for better schools has increased and its isolation has deteriorated: when the United States concluded the celebrated "wheat deal" with the Soviet Union in 1963, Senator Frank Carlson of Kansas, a healthy conservative Republican by anyone's standards, supported it— for obvious Kansas reasons.

And yet, despite Bolton's instincts, despite the increasing contacts between the Midwest and other sections of the country, despite DuPont cellophane, the Menninger Foundation, and the Air Force, Topeka and Kansas and a great portion of the Midwest have escaped neither the traditions nor the restrictions of

the past. The state is still dominated by Republicans—and even
the Democrats tend to be conservative; the wctu and the oil interests and Protestant fundamentalism are still forces to be reck-
oned with, though all of them appear to have a decreasing influence, and when the farmers speak through the Farm Bureau and
the Grange, the legislature listens. The legislature is still oriented
in favor of the rural areas, with House seats based on a county
system; a recent reorganization of House districts gave the cities
a little more influence, but not enough to offset rural domina-
tion. (The State Supreme Court recently ordered House reap-
portionment by April 1966.) It is still impossible to buy a drink
in a Kansas restaurant, although some will allow customers to
bring in bottles under their coats; and it is still difficult for the
schools to obtain an adequate program of state support. "The
legislature will take hours debating laws about fences," said a
Topeka lawyer, "but they rarely pay attention to the problems
of cities." When C. O. Wright, the executive secretary of the
Kansas State Teachers Association, attacked the state's educational conservatism, the legislature immediately prepared to investigate, not education, but Wright and the ksta. Even relatively
enlightened Kansans tend to be suspicious of school consolidation and centralization. "Diversity made this country great," said
the lawyer quoted above. "The more we centralize, the more educational policy will be dictated by someone in Washington. . . .
By whom? By the National Education Association or the Office
of Education—it's all the same." "When people start coming
back to the farm, as they surely will," said a letter writer in the
Topeka Capital, "then we'll need these [small rural] schools
right where they are."

Although Topeka has moved well beyond old style Babbittry
and small-town parochialism, it is still a place with provincial
concerns, tax-minded businessmen, and budget-minded public
officials. "You have to see that you get your money's worth," said
Oscar Stauffer who, as publisher of the two papers, is usually
considered a spokesman for business. "A few years ago we had no
bonded indebtedness for the schools. Now we're going like the
federal government. Taxes hit downtown Topeka pretty hard."
Stauffer is also worried about the changes in textbooks. There
was a time, he said, when the texts devoted considerable atten-

tion to Patrick Henry, Henry Clay and the stories of Horatio
Alger. "They don't do that as much any more. Patriotism is an
important thing, and it's important for the schools to teach it."
Although Stauffer's concerns are shared by some other Topekans,
the city has never been subjected to any textbook investigations
or to teacher purges; it has few, if any, vocal John Birchers or
religious reactionaries. "The Bible issue around here," said
Wright, "is pretty much of a dead cat." Nevertheless there is con-
tinual pressure to hold the line on educational expenditures, a
lingering suspicion of federal funds and a reluctance to take on
anything that seems too big or too progressive. At least one member of the board is strongly opposed to federal school aid while
the board as a whole has been attacked for being too concerned
with the status quo, with the budget, and with economic values,
rather than with the development of an outstanding educational
program. "The schools won't move unless there's pressure," said
a critic. "The board is identified with the Chamber of Commerce, so there's tax pressure but no real pressure on the curriculum."

The resulting vector of these forces produces an academic
course, a direction that is fairly near the center of contemporary
educational practice. While Topeka has generated no radical departures, while many of the ideas borrowed from elsewhere affect only a minority of children, and while there is still a tendency to think small, the city has moved a long way from the small
midwestern town of thirty years ago, and even a longer way
from rural Kansas. Gone are the days when textbook adoptions
hinged on a hunting trip with the book salesman and the casual
gift of a new shotgun; gone are the days when teachers worked
for insurance companies every summer as "hail adjusters"; gone
are the days when a few pinches of morality and the three R's
comprised the substance of schooling. The very fact that there is
talk of compensatory education, that the schools—and the community—are being persuaded that equality doesn't stop at the
school door, that C. O. Wright can refer to classroom Bible reading as a dead cat, the fact that Marjorie French and Otto Bodenhausen are *there*—all these things are indications that all of
American education has come a long way.

III

The old roots of American education are still visible on the landscape beyond the cities. While districts are being consolidated and the smaller rural schools are slowly being closed, many towns proudly continue to operate separate systems for the education of a few hundred students—some of them with high schools graduating classes of three or four seniors. Pressure to unify school districts and raise standards generates violent local animosities, not so much between communities as between local interests and state authorities. The Iowa legislature was recently urged to investigate the State Department of Education because the department had been considered too harsh in forcing consolidation. The elimination of schools not only offends local pride—and that can be fierce—but it arouses well-developed suspicions and fears—fear of remote control, suspicion of new courses and teachers, and anxiety about excessive exposure to the modern world. The farmers of Iowa and Kansas and Nebraska and Wisconsin have heard about juvenile delinquents, about discipline problems in the schools, about all the things happening in New York and Chicago, and even in Kansas City, St. Louis, Topeka, and Milwaukee. Many of them are proud that their schools build character, that their students are well behaved (and *that,* after all, is what schools are all about) and that they respect their teachers, their parents and their community. Some are willing to forgo classes in French and modern mathematics in return for "character," and are not convinced that they can have both. There are communities which have erected highly modern schools that employ the latest pedagogical devices, but there are others still committed to traditional techniques and traditional attitudes.

This is where the American school came from. If one goes to some of the smaller towns in the Midwest (and in the East as well) one is sometimes reminded of descriptions of the New England school of the last century—of McGuffey's Readers and Horatio Alger, and even Webster's spelling book. Although these documents are no longer used, despite the efforts of a few isolated communities to restore them, there is a quality about the schools, the teachers and the community that is sometimes more reminiscent of the nineteenth century than the twentieth.

Listen at the first grade door and hear the kids drilling, speak to the older teachers and administrators about discipline, look at the equipment, the budgets and the buildings. Phonics—learning to spell and read through the study of the sounds of letters and syllables (as opposed to the so-called "look-say" method which stresses complete words) is employed in many schools. But in the more traditional classrooms phonics receives special emphasis. In an elementary class:

"B says buh-buh-buh
"C says cuh-cuh-cuh
"D says duh-duh-duh"

It is all done in unison under the direction of a red haired woman of about fifty. "Take out your word sticks," she says, "and let's do our A and P. Let's put our C by this and we get? . . . John?"

"Cap."

"Our L. . . . Julie?"

"Lap."

"Our M. . . . Jody?"

"Map."

"John, what happens to 'cap' when you use the magical *e*?"

"It makes the *a* say its name: cape."

"It's easy to learn to spell when you know some phonic sounds, isn't it?" she asks the class, which answers in unison: "Yes, Mrs. Griner." Then she turns to the visitor and says, "This is a wonderful school in which to teach. We have so few discipline problems."

Mrs. Griner is one of thirty-five teachers at the Jesup Community School in northeastern Iowa, an area of family-size farms devoted to corn, alfalfa, cattle, and dairy products. The town of Jesup is slowly falling into the shadow of neighboring Waterloo, about fifteen miles away, where some of its 1500 residents commute to work in the John Deere tractor plant and at the Rath Meat Packing Co. But the surrounding country is still agricultural, physically and spiritually, and it demands approximately the same things of its schools that it did a half century ago.

The sign over the doorway simply says "school," a redundant announcement alongside the flagpole, the swings and the jungle gym in the dusty front yard. The main building, erected in 1916, is red brick, three stories high and behind it, like an odd collection of children's blocks, is a patchwork of additions and alterations constructed in later years. Behind them, and across a paved road, the cornfields begin. The school, which has been growing, educates 800 children from the town and the surrounding countryside in 12 grades and an all-day kindergarten—what the trade calls a K-12 program. It offers a conservative program of academic courses—two years of French were recently added, partly under state pressure—as well as vocational agriculture, business education, physical education and band, and it tries to provide a reasonably full program of extracurricular activities and athletics. But its most important program is character and discipline.

"The school prepares them to be decent citizens," said Burton North, the stocky country moralist who has been superintendent since 1951. "We use corporal punishment when we have to. The parents come in to thank us for the discipline. Our biggest problem these days is to overcome the effect of the lackadaisical attitude of some of the parents. I had a mother who asked that we give her boy some better grades to encourage him. If I did he'd know me for a liar. He knows better what grades he should get than his teachers do. Another one complained that we hadn't given her boy enough preparation for college; I told her that if he knew what was in that textbook he'd have no trouble. This community lives pretty well without much sweat, and our only trouble is that kids aren't aiming high enough. They're not shooting for the stars." North, who has been an Iowa schoolmaster for nearly forty years (he was to retire in 1965), is proud of the good character of his pupils, and of the community's respect for the school, of the way he saves money by constructing and repairing his own facilities, and of his success in teaching the three R's. "I'm going to teach phonics and I don't give a damn what anybody says. The teachers are pleased with what we're doing: I give them all the equipment they want—the best materials. They've got no complaints. We have an all-day kindergarten every day, and when those kids come to first grade, they're ready to *read*." At the same time North remains unimpressed by the national courses in mathematics and science (one of his critics said he doesn't understand them) and cautious about any major departure from the traditional program. "I'm not excited about the new physics and the new biology," he said, "and I think the new math is the biggest waste of time I've ever seen. I want these kids to learn their multiplication tables. They have to know how to add and subtract." Jesup's high school program includes courses in physics and chemistry—the latter was recently added —but both are taught without much regard for newer methods or for modern scientific concepts. For the most part they are devoted to the memorization of formulas and to the process of learning to use them to get "answers" to well-defined numerical problems.

"Mechanical advantage depends on the number of ropes you use," says the physics teacher, looking at some diagrams of pulleys and inclined planes he has drawn on the board.

"How much force is required to move a wagon with a hundred pound weight?" a student asks.

"That depends what you try to pull the wagon through," the teacher answers. "If you push it through soft sand it would take more than if you pushed it on a paved road. . . . You do a lot of work getting the block into the wagon. . . ."

"If you put the block in a wagon," the student says, "you can pull it around all day. Why is that?"

"A lot of it is weakness in yourself. It's easier to haul the block up than carrying it up the stairs. When you lift it straight up, you're doing all the work at once."

There is a kind of somnambulistic unreality about it all, as if school were somehow detached from the world that surrounds it. Despite some able teachers, many students behave as if attending class were an unpleasant duty that life has imposed; they don't always know why they're there, but are sufficiently well behaved not to ask any irreverent questions. Although North reports that all his pupils read well at the end of the first grade—he has instituted the best phonics method available, he said—some of his own teachers feel that the constant drill stifles curiosity and that, beginning in fifth grade, the children in Jesup fall progressively farther behind in their reading ability. (North points to test scores indicating that this is not the case.)

Hadley Castor's sixth graders sparkle with questions about nutrition during their health lesson, but a so-called "bright" eleventh grade English class displays considerable ignorance about the meaning of words, of the news from the outside world, and a virtually total barrenness of even remotely interesting ideas. Giving a set of "impromptu" speeches, some of these sixteen-year olds show nothing so much as pride in their incompetence and delight in their immaturity. The teachers are discouraged from discussing evolution or sex in deference to the region's religious fundamentalism ("I know evolution is correct," one of the teachers said, "because so many babies are born with tails, which the doctors cut off"), and they have little access to the literature and ideas of the outside world. Although North encourages them to attend summer institutes and courses at the State College in Cedar Falls, and although the school itself is increasingly subject to standards imposed by the State Department of Education, Jesup as a whole remains intellectually self-sufficient, trusting to the good sense of its farmers and small businessmen—to a folk intelligence—rather than depending on continuing contact with any larger intellectual or cultural community. Even though farming is a declining source of local employment, the Jesup School, directed by North and a farmer-dominated school board, remains strongly oriented to the attitudes and practices of an agricultural community. Fifty of Jesup's 250 high school students are active members of the local chapter of the Future Farmers of America, and its program of vocational agriculture continues to thrive. The FFA chapter conducts regular meetings every two weeks, with field trips to neighboring farms, packing plants and feed companies interspersed between them. At each meeting a student recites the FFA creed:

> I believe in the future of farming, with a faith born not of words but of deeds . . . achievements won by the present and past generations of farmers; in the promise of better days through better ways, even as the better things we now enjoy have come up to us from the struggles of former years.
>
> I believe that to live and work on a good farm is pleasant as well as challenging; for I know the joys and discomforts of farm life and hold an inborn fondness for these associations which, even in hours of discouragement, I cannot deny.
>
> I believe in leadership from ourselves and respect from others. I believe in my own ability to work efficiently and think clearly, with such knowledge and skill as I can secure, and in the ability

of organized farmers to serve our own and the public interest in marketing the product of our toil. I believe we can safeguard those rights against practices and policies that are unfair.

I believe in less dependence on begging and more power in bargaining; in the life abundant and enough honest wealth to help make it so—for others as well as myself; in less need for charity and more of it when needed; in being happy myself and playing square with those whose happiness depends upon me.

I believe that rural America can and will hold true to the best traditions in our national life and that I can exert an influence in my home and community which will stand solid for my part in that inspiring task.

This recitation is followed by a discussion of chapter business, by announcements of local agricultural events, and by talks and films on such topics as fire safety, rodent control, use of pesticides, "earnings and savings," and "the meaning of Christmas." Students report on the progress of the livestock they are raising, on the nutritional yield of various feed mixtures, and on other farm-related projects.

Activities of the FFA are closely integrated with the formal four-year course in vocational agriculture directed by Marshall Grosscup, a patient, soft-spoken teacher who is entirely committed to the improvement of agriculture, and who feels—all statistics to the contrary notwithstanding—that there will always be jobs for his graduates, either on the farm, or in the growing area of farm-related employment. Grosscup's classroom is covered with charts and diagrams about feed prices, anatomical diagrams of cows and announcements of stock sales:

Rath Packing Co. will sell from
their swine farm to Jesup FFA members:

1. Mature bred sows for February litters.
2. October farrowed market barrows

For Sale: Purebred Angus heifer
Hampshire Ewe Sale, December 5, Waterloo

Grosscup's courses are part science, part intuition, and part inspiration, and the problems he gives his students can be solved only by using the correct combination of the three: they concern feed efficiency and nutritional components, farm organization and management, budgets and marketing, crop identification and weed control, farm mechanics and soil conservation. Each course involves special projects as well as shop work, visits to stock sales and farms, and reports on individual agricultural activities. "The essence of this problem is half calculation and half hunch," he says to a student. "This is an input-output problem," he says to another, discussing the nutritional content of various feeds. As the class works he goes from student to student with comments about the relevance of the immediate problem, and with occasional announcements about local agricultural events, and with admonitions: "It wouldn't hurt for some of our members to invest in some good breeding stock. . . . There's a couple over here who raise real good hogs. We're going to go out there Saturday and we'll be back by four thirty so you can get the chores done. . . . Nowadays you have to do a little figuring. This is a dairy feeding problem. You want to know how much of each to feed the cow."

Whenever Grosscup is challenged about opportunities in farming, and about the exodus of young men and women from the farms to the larger towns, he says that many people in this country still "have jobs related to agriculture" and that salesmen and manufacturers of feed and tractors, of fertilizers and machinery, still have to be conversant with the problems of the farm. "We're getting to the point where some people feel you have to have a test tube in every kid's ear and a math book under every kid's arm. The college people are getting everybody excited about these things but they haven't paid much attention to the rank and file kid. We're entering the biggest era of vocational work you've ever seen, and I don't think everybody's got to have twenty-five years of math to get along." Grosscup feels that the shop work he gives his students—building feeders, for example —will teach them the fundamentals for many other trades, that there is a universality about vocational agriculture that extends far beyond the farm. When he wants to describe his ideal graduate he gives his questioner a reprint from *The Stockmen's Journal:*

> The farmer must be engineer enough to run $20,000 or more worth of machinery, and blacksmith enough to fix it. He must

be economist enough to know when to buy and sell, bookkeeper enough to spot the weak points in his operation, gambler enough to interpret weather and prices, and veterinarian enough to spot disease or stick a bloated cow.

The farmer doesn't have to be a chemist, agronomist, or diplomat, yet he should know what's in his fertilizer formulas, which crop variety is best and when to plant it, and he may have to convince his wife that a one-man hay baler will increase farm profits enough to buy her that long-awaited dishwasher.

The farmer must have brains enough to make dozens of decisions a day, and brawn enough to toss around bales of hay and bags of fertilizer. And with it all, he must be able to walk into his bank and ask for $20,000 to $100,000 without batting an eye. . . .

In such a description—and Grosscup's view is probably shared by many other people in Jesup—the function of the school is to produce an American yeoman, a neo-Jeffersonian individual capable of mastering a variety of practical problems, a self-sufficient man, part craftsman, part farmer, part capitalist. He will live in a world small enough to respond to his techniques, and direct enough so that he will understand it. Jesup is still such a world—a place where Burton North is personally acquainted with the family background of many of his eight hundred students, and where he can go from house to house discussing the inhabitants, their jobs and their interests—but the limits of Jesup township no longer encompass the world or even Iowa, and the skills of the farmer no longer control all of life.

Some of Jesup's teachers are bravely battling this problem in their classrooms, trying to make connections with the larger society, just as vocational agriculture makes connections with the local countryside, fully aware that education *in* Jesup is no longer education only *for* Jesup—that many young people are leaving for the larger towns and cities, and that the teaching which was once adequate for the rural community is insufficient for Chicago, or even Dubuque and Waterloo. One of the most exciting and competent of these teachers is Donald McCulley, an ex-Marine captain (North, introducing him, generally promotes him to colonel) who is a graduate of Cornell College (Iowa) and is now taking further courses toward his master's degree at Cedar Falls. McCulley teaches American history and French. In a United States history class:

Q. Do you feel Americans are as patriotic today as they were in the national period after the War of 1812?

A. There's a veneer of indifference [says a girl, who is later identified as one of the brightest students in the class]. We complain about the government but underneath we're as patriotic now as ever.

A. We take freedom for granted; we don't realize what freedoms we have. We can't imagine kids in the Soviet Union.

Q. Do you think we have to wait for an all-out shooting war to prove our patriotism? Aren't there conditions existing inside our country that require patriotic effort? [There is no response, so McCulley rephrases the question.] Isn't patriotism also involved in working for a good cause? What conditions do we have that need changes?

A. Slums.

Q. How many of you have been in one of the big cities? [A few hands go up—perhaps ten out of thirty-five.] We tend to take our luxuries for granted. Doesn't it take an element of patriotism to fight for better conditions in your own country?

A. There are people fighting for this.

McCulley continues to press, encouraging students to speak about the space program, the assassination of President Kennedy, Cuba, and about the 1964 election (which, one of the students felt, was a low point in American patriotism because of all "the partisan mudslinging"), trying to make connections between historical experience and contemporary events and, in some way, between the morality of the nineteenth century and that of the twentieth. Although McCulley is young, energetic and, in most respects, a thoroughly modern man, the question remains whether he can make those connections, and whether the contemporary world can ever be controlled or understood with the ideas and techniques of an older America.

That older America is still plainly evident in the community, its institutions, and the surrounding countryside. A ringing telephone on the party line is a signal for everyone on the line to start listening—"sometimes there's so many people on the line," someone said, "that I can't hear the person who's calling" —and lights burning next door after ten o'clock are enough to start a rumor that the neighbors have joined "the drinking crowd." But the inquisitive people next door also offer help when someone is sick, bring cookies around at Christmas, greet strangers like old friends, especially at the church door, and take great pride in the accomplishments of the kid down the block. Although Jesup residents get better reception on their television sets than many people in New York, communication with the world outside is limited. Each morning at seven a passenger train called "The Land of Corn" roars through town—a dangerous grade crossing has resulted in several deaths—and every now and then, according to local residents, some noisy kids from Waterloo create a little disturbance at Hummel's Cafe, the only eatery open after two in the afternoon. But for the most part the town lives a quiet life. Taxes are low, church membership is high (one third of the area is Catholic, and Catholic children attend parochial schools, thus making the public school smaller than it would otherwise be), and although business is not nearly as good as its merchant would wish—every year Waterloo encroaches a little more—Jesup gets along. And Jesup clings to its religious fundamentalism, and to a native anti-intellectualism. A Protestant clergyman—who is probably among the most liberal thinkers in town—said that there is strong prohibition everywhere against discussions of sex or evolution ("people are afraid that science has disproved the Bible") and that even a reference to adultery in one of his sermons produced hostility. At the same time, he said, there are people in Jesup who seem to be proud of their limited interests. "Why I haven't read a book in twenty years," was the way he quoted one of the more distinguished local ladies.

And the school reflects the town, reflects its good sense as well as its isolation, its frugality along with its agrarianism. Burton North, known as "an unusually economical administrator" has a well-developed passion for avoiding academic frills, and for keeping his buildings in shape and his kids in line. He has assembled all the equipment for maintaining his own buses, is frequently tearing down and rebuilding partitions and walls inside the school, and forever urging teachers to turn off classroom lights on sunny days. The teachers are encouraged to attend church, and although there are no devotional services in the classroom, there is an annual baccalaureate in which local clergymen are invited to participate. Despite the fact that there are some pre-marital pregnancies almost every year, discussion of sex in the classroom—or anywhere else—is strictly taboo.

Jesup, which draws its teachers primarily from small colleges in Iowa and neighboring states, pays reasonably good starting salaries, beginning at about $4800 (1964–1965), but its increments are small. The highest paid teacher is Grosscup, who earns $7700, more than the high school principal. As a result, most of the teachers moonlight ("Last year," said a member of the school board, "three of the seven men on Everett Sherman's street construction crew had master's degrees") and only a few are interested in spending much of their spare time developing new courses or in improving their teaching techniques. At the same time some of the teachers feel that North and the board have been too parsimonious not only with their salaries but also with educational materials and other equipment. "The textbooks are old, and the plant is poor," one of them said. "Why North even has us use handed-down football equipment for the junior high football team. The helmets don't fit, they turn around on the players' heads, and that's dangerous." Nevertheless—and despite their complaints—many of the teachers say they like Jesup, like life in the small town, the discipline in the school, and the hunting in the surrounding countryside. If they could only get a little more money . . .

Most of Jesup's parents and voters appear to be equally satisfied. Although some of them complain that North is something of a dictator, they are pleased with his economy and his discipline, and with the fact that Jesup's school tax is one of the lowest in the area. Many of them are graduates of the school, and if they don't recall the academic program as having been very exciting, they do feel that the school has always produced decent citizens. "I don't think we need to feel ashamed of our school," said Gilbert Stoddard, a rural mail carrier who sits on the school board. "We have few complaints from parents; the ones we get come from people who corner you on the street and growl. Many parents say we do more for their children than other schools."

And yet Stoddard himself is anything but smug. "I know that today's kids are going into a world much different from the one I did, even if they stay on the farm," he said. "I think maybe the school hasn't changed as much as it ought to. The problem in a school this size is that we don't have the resources we need and so we have to find some way to help the kids dig it out for themselves. What we need is a better library in this school, and a librarian and a counselor. Once we have them it's almost unlimited what a kid could dig out for himself. . . . Many people around here don't have an opportunity to get around. The farm family can't take a vacation, so it's the school's responsibility to give the kids an idea of what goes on." Stoddard recognizes the moonlighting problem but wonders whether increased teacher salaries would make much difference. "We'd still have the people we've got now," he said, "and I'm not sure they're all worth big raises. Then the money would be wasted."

Although there is some criticism of the school's failure to try more modern methods, and occasionally a parental complaint that its college preparation is inadequate, North feels that the school has made substantial improvements during the past decade. "We bought movie and slide projectors and tape recorders," he said, "and we're getting into some calculus in the high school. Dick and Jane readers? . . . We threw them out five years ago. We've got better material now, we've got the best phonics material available." North believes that his graduates—about one fifth go on to some further education—do well in college, and that those who don't go on have little trouble finding jobs. "They can all get work, on the farm, or driving trucks, or in the plants at Waterloo. When we get to talking college we have a hard time with some of them. Why should they go to college—just look around—now here's a fellow who graduated from this school and went into the plumbing business. He must be making ten thousand; and down the street there lives another man . . ."

Despite North's satisfaction with the school and the community, and despite his obviously good sense in rejecting a standard mold for the education of every student, self-sufficiency is evaporating under pressure from modern technology, and especially from the automobile. For every Jesup graduate who tries to find a job on the farm or in the community, there is another one plan-

ning to leave, usually for work in a larger city. More and more
people owning farms have given up full-time agriculture to take
jobs in Waterloo, Independence, and Cedar Falls, while several
of the young men and women who have gone to Chicago or Des
Moines reported that their schooling was often inadequate for
some of the state colleges, and that the preparation provided by
those colleges left them at a disadvantage in competition with the
graduates of the Harvard Business School, Northwestern, or
Michigan. Several of Jesup's little businesses have closed during
the past decade and more are likely to close in the next few years.

Thus the town, like many other small American communities, is confronted with a difficult choice: it can continue to educate its children for life in the small town, or it must make a
major effort to bring the news of the modern world to the classroom, to educate for an impersonal, technological society, and
thereby generate even more impatience with the small town, its
virtues as well as its limitations. If it does this, it will, like the immigrant father, measure success by the cultural space between
itself and its children, and that involves nothing less than a conscious decision to cease being what it has always been. A few
miles to the north, a community of Amish families is trying to
cling to its traditional ways, driving black horse-drawn buggies,
rejecting the automobile and television and much of the outside
world. The Amish children still attend school in one-room buildings, learning the three Rs, and ending their formal education
at the eighth grade (a few orthodox families have had a running
battle with the state in defense of separate schools, employing
eighth-grade Amish girls as teachers, in violation of state teacher
accrediting laws). But Jesup, unlike the Amish, long ago accepted
the technology of the modern world, giving up the attempt to
be commercially self-sufficient, and thus there is an ironic aspect
to its good natured but somewhat condescending references to
the "Hookeys" (so named for the hooks and eyes on their
clothes). The Amish are trying to preserve their culture by rejecting at least part of the surrounding technology. Jesup is still
trying to have the technology without some of the culture and
attitudes that it ultimately demands.

Every school system has about it a kind of internal perfection. The technology, the education and attitudes of the community, the salaries paid, the competence of teachers and administrators, the social, cultural and political views of parents and school boards—all these things tend to be internally in harmony, and to reinforce each other. Where a substantial number of people in a community—as in Topeka—make a conscious effort to be conversant with the ideas of the outside world, those ideas will ultimately appear in the classroom, and they will reflect themselves in the teachers and administrative staff. Where the community looks entirely to itself, trusting to the experience of the past, it will educate for the past. This is not to say that the local situation, and the varied backgrounds and abilities of children, can be disregarded. Neither Jesup nor Topeka can operate schools like New Trier or Scarsdale or Newton. There is no formula. And yet every community is educating children who will live and work somewhere else, who will share the problems and possibilities of a common civilization. This land *is* your land and my land, and none of us can plan on confining ourselves to some little corner of it. This makes it just as dangerous to ignore the tremendous new developments of modern education as it is foolish to regard a successful school somewhere else as a complete model.

The American Midwest is not a perfect microcosm of all America. Its small towns and cities are often closer to an older and more rural style of life. And yet even the rural communities are a far cry from what they were thirty or forty years ago. Most American farming, unlike Jesup's, is carried on in large units; it is highly mechanized, and it is as much committed to station wagons, washing machines and television sets as the commuter suburb. At the same time, no city is more than an hour or two from a major university, and from other centers of intellectual and scientific power. Many communities have come to understand this, and to take advantage of it, making the expertise of the university, and of people like the Menninger psychologists and psychiatrists a part of the local system. By its very nature this expertise, speaking for the modern world, will tend to conflict with the traditional sense of things. It will insist on cosmopolitanism and sophistication, on a focus *beyond* the local community, while the latter will continue to restrict itself to more limited definitions. That traditional sense still has a great deal to say, as in Jesup it always has. Its somewhat suspicious conservatism may help check us from rushing headlong into some kind of meritocracy by reminding us that not every kid was meant to have a test tube sticking out of his ear. It may also demonstrate that certain traditions of service and loyalty will never be irrelevant, and perhaps even by showing that the missing link in our chaos of unemployment, affluence and obsolescence is the small craftsman, the fellow who used to *deliver* the groceries, to bake decent bread or do a reliable job repairing the roof. But to disregard the modern world, or to try to separate its styles of thought from its technology, is a dangerous—and probably an impossible—enterprise. By looking outside as well as inside, the local school system may, in some degree, be able to combine the best of both worlds, and thereby find a way to an exciting and more relevant education.

2

Saving the City

CHICAGO—as the cabaret on Wells Street reminds you—is America's Second City. But in the magnitude of its school problems, in the salary it pays its superintendent, and in the controversies he has helped generate, it is undoubtedly the first.

Because of its location in the Midwest, and because of the Board of Trade, the Merchandise Mart, the stockyards and the national transportation system, Chicago is everybody's Big American City. Speak of New York or Los Angeles and people take exception because of the Jews, or the immigrants—of which Chicago has as many as New York—or Hollywood or freeways, but mention Chicago and there is general assent. If Chicago isn't American, what is? This is the city of Theodore Dreiser and James T. Farrell, the birthplace of Hemingway, the home of the mail order house, Rotary and the American Medical Association, a city offering good music and good steaks, and a major university center competing with Cambridge and Berkeley in the prestige of its academic menu.

No longer the spiritual center of American isolation that it was in the days when Colonel Robert R. McCormick ran the *Tribune,* Chicago is, in some respects, a big rambunctious village rather than a well-planned metropolis. Its main focus is the commercial area of the Loop, and its largest expanse of green space is stretched like an awkward barrier between the city and Lake Michigan. The hipsters say that when Orlando Wilson, the police commissioner, began to make it tough on the call girls, the convention business hit hard times, and the taxi drivers are perennially angry because someone is either tearing up or parading down Michigan Avenue, one of the few north-south arteries around the downtown area. In the devil's dictionary Chicago will always be the place of the fire and the gangsters; but it is also the nerve center of rural innocence, where the future farmers come to see the stock shows, thinking they're in a real evil city, where the mayor once denied the existence of slums, and where, in many places, the principle of the "neighborhood school" is the only vestige of the neighborhood that still remains.

Chicago has managed to develop some stable integrated areas, as in the Marynook Community on the extreme South side, and in the low-to-middle income Michael Reese and Lake Meadows housing developments. But usually the different parts of the city are as stratified economically and racially as they are in every other American metropolis. As a result Chicago, like most of its urban peers, operates what often seems like two school systems, one for a declining number of whites, the other for a growing proportion of Negroes. Ninety per cent of the public schools are more than ninety per cent white or ninety per cent Negro, and although they are operated by the same hierarchy they have generally different functions, different kinds of personnel, and vastly different problems. (There is also a large parochial educational establishment with which the public schools are now carrying on a shared-time flirtation: the plan is to have some parochial students take shop, science and vocational courses in the public schools, the other subjects in the Catholic schools.) Of the half million children in the city system—a school population roughly equivalent to that of Norway—approximately half are Negroes; the remainder are "whites" of every description, from upper middle-class children of university teachers and professional men through Puerto Ricans, southern mountaineers and Mexican-Americans. The differences among them encompass the full spectrum of American experience and background: the Mather High School on the North side is a great deal closer to suburban Evanston—geographically and socially—than it is to Du Sable or Englewood or John Marshall, all of which are black ghetto schools; and the population of the Goudy School, composed of the children of Tennessee and West Virginia immigrants, has more in common with the mountain schools of those states than it does with that of the modern all-Negro Beethoven School on the city's South side.

Despite their internal differences—differences in staff, in

equipment, in children—despite the fact that there is a growing Negro middle class, and despite the presence of many lower class whites, the schools are known more for their racial differences—for the segregation problem—than for anything else. Those differences are statistically apparent: they show up in test scores, in teacher assignments, in the dropout rate, in college attendance—in almost every measurable characteristic of any relevance whatever. *On the whole,* as almost everyone knows, the children of culturally deprived families, and of Negroes in particular, are less ready to attend school when they get there, perform less well in their classes, and are more likely to drop out or be forced out before they finish. The children bring to school all the problems of the slums, of the housing projects, of unemployed or nonexistent fathers, of the street gangs, and of loneliness and deprivation and confusion, burdening the schools with problems for which they are not prepared or financed, and which many people are not yet really willing to confront. In response, many whites have either erected economic and social barriers, hoping they can stop this cultural glacier, or they have fled to the more salubrious suburbs. Of Chicago's 3,500,000 people, about 1,000,000 are Negroes, and their number is growing. By 1970, if the present trend continues, Chicago, like Washington, D.C., will be educating a school population that is overwhelmingly colored.

Now the schools are being asked to help reverse that trend, to become vast social agencies, to provide programs for three-year olds, to break down neighborhood segregation patterns and to do what no educational system has ever been asked to do before. They are supposed to help save the city. In a recent study of the Chicago system headed by Professor Philip M. Hauser of the University of Chicago, the board of education was reminded that:

> Programs to effect school integration must reckon with the fact that the white elementary school child is already in the minority . . . and the time is not far off when the same will be true of the white high school student. Unless the exodus of white population from the public schools and from the City is brought to a halt or reversed, the question of school integration may become simply a theoretical matter, as it is already in the nation's capital. For integration, in fact, cannot be achieved without white students.

Rarely in history have any communities been faced in peace
time with as grave and serious a problem as now faces Chicago
(and other great metropolitan centers), a problem which threatens the very future of the City and contains portentous implications for the welfare and security of her people . . .

Without the resolution of the problem of school integration
and without improvement in the quality of education . . . the
future of the City of Chicago and of other great metropolitan
areas will be seriously jeopardized and the interests of the entire
nation may be impaired and imperiled.

The Chicago schools have been boycotted and picketed;
there have been suits and petitions, protests and studies. Plans to
combat segregation have been met by counter-plans, by invective
at meetings of the board of education, and then by new studies.
But in each instance, the focus of the controversy ultimately falls
on the stormy, strong-willed, but capable individual who has
been superintendent of schools since 1953, Benjamin C. Willis.
Willis has been accused of being a racial bigot, a tyrant and a tool
of the banks and real estate interests. He has been hailed as a sav-
ior of the neighborhood schools, and cheered by frightened white
property owners to the chant of "We Want Willis." He once resigned his job when the board that hired him issued orders that
he considered excessive (and then returned when the same board
asked him to come back), and he held—for a period of several
years—a second job surveying education for the Commonwealth
of Massachusetts. Until that survey was completed he was the second highest paid public official in the United States.

Willis—sometimes called Uncle Ben behind his back—is a
manager, and a brilliant one. Ask him about the problems of education, and he will remind you that in the past decade he eliminated double shifts in the city's schools, reduced the average class
size, constructed 4800 new classrooms in 236 new buildings and
additions, increased teachers' salaries, added new programs for
culturally deprived children, advanced students and vocational
training, built a brand new Teachers College, introduced nongraded classes (called the Continuous Development Plan), instituted new courses and educational television, enlarged the school
libraries, and reestablished tuition-free summer schools. And, he
will point out, this was accomplished even while the school popu-

lation grew from just under 400,000 to over 560,000. To Willis
every educational problem is ultimately a problem in management and finance. "Put a cop on a corner with 5000 cars and he
looks like a chump," he said. "Give him 25 cars and he looks pretty good." Thus cultural deprivation becomes a problem in class
size, budgeting and personnel, and segregation a special aspect of
school construction and space allocation. Negro demands are a
healthy sign: "They see education working," he said. "It's the
American solution to economic stratification." But as far as the
militant integrationists are concerned—"I don't think they've
even thought about what they want in the way of education." To
Willis, the problem of segregation can be met *inside* the classroom, but he is not prepared to use the schools to save the city
and, moreover, he does not seem to be willing to discuss it. Each
time he is asked about segregation or about inequities within the
system, he produces a set of figures, a new plan, or a report calling
for millions of dollars (and sometimes billions) in new appropriations. His responses to civil rights pressure, and sometimes to
questions from members of his own board of education, are frequently made in tones of impatient contempt. *He* is the professional, *he* will make the decisions, and *he* will solve the problems,
if only the citizens, the NAACP, and the Urban League, and all the
other muddleheads will let him.

But Willis' public relations problems—the animosity that
some people feel toward him—are only a small part of Chicago's
dilemma. (Someone once suggested that if "Uncle Ben would
only put a couple of those cute Negro secretaries into his front
office all his troubles would be over.") Many of his enemies, who
include a large part of the vocal Negro community, feel that no
educational or racial progress can be made until he leaves his job
(his contract expired in August 1965, but he has been reappoint-
ed.) Many of his friends believe that he is a good superintendent,
while some of his other supporters consider him the last and best
defender of neighborhood schools, the bastion against integration, "the man who will save the city from the Negro." Thus
Willis has become a symbol, and thus the schools have become
the prime sociological battleground of the city. The issues in
this battle involve not merely problems of segregation and
integration, special programs for culturally deprived children,

improved vocational education, and other special types of training, they also involve the vastly more complex question of function and purpose. Should the city commit itself to the principle
of the "four walls" school devoted exclusively to the best possible
teaching, or should it consider its educational system as a huge
agency fostering everything from social welfare to urban rehabili-
tation? In *The Public Schools of Chicago*, the second major
survey made for the board of education in the last few years,
Professor Robert J. Havighurst, a University of Chicago social
scientist, described the choice, and then came out squarely for
the second alternative:

> There are two opposite schools of thought among educators
> concerning the conduct of public schools in the big city. One
> may be called the "four walls" school. The basic principle is
> to do the best possible job educating every boy or girl who
> comes into the school, whoever he is, whatever his color, na-
> tionality, IQ or handicap. This means building good school
> buildings, equipping them well, and staffing them with well-
> trained teachers. . . .
>
> The four walls type of school system works for efficiency and
> economy, and attempts to free the creative teacher to do the
> best possible job of teaching under good conditions. The com-
> munity outside the school is regarded as a source of complexity
> and of tension-arousal if the boundary between community and
> school is not clearly defined and respected.
>
> The other school of thought may be called the "urban com-
> munity" school. The educators who advocate this believe that
> the big city is in a crisis which . . . requires the active participa-
> tion of schools in the making and practicing of policy for social
> urban renewal. This big-city crisis is reflected in feelings of un-
> certainty and anxiety on the part of parents and citizens. There
> is danger of a collective failure of nerve which saps the vitality
> and flexibility of the city's efforts at urban renewal. . . .
>
> The urban community school attempts to act constructively
> in this crisis by involving the parents and citizens in the deci-
> sions about school policy and practice. The educator accepts
> the frustrations of working with people who themselves are con-
> fused and uncertain about the schools, believing that the only
> way to solve the problems of the city is to work on a give-and-
> take basis with citizens and community organizations.

The Havighurst report strikes squarely at Ben Willis (Willis himself was theoretically a member of the study group but he rarely attended its meetings; in effect he boycotted the whole project). It is Willis who appears reluctant to involve "parents and citizens in the decisions about school policy and practice," who has declined to face the issues that most annoy his critics, and who refuses even to give out the telephone numbers of the individual schools. Willis sometimes lectures his own board of education like a group of slow-witted schoolboys, reading reports which, for some reason, are rarely distributed to the board before the meetings. Thus the men and women who have hired him often sit at bare desks listening to the superintendent discuss something which they will not be able to study until after the meeting.

But Havighurst is also striking at something else, something far more profound. Between the lines of his report is a conception of public education that has hardly even been mentioned. According to Havighurst the school must become one of the prime agencies for preserving and stabilizing neighborhoods, functioning as a magnet to hold and draw back the white middle and upper classes, and as an instrument—perhaps *the* instrument—to preserve and restore the city. In such a conception, the school becomes not only a social agency, it becomes the keystone, the essence of the community itself.

II

The Jean Baptiste Point Du Sable High School, which occupies a long ugly block of South Wabash Avenue, looks, and sometimes feels, like a prison. Its long locker-lined halls are constantly patrolled by teachers stationed in such a manner that they are always in sight of each other; reinforcing them are two uniformed policemen. Wherever one goes in the school there are locked doors, keys, and patrols. The school's administrators emphasize that these precautions are designed mainly to control pilfering and disturbances generated by outsiders, most of them former Du Sable students who have dropped out, but they also concede that places like the cafeteria could be powderkegs without the cops, and that the teachers' desks are likely to be cleaned out if they are left unlocked or unguarded. At the same time Du Sable is almost hopelessly overcrowded; it lacks adequate gymnasium facilities and laboratories, and although its ninth graders have been forced into other buildings, it must still conduct classes on the gymnasium floor—sometimes several going on side by side—because all the classrooms are filled.

Du Sable High School—adjacent to the Du Sable Upper Grade Center, a Willisism for a two-year junior high school—educates 3500 Negro boys and girls in the tenth, eleventh and twelfth grades. There are no whites; the last one dropped out in 1963. "This area," said the newly appointed principal, a Negro named Byron C. Minor, "has all the characteristics of slums all over the world, plus some gimmicks no one ever dreamed of. This is one of the few areas in the United States where the median income actually went down between 1950 and 1960; it approximates rural South Carolina in income and in the number of years of education completed by adults." Du Sable's students, Minor said, come from two public housing projects and from a section that still has some "private" homes. One of the housing projects was opened at a time when the Chicago Housing Authority still screened applicants; the other, opened later, is occupied by unscreened families (the CHA had by then decided that screening was too expensive) and represents the more extreme social misfits. "No one owns anything in these projects," Minor said. "They can't even put picture hooks in the walls. Thus there is a serious lack of initiative and interest, with thousands of boys who don't know how to use a screwdriver, tighten a hinge or fix a doorknob. There is no pride of residence; they have contempt for themselves and everybody else."

That self-contempt and the corresponding lack of motivation is the school's paramount concern and its most contagious disease. "My friends told me not to come here," said a young teacher with barely a year's experience. "Some people here are discouraged. They come to class late, sit and smoke half the period, and dawdle over lunch. You have trouble getting books—usually they arrive late—and sometimes you suspect that they're the culls from other schools." The brighter and more ambitious students—and some are *very* bright and *very* ambitious—concur. "Sure we get the worst books," one of them said. "They say we don't take care of the books, but that's a lot of baloney. Most people do. Many of the good teachers don't use the books much; they try to get you to work with other materials." The students also agree that some of the teachers have lost interest, that they appear late for classes, and that other schools "try to bribe the good teachers away." The better teachers, one of the boys said, are strict. "At Du Sable," he added, "caring and being strict go hand in hand.... There are some teachers who don't care, and some who tell you 'I'm not here because I like it—as soon as I can I'll transfer to a white school.' "

Du Sable's student population, like its staff, falls into two general categories. Although one teacher called it "a remedial high school" in which 65 per cent of the students are enrolled in remedial or "basic" English courses, there is a sizable minority which plans on further education—usually at one of the city's public institutions—which reads James Baldwin and Richard Wright, complains about the poor science laboratories, and becomes passionately involved in civil rights activities. Some of them have picketed their own school, asking for better books, and a few occasionally rush downtown after classes (*on their own*) to attend the meetings of the board of education. "There's two kinds around here," one of them said. "There's the gousters and the ivies. The gousters have the process hairdos, the leather coats and the black stockings. Some of them are winos or addicts. The ivies have short haircuts, they wear ordinary skirts and sweaters —you know, they look like everybody else." Most of the students in his crowd, obviously, were ivies, but when he was asked he identified himself as a "Whig.... That's spelled wwig—wear what I got."

Of Du Sable's remedial students, some are almost as highly motivated as those who are reading and working up to grade level. They are aware of their deficiencies, of the value of education, and of the crimes that the school system has perpetrated on them since the first grade. But many are already sullen, defying their teachers to teach them anything, waiting until they have escaped the compulsory attendance laws, or simply disappearing into the ghetto whence they came. A guidance counselor tells the story of a chronically truant girl who was threatened with confinement to a correctional home if she did not attend school. "She just smiled," he said. " 'You can't do that any more,' she told me. 'I'se pregnant.' " The attitude of such students, the neighborhood surrounding the school, the lack of facilities, the whole environment of South Chicago (even to the Du Sable parking lot, where the dropouts like to slash the tires of the teachers' cars) ultimately have their effect on teaching morale. The Negro high schools have a lower proportion of permanently assigned teachers, they have more trouble getting substitutes—and sometimes can't get them at all—and they have, in comparison to the white high schools, a far greater percentage of people who have given up, time servers, cynics, sadists, and world-weary individuals who are permanently enrolled on the transfer list. But, strangely enough, they also have a surprising proportion of dedicated, and sometimes brilliant individuals, people like Katherine Bogan, a Du Sable guidance counselor, who treats the students she calls "my children" with an earthy and intelligent affection, and who remains a counselor to many of them long after she has helped shoehorn them into college; Luke Helm, a big, affable Negro history teacher whose classroom barbs inevitably turn out to be the spurs of motivation rather than the insults of contempt; and Joyce Lanahan, a young, attractive teacher of geography who went from the affluent North Shore to Carleton College and then went beyond both to accept the delights of teaching in the ghetto. The materials with which such teachers work are sometimes inadequate, the classrooms are drab—usually brown or green—and the books often fatigued and irrelevant. Their official social studies syllabus includes such items as (in Contemporary American History) "The Relation of Good Family Living to National Defense and Welfare," "Explain the Administrative Organization of the Chicago Public Schools, showing in what respects we attempt to secure unity without uniformity," and "Have a panel on 'Intolerance threatens the prestige of the United States in world affairs.'" The textbooks in American history—and in other subjects—devote little attention to the Negro or to the problems of civil rights, segregation or the slums, forcing them often to improvise or to find bootleg materials. And yet even those who adhere closely to the book sometimes manage to produce interest in altogether improbable subjects. For some teachers, apparently, no limitations of subject or reading matter are so overwhelming as to preclude effective classroom operations.

The twenty-five students in Luke Helm's world history class

are sitting in no discernible order whatever. The chairs scattered around the room are arrayed in miscellaneous directions, most of them facing forward. It is the Monday after Thanksgiving.

"Have a nice weekend?" Helm asks.

"I ate too much," says a boy.

"My sister was there," says another.

"You don't like your sister?"

"No."

"Do you know what sibling rivalry is?" Helm asks without waiting for an answer. "Who else had a lousy time?"

"I had the flu," a girl answers.

"How many of you picked up your history book over the weekend?" One limp hand goes up. "I guess the little points on the top of your heads were smoothed down. . . . Now who was Richelieu governing for?"

"Louis XIII," a boy answers.

"Jesse has reformed," says Helm. "He knows something. He deserves a round of applause." They applaud.

"What did Richelieu do that was unusual?"

"He fought on the side of the Protestants."

"He did? Ridiculous. A cardinal of the Roman Catholic Church fighting on the side of the Protestants . . ."

"That's what you said." They all agree. That's what he said.

"I was lying."

"If he was fighting on the side of the Protestants he could fight France and Spain."

"Who was on the throne of France and Spain?"

"The Hapsburgs."

"So he wasn't fighting a religious war; he was fighting for political power."

"Why did Marie de Medici appoint Richelieu?" a girl asks.

"Maybe she felt he could do a better job," Helm replies.

"Maybe she had a crush on him," a girl suggests.

"Well, there's a way to find out. I hope the question burns in your pea-pickin' heart until you burst into the library and shout 'Miss Clark, give me a book about the Medici family.' "

Does anyone in the Chicago ghetto care about the Medici family, or about the mercantilism of Colbert, the rise of the middle class, or even about the French Revolution? In Helm's class, apparently, they do. They care about it because Helm has made it into something of a personal affair, almost a form of hipsterism in which the squares are the ones who don't know what Richelieu was up to. "I want you to see that history is a chain of events," Helm says, implying that to understand that chain is somehow to control it, and implying further that if you want to amount to anything, you have to learn the acceptable means of social control.

For Du Sable High School, Helm is an unusual man with an unusual group of students. Most are not as bright and not nearly as well motivated (many teachers would think it absurd even to ask if anyone had cracked a book over a weekend). And yet almost all the teachers who seem to be successful, whatever their official subject matter, are those who implicitly, and often explicitly, deal with the one topic that really seems to matter: the power of the individual—and particularly the underprivileged individual—to survive in a hostile and confusing world.

Raymond L. Neubauer, a young Dartmouth graduate with a concern for the problems of the inner city, teaches courses in Essential English, one of Chicago's euphemisms for remedial work. His thirteen students—tenth graders—read at about fifth grade level. The problem for Neubauer is to find appropriate material, material that will be interesting as well as comprehensible. For his current text he has chosen a little pamphlet prepared by the state's attorney general and entitled *Your Rights If You Are Arrested.* The students read portions of the booklet aloud in class, and then Neubauer asks questions about the passage just completed:

"How much force can a policeman use to make an arrest?" Neubauer asks.

"Sometimes they use more than they need to," a girl says.

"Man, that's no joke," a boy says.

"Do you know what a search warrant is?"

"The search warrant," a student says, reading from the pamphlet, " 'is an order issued by the court after a complaint and verifying affidavit have been filed. The warrant must describe the property which is the object of the search and the premises to be searched. The officer may use force to gain admittance, if after notice . . .' " The reading is slow and painful.

"Do you know what premises are?" Neubauer asks. There is some discussion and explanation. Finally a boy says:

"You mean it's like a raid. They come in and say 'all the girls on that side and all the boys on this side.'"

"They're supposed to have a warrant, except in special cases," says Neubauer.

"They never got a warrant."

"Do you have to answer questions when you're arrested?"

"No," a student answers.

"What protects you?"

"The Fifth Amendment."

"They hit you if you don't answer their questions."

"You answer questions," a boy adds.

"Or else," says another.

Neubauer reads: "'You are under no duty to answer any questions directed to you by either the arresting officer, or the court, nor are you bound to sign any statement if you state that you are relying on your constitutional right to do so.'" There is a moment's pause, and then he continues. "'The use of force or intimidation to coerce a statement from you should be reported promptly to the court, the State's Attorney, and to your lawyer.'"

What Neubauer is doing is not part of any official curriculum; like many other teachers of similar students, he has struck out on his own. "The regular things won't work," he said, "so I try a few new ideas." To teach grammar—or "structural linguistics" he uses jive talk, making the students compile a dictionary:

Can Opener
    Noun: cook
    My mother is the can opener in our house.
Boss:
    Adjective: fine, good
    We are having a boss time.
Scratch
    Noun: money
    Can I borrow some scratch?

And to teach literature he has students read *Raisin in the Sun* (which they act out in class) and other works of Negro literature.

He talks about life in the ghetto, and tries to convey a sense that, despite its complexities, life can be managed in the city, and that there are acceptable means of controling it.

The common course, and certainly the common topic of conversation, is civil rights, human rights, and the socially tolerable methods of self defense. (Many students have learned other means of self-defense.) "Race relations is always the first topic they want to talk about," a teacher said. "They even talk about it in Spanish class." On the blackboard in a civics class the assigned readings are always posted: *Black Boy,* by Richard Wright; *Slums and Suburbs,* by James B. Conant; *Why We Can't Wait,* by Martin Luther King. Du Sable has an active Human Relations Club, and a Negro History Club, and some teachers who don't hesitate to speak freely about the injustices suffered by Negroes and about the inequities of the school system. "This place looks like a federal prison," one of them told a class. "And that's typical of the treatment of the Negro people in this country." But many are also quick to confront students who begin to feel sorry for themselves, who feel that discrimination is a legitimate reason for resignation, saying that the situation stinks, but is not irrevocable. "You can move up," said the teacher quoted above. "You can come out of the ghetto and still get to the top. Many positive things are going to take place for Negro Americans in the next few years." In the ghetto, civil rights is the core curriculum.

No one can estimate what the impact of these discussions will be, or how many students become involved. Clearly there are many teachers who try to operate in a conventional way, speaking about things that have little relevance, following the textbook day by day. And there are others who have given up, who express their contempt for the students (the Negro teachers are usually the worst offenders), and who sometimes fail to appear in class until the period is half over. Even the best teachers agree that the optimum homework assignment in a history text is about five pages a night. ("If you assign more than eight pages," one said, "they won't go near it.") It is futile to expect even that much from the less motivated students. Many of these students are unbelievably wily in the ways of the street and incredibly naive about the rest of the world: in one class of thirty-five kids there was not one who came within 100 million of guessing the population of the

United States, and only two or three who had even been inside Marshall Field's or Carson Pirie Scott, the two large downtown department stores. "The problem," said Byron Minor, the principal, "is to make the curriculum fit their levels. We're trying to expand the industrial arts program—recently we started an auto shop—just to get them involved."

Most of the students who come to Du Sable are hopelessly far behind, and many have already been sapped of the motivation and self respect that Minor and others would so desperately like to instill. The median reading level of its tenth graders is a little over seven years; the average daily absence rate is fourteen per cent, and the chances that a tenth grader will finish school are about one in two. But all these characteristics are merely projections of what has been going on in the elementary schools, in the Upper Grade Centers, at home, on the street, in the elevators of the housing projects, in the alleys and in the pool halls. Despite some notable exceptions, student apathy and hostility infect teachers and principals who, in turn, infect still more students. Children recognized as psychiatric or emotional cases are pushed in with slow readers, and slow readers with average students. Because of overcrowding kids are moved from school to school, from high school to Upper Grade Center, from teacher to teacher, from classroom to classroom. Among the more flagrant examples is the so-called Forestville Compound, a cluster of academic tombs on South Saint Lawrence Avenue. In the summer of 1964 a group of parents, all of them Negroes organized a protest and issued a statement describing the situation:

> "The Forestville Compound," the name used by Supt. Willis to describe the Forestville School, actually consists of three different schools. They are Forestville South, Forestville North, and a 9th grade branch of Du Sable High School. Forestville South has a pupil enrollment of 2200; Forestville North's enrollment, which consists of 7th and 8th grade students, is approximately 1200; while Du Sable's branch has a student enrollment of 420.
> Over a number of years the problems of the "Forestville Compound" have become more serious. These problems were largely generated and fostered by a system of de facto segregation with

its characteristic by-products of overcrowded classrooms and unequal education. The quality of education became a central issue when the parents began to recognize that segregation of
their schools, whether deliberate or by chance, had lowered the
quality of education in their schools.

The parents for many months have attempted to get improvements and change through their PTA body, the local school
administration, general school administration, and finally, the
Board of Education. In all efforts they were at best tolerated but
more frequently ignored with their grievances falling upon deaf
ears.

There are many problems at the "Forestville Compound,"
with many questions that remain unanswered. Taking a look at
the major grievances—low achievement levels, the Du Sable
High School Branch, lack of and inadequate E.M.H. [educable
mentally handicapped] classes and facilities, poor and inadequate books, insufficient library facilities, overcrowding, and an
insensitive administration—the parents have formulated the
following specific indictments:

At Forestville South, with an enrollment of 2200 pupils, some
of the kindergarten through 3rd grade classes are located in a
CHA Hi-Rise Building (Washington Park Homes). The Forestville North Upper Grade students use the classroom space that
should be utilized for Forestville South, which is a kindergarten
through 6th grade school. In turn, the Du Sable High School
Branch takes up space in Forestville North. It is a regular game
of musical chairs.

In addition, Forestville South has no lunchroom for the children. The original one was destroyed by fire five years ago, and
rather strangely, the principal at that time refused to allow the
lunchroom to be rebuilt. At present, pupils from the Forestville
South School must fill out special forms to use the North's lunchroom facilities because of the overcrowded conditions and lack
of necessary facilities to handle all three schools. One of the
school's binding rules states that children from South building
cannot use the North's lunchroom unless proof is presented that
both parents work during the day. This ruling, of course, leaves
the local candy stores and "greasy spoons" as lunchrooms for
hundreds of boys and girls.

Pupils are not allowed to take textbooks home. Instead, the
principal offers to sell the parents outdated texts or texts that
are not used in the class. The parents are also concerned about

the fact that children cannot enter school before the bell rings. Whenever there is rain, snow, or sub-zero temperatures, the children have to stay outside and suffer.

Efforts to ameliorate and find solutions to these problems through some kind of cooperative efforts on the part of the parents and the local administration have failed abysmally. The principal has been uncooperative, patronizing and condescending in his attitude toward the parents. Many parents state that his "you people" attitude is intolerable, and he has shown almost "total disregard for the problems of the school and the community." He has thus fostered an atmosphere of hostility and alienated all parents who have sought to improve their school.

Achievement data compiled in 1962 indicated that four out of five students from Forestville North were being graduated with achievement scores that were below the level at which they should have been, two out of five students graduating from 8th grade had reading scores of 5B or less. Recent evidence would appear to indicate that this tragic situation has changed little.

In the Du Sable Branch at Forestville North, where school drop-outs are made and not born, the students are angry, hostile, and miseducated. They say that the students cannot learn at Forestville North High School. Ask the so-called high school students and they will tell you in their best language, "It's different from a real high school. The teachers are too young, and besides, they don't know nothing." In addition, they add, "They never stay long." Of the 18 teachers, there exists only one teacher with assigned status.

At the Du Sable Branch, from September, 1963 to December of the same year, a game of "musical teachers" was played. During that period, the faculty mortality rate was so high that in one class the students experienced a new teacher on four (4) different occasions.

The overall quality of teaching at the branch has been described as substandard and archaic. One administrative source has stated that in the Du Sable Branch, "The teachers in all cases are inexperienced and ill-prepared to attack the problems or reach their students."

The high school branch has only an inadequate library that is a cramped section roped off in the Upper Grade Center. It is a library with far less facilities than one would find in the most backward of segregated high schools in America. The list of wrongs is long: filthy classrooms; a frightened and insecure faculty; inadequate textbooks; no art classes; no history classes; no shop classes; no typing; and only limited science equipment and materials; and classrooms are overrun with E.M.H. students who are present because of the total absence of E.M.H. classes. All of these point to the shocking abuse perpetrated upon children in the Du Sable Branch of the "Forestville Compound."

At the bottom of this shabby foundation we find a principal, frightened and bewildered by the complexity and futility of his task. As one parent puts it, "Ben ordered him to make a High School—and in nothing flat and out of nothing, he made a high school."

The mood at Forestville North ranges from dogged optimism to utter despair. "I'm telling you about a Negro who won a world's championship," says a teacher, almost shouting, "and you're not listening." In another classroom, the teacher tells the visitor—about halfway through the period, "Oh, we're not doing anything. We've finished our work and we're just killing time," and in still another classroom the teacher is telling the class, "Tomorrow we'll have a test for sure," almost as if she were trying to reassure herself. Her blackboard carries signs saying "Everyone has the Right to Free Choice in Employment" and "All Are Equal Before the Law," but the real motto has been scribbled inside one of the lift-top desks:

> Cool and mellow
> 2 in a car
> 2 little kisses
> 4 weeks later
> Mr. and Mrs.

The school's principal, Herman R. Margolis, a conscientious school man, is a good example of Willis' overworked traffic cop, a man who is the academic counterpart of a floor manager at the opening of a big sale in a department store basement. "It isn't all poor teaching," Margolis said. "There are sixteen-year-old kids here from Mississippi who couldn't recognize 'cat' and 'dog' when they came to school." Margolis is perfectly aware that the school graduates students who don't read as well as most ten-year olds but, he said, "if you applied the same standards you'd have young-sters here who are eighteen or twenty years old. The whole prob-lem is knowing how to hasten the process of education." Would it help to get some community volunteers to tutor the children? "Yes, it certainly would help, but I have no authority to ask for outside volunteers."

Like many other south side schools, Forestville North does have a tutoring program staffed by teachers engaged by the system to stay after school and assist children who ask for help; but that program is marginal. Most teachers in most South Chicago schools fly out the door when the bell rings. Many have been told that it's not safe to stay after four o'clock, that they will get their tires slashed, that they will be attacked, or simply that they must vacate so that the buildings can be cleaned and locked. And even those who might be tempted to stay, to work late, to discuss common problems, or to meet with students, often cannot: they have sec-ond jobs at other schools and must tend to their moonlighting.

The sources of South Chicago's educational problems are in-credibly complex, but as one goes from teacher to teacher, from block to block, from school to school, it becomes apparent that this, too, is a perfect system in which almost all the elements are well suited one to the other. Children from poor backgrounds are exposed to poor teachers in dingy schools; are often discouraged from continuing by their peers, their parents, and their formal classes; are given poor and irrelevant books which, in some cases, they are not allowed to take home (because, the administrators say, they'll get stolen or damaged, and won't be read anyway); are harassed by all of the official machinery of the community; are constantly reminded of their inadequacy, and are finally sent or thrown to the world to raise *their* children. In the meantime the teachers begin to select themselves out, and so do the schools. Un-less they are unusually dedicated and specially trained most of them have no inclination to stay in the ghetto very long; the prob-lem of bridging the space between your world and their world, of confronting those kids, and of handling the official apathy is usu-ally too much. The better teachers are transferred and the poor ones stay. In some schools it is impossible for the principal to get substitutes, and in a few the elementary classes are supervised by a librarian, and sometimes even by an older child. (Classes are

rarely consolidated because the principal's salary is based on the
number of classes in his domain.) And as the ghetto areas become
more crowded, so do the schools. Although Chicago uses hundreds of mobile classrooms (sardonically labelled Willis wagons
or ghetto carts) it is constantly shifting slum kids from school to
school and from teacher to teacher. "I know a kid seven years old
who's been to four schools," said a Negro mother on the South
side. "She started kindergarten at Oakenwald, then was moved
to Oakland—to get there she had to cross Drexel Avenue, which
is a dangerous street—then she went to the school in the high rise
(where the board of education is renting space) and now she's at
Doniat, and has to cross Drexel again. Her mother can't take her,
because she's in a wheel chair." At the same time some parents—
either because they are dissatisfied, or because they move—are
constantly withdrawing their children from one school and en-
rolling them in another. "Under circumstances like that," someone said, "you can't blame the kids for becoming schizophrenic."

The system—community and schools—sometimes functions
so as to embarrass or intimidate conscientious parents, to scare
away protests and to discourage interest in education. "You know
your child can't read and write," a parent said, "but you think it's
just your kid reflecting your own inadequacies. You think he's a
freak, so you don't say anything. It wasn't until someone stole
some of the reading scores from one of the schools that we discovered that everybody was in the same boat. And if you do take an
interest in the school they have a way of making you feel so inferior; they're so condescending. I haven't got much of an education; but I did go to high school, and I know that my kids
weren't learning."

Accumulating pressure from the Negro community—and
from many whites as well—has generated new efforts to provide
more compensatory education and other extra services designed
to overcome the handicaps of culturally deprived children. Willis
himself was one of the instigators of the Ford Foundation Great
Cities Project, a program to motivate children who have a history
of failure. The board of education is also sponsoring after-school
reading classes, is providing extra professional services in some
problem schools, has set up special night classes for "drop-ins,"
youths who have dropped out of school and now want to continue

their education, and is experimenting with preschool programs for three- and four-year olds. But its most significant ventures to date are the so-called Doolittle Project—an intensive elementary school program whose central purpose is to give both children and parents a new sense of self-respect—and the Vocational Guidance Centers, a half-dozen schools established for overage elementary students, most of them over fifteen years old. At the Drake Vocational Guidance Center, the original, and still the model, school in this program, 300 of Chicago's 25,000 overage elementary school children are being given intensive teaching and guidance to bring their academic competence to high school level. The average rate of progress at Drake is about one year in a five-month period; students remain there until they can read at the sixth grade level—the average stay is about eight months—and are then encouraged to enroll in a regular high school. "The parents originally thought this was a dumping ground," said David Helberg, the principal. "But they learned that some of these kids progressed the equivalent of two or three years time." Helberg and his staff are operating on a ratio of fifteen to one, counting all professional employees, and with an average classroom size of twenty students. They have been able to attract some outstanding teachers, who work with a strange and varied collection of materials—including McGuffey Readers—and they have somehow created the atmosphere of a decent high school, rather than that of a prison or a nursery. "They're treated like high school kids," Helberg said, "and most of them call it a high school. But you have to be honest with them—tell them where they stand. There's no point in going through the business of the robins and the wrens" (the local terms for different elementary school reading levels).

The key to Helberg's success is a work and vocational training program which enables students to learn tailoring alterations (several now have regular employment in coin-operated dry cleaning establishments), millinery work, cafeteria and restaurant salad work, simple maintenance jobs and a number of other semi-skilled trades. The school helps them find part-time jobs, arranging their schedules so that they can work on the outside while continuing their studies at the school. Its full-time employment coordinator travels all over the city to speak to businessmen, arranging for student placement, encouraging cautious bosses to take a chance with a kid, or to take another chance, or even to take a third chance. No one assumes that this training or the jobs are the beginning of a lifelong career in that particular trade (many are already marginal), but they are the start of motivation, and the beginning of a perception that those middle-class values and the education they demand make some sense after all. "The important thing about these kids is that they didn't drop out, even though some of them flunked their reading tests," Helberg said. "We group them according to their physical size and their academic level, and we give them the incentive to do something. It's amazing. Their attitudes and their appearance change; the patent process haircuts and the brush cuts seem to go. I wish we could take their pictures before and after. We even get to the point where we get some homework out of them." Helberg and most of his teachers believe that their students can learn, and they seem to act on this belief. Some of the teachers are moralists, falling back on the Horatio Alger maxims of the nineteenth century, some are not; but almost all of them operate as if the children mattered, as if the whole enterprise mattered. They have been given smaller classes, assistance from guidance personnel, and a great deal of support from their principal, but their prime strength is simply their attitude: they are not conspiring with their students to defeat the program.

In his report on the work of Harlem Youth Opportunities Unlimited (Haryou), the psychologist Kenneth B. Clark said:

> The tendency on the part of some educators, and others, to lump all children in a racial ghetto as "culturally deprived" and therefore "uneducable" is an insidious form of stereotypic thinking and is a contemporary version of the earlier contentions that Negroes are innately inferior. The educational effects of the arguments for cultural inferiority are the same as the earlier and more primitive assertions of racial inferiority. Both points of view lead to the development and implementation of educational procedures which stunt the ability of the child to learn and result in the self-fulfilling prophecy that he does not learn. If it is assumed that a child cannot learn, and if he is treated as if he cannot learn, he will not learn.

Helberg's school seems to demonstrate the validity of that

contention. And yet no school system, no group of teachers can act as if children from the ghetto were just like children from the suburbs, expecting them at the age of six to be ready for the middle-class oriented primers, for Dick and Jane readers, or even for the social atmosphere of the normal classroom. Someone in Chicago pointed out that "the survival technique in the slums requires a hell of a lot more brilliance than learning to survive in a middle-class home. When a kid from the suburbs loses his lunch money the mother calls up the principal and says 'please loan my child a dollar.' The kids in the ghetto have to know how to survive without those little perquisites." Thus the school must make the middle-class world relevant, it must teach that jobs and hard work, honesty, education, decent manners, and all the rest, have something to do with life as slum kids know it; that the city with its policemen, employers, social workers and bureaucrats is not altogether capricious, and that society is something more than a jungle. It means taking children who have rarely heard a complete English sentence, who sometimes don't even know their full names—having been addressed as "Junior" or "Sis"—and building their vocabularies to the point where the words in a reader or a spelling book or in a teacher's classroom instructions are familiar and correspond to something in the child's experience. It also means working with children who systematically tune things out, who have grown up amid so much noise and shouting, that they have *learned* not to listen. By the time some of them begin kindergarten they are already behind.

"What we're trying to do," said Lloyd J. Mendelson, the principal of the Farren Elementary School, "is to make school important in the lives of the children." Farren faces the Robert Taylor homes, a monstrous cluster of thirty-two high rise buildings which constitutes the world's largest public housing project. All of Farren's 1600 children live in five of those buildings. "There used to be walkups over stores around here," Mendelson said, "and there were some real transient elements. Now we're more stable than we've ever been. Our turnover is only between ten and twenty per cent per year."

Mendelson's mission is to overcome the handicaps of a group of children whose day is spent going down an elevator, crossing State Street, sitting in a classroom for six hours, crossing State

Street again, and going back up the same elevator. Thus he is trying to add what he calls "a lot of visual motivation" and a lot of
extracurricular activities. The school runs cultural enrichment
trips not only for its children—to the ballet, recitals, the sym-
phony—but occasionally for their parents as well. It is trying to
build up rapport with the community (though most of the time
it seems to be telling rather than listening), and it collaborates
closely with workers from various social agencies: Mendelson said
he meets with twenty social workers each month. Farren has
mathematics and science clubs, a school paper, a drama club, an
art fair, a cultural enrichment club, and a great number of other
activities, displays, shows and performances, all of them designed
to compete with the deadening effect of the normal environment
and to involve children in the official and accepted activities of
the school and the culture. In addition Farren has some magnificent teachers—people like Phala Daniel who works with a kind
of modern mathematics, getting children to *discover*, for example, that multiplication is just repetitive addition—and it is expanding its ungraded primary classes, allowing children to progress at their own pace. Its chalkboards and bulletin boards are
covered with drawings, with accounts of "Our Walking Trip" to
the police station, the public library, and to various other points
of interest, and its reading and social studies materials are slowly
being bolstered with books relevant to the city. Although the pupils still have to read about little white houses with little white
children, they are also beginning to get the first copies of a series
of social studies books by a Chicago teacher named Muriel Stanek
called *How People Live in the Big City*, attractively illustrated
volumes about the cultural and economic varieties of the city:

> In this neighborhood there are big houses, little houses, apart-
> ment buildings and factories. Many of the people living in this
> neighborhood work in the factories.
> Some neighborhoods are noisy and dirty.
> Others are quiet and clean.
> Wherever you find a big city, you will find these many dif-
> ferent neighborhoods with their big, small, old and new
> houses . . .

The books still ring with the old textbook tones—saying, in

effect, that everything is just wonderful, and not explaining why some neighborhoods are noisy and dirty while others are quiet and clean—and indicating by their style that whatever is, is right. But these books are still several steps ahead of Spot and Susan, the visit of wonderful old grandma (what normal child wouldn't love grandma?), the trip to the beach and the white father's departure for the office. "Why," said an officer of the Urban League, "can't a Negro ever carry a briefcase?"

And yet, despite its materials, its activities, despite Lloyd Mendelson, Farren has not surmounted the handicaps of the system. It still has anxious teachers who tell their students that "you'll be in trouble if you do pages in the book that you're not asked to do," and who are convinced that only rigid rules will produce a successful classroom. And although Mendelson said that "the policy downtown is to encourage us to play a role in the community" it is perfectly apparent that the role is to be that of preceptor rather than partner, and that parental activities at the school attract only the smallest minority. Mendelson's trips and clubs, his bright building, and his teachers undoubtedly have a major effect. But they are not enough. When the sixth graders leave Farren, they are just about a year behind the national average.

Every articulate critic of Chicago's Negro schools—and of the other schools as well—has his favorite atrocity stories, and everywhere one goes in Chicago there is some evidence to support them. "You ought to see their compositions," said a junior college teacher, "and we get some of the best graduates of these schools.... Du Sable? I don't know anything that's right with the place." The median dropout rate for Negro schools is about double that for the white schools; and the median reading level at sixth grade is approximately eighteen months behind the white average. "Our shops," said the principal of a Negro high school, "are antediluvian. To teach the needle trades we have to use the same kind of sewing machines as the happy housewife, and our typewriters for the business courses are falling apart. Right now we're short ten or twelve teachers; we have some people teaching six or seven periods, and more than half of them are on temporary certificates. What shows up as savings in the budget is achieved with the blood of other people." Dunbar High School, a highly promoted, modern-looking all-Negro vocational school, has a well-justified reputation in many of its courses, but it also offers obsolete training in dressmaking because the teachers have tenure; it has a course in printing but no training in modern offset processes because the necessary equipment, long asked for, has never been provided. It offers no courses whatever in electrical work because "these kids (i.e. Negroes) can't break into the field." Despite such situations most principals are reluctant to complain. Protests about the difficulty of getting substitutes is likely to impede promotion. "This town is full of suitcase principals," someone said. "A principal is considered a failure if he's not moved in three years. So they keep quiet until they're sent somewhere else."

And while some schools are understaffed and others offer irrelevant courses, many piously pretend that their students are learning even though the teachers and the student know that they are not. It was that pretense which was the cause of the Forestville protest; when the parents discovered that they were "all in the same boat," that none of their children were learning; they demanded that their kids *not* be graduated or promoted until they knew how to read and write. "A Negro can graduate from high school with honors around here, and then take remedial reading in junior college," one of them said. "The Negro parents want tougher standards."

The militant Negro organizations—and they do not represent the entire Negro community—have lost no opportunity to remind Willis and the board of the inadequacies. Most of them feel that Willis is a symbol of segregation, and that little progress will be made until he goes. At the same time they never cease reminding the superintendent, the board, and Mayor Richard Daley, who appointed the board, that there are inequities, and that Chicago is losing rather than gaining in the matter of integration. "We used to need a lot of illiterate people in the economy," said Edwin C. Berry, the director of the Chicago Urban League. "They just forgot to change the program when the situation changed." Berry is no flaming radical; he has discouraged as many protests as he has helped organize, but he is under no illusions about the schools. "There's always an administration excuse: the Negroes are primitive, they have no discipline, they steal books, and they always say they come from Mississippi. In some cities there's an attitude of wanting to do something about Negro education; here the attitude is to be primitive. You can't have any progress here because they're never willing to admit that there's anything wrong. Right now, of course, Willis couldn't satisfy the Negro community even if Jesus came down and threw his arms around him." Berry said that he has "never been on record in favor of bussing for bussing sake" but he feels "it's time that they gerrymandered school districts in favor of integration, that we begin to use the under-utilized schools, and that we integrate the teaching staffs." At the same time he wants more compensatory education. "We have to do both—start integrating and provide more compensation. Even if we decreed an open housing market most Negro children would still be going to school in the ghetto." Would integration of culturally deprived children and middle-class white children inevitably lead to resegregation according to ability tracks inside the schools? The answer is no. "The old time teachers did it instinctively. There were smart and slow kids in every class. There are a lot of ways that there can be compensation. You do it with imagination and a little love. The attitude is the most important thing of all. Many white middle-class teachers never can quite make it because the kids can't turn white; the teachers have to be trained to understand what's going on in contemporary urban life. The children can learn a little democracy by example and by the teacher's attitude. Instead they learn arrogance, lying, and apathy."

To many Negro militants, the problem of school segregation is a problem of political power. As far as Berry is concerned the top leadership in business has started to "become enlightened on the race issue," but even he feels that "everything is a matter of wringing concessions from some power structure." Many other Negro leaders agree. "The entrenched forces rarely respond to moral pressure," said the Rev. Arthur C. Brazier, a Pentecostal minister who is deeply involved in a number of South Chicago community organizations. "Persuasion rarely changes minds. You have to have leverage." In his view Negro demonstrations, boycotts and legal action were responsible for the various surveys of the segregation problem and of the school system in general (e.g. the Havighurst and Hauser studies), and for that reason they were useful. But now, he feels, "we have to do more than demonstrate and so we're putting a greater effort into voter registration and voter education. Right now Chicago is a one party city, and we have no place to go. The Republicans can't win. But at some point there's going to be a real challenge. We don't have to win; and if the Republicans put up a strong man we can come close." One of Brazier's targets will be William L. Dawson, the 79-year-old Negro congressman from the First Illinois District who, next to Willis, is a favorite villain of certain Negro leaders. Among his critics Dawson is considered a machine politician interested in perpetuating his hold on his South Chicago fief—the Adam Clayton Powell of Chicago—and is often regarded as a traitor to the cause of civil rights. Despite that hold, Brazier expects "great changes in Negro voting patterns." Negro voting registration is not as high as that of the whites, but it has been growing, and Negro leaders expect that it will grow faster in the years to come.

People like Dawson, Mayor Daley and Willis represent a system of power and control which, many Negroes believe, was designed to frustrate educational and racial progress. They feel that they represent the big real estate interests (which, until a few years ago, kept careful maps of those blocks in which they would allow Negroes to buy or rent), the banks, the Democratic machine, and "the power structure" generally. They feel that Willis is a southern segregationist—he originally came from Baltimore—and that he is an agent of big business, that some South Chicago ward bosses and aldermen have traded the interests of their community for political patronage, and that even politically innocuous projects are frustrated by politicians who control building inspectors, policemen, and welfare distributions. The frustration is typified by the experiences of people like Hattie Williams, the wife of a Negro postal clerk and a leader in the Forestville protest. Mrs. Williams and a number of other Negro women run the Eleanor Roosevelt Oakland Study Center, described by her as "a place where children in the community may do homework, and receive tutoring in reading and math." The Center operates in a little South Chicago store which has no adequate heating system, and only the most minimal electric lights. A grant of a few hundred dollars from the Eleanor Roosevelt Foundation pays the rent. "We asked some of the ministers around here if we could use their churches for the tutoring center," she said, "but most of them turned us down. One was willing to rent us space. But as soon as we moved in the inspectors came around and said the place was unsafe for a school, that they'd have to install a sprinkler system, so we had to move out. There is a tutoring project in the Washington Park Homes (a housing project) but when we tried to get the meeting rooms in one of the high rise projects near here we were turned down. It's all according to who you know. If the Democratic precinct captain wants to have a meeting there he can have it. . . . We told them we weren't affiliated with CORE or SNCC but that didn't make any difference. They just don't like anything that smells of thinking or independence." Mrs. Williams said she was offered help by a student group at the University of Chicago, but "they wanted to stack our board with their people," and since the Negro mothers wanted to help themselves, they went their own way. So the Center moved into the store, paying rent to "a landlord who lives on the North side and won't give us much help. We cleaned the place, painted it, and had electricity installed. The fathers helped us haul all the junk away. But the heat still breaks down." The mothers have collected books ("We have to chain the Dr. Seuss books to the wall") and are now tutoring 120 children three times a week; the center is open every day but can only accommodate 60 children at a time. Twice a week a "Mothers Club" operates a small preschool program. "You can criticize as long as you want," Hattie Williams said, "but unless you do something you won't get very far. We haven't got any money to send our kids to private school so we have to help them, and we have to depend on the public schools. We want our children to learn, and we want to motivate them to learn. But I wish we could find a better place. We've already lost about nine days this winter because the heat broke down."

Not all of Chicago's Negroes share the views of men like Berry and Brazier; people like the Rev. J. H. Jackson, a Baptist minister, and Mrs. Wendell E. Green, an upper middle-class Negro who sits on the school board, are defenders of the administration and of Willis' competence as superintendent. They feel that the schools are being blamed for social evils for which they are not responsible and that great improvements have been made in the past decade. It seems doubtful, furthermore, whether even a size-

able minority of Negroes on the South side and the West side—
the two major ghettos—is interested either in breaking down
the patterns of the neighborhood school, in bussing, or in any
form of militant action to achieve school integration and higher
academic standards. Although Brazier feels that an integrated
school improves automatically—partly because the white children represent hostages for academic ransom—and although
most Negro parents perceive the importance of education, many
are not yet aware of, or interested in, the difference between
good, mediocre and inferior schools. In a sense they not only tolerate but encourage the patronizing attitude of the administration. (Many middle and upper-middle-class Negroes, moreover,
have little interest in the problems of the slums. "They've just
made it themselves," someone said, "and they're the last ones that
want anything to do with the ghetto. It's pretty hard for the white
liberals to be convincing until the well-to-do Negroes become
more active.") Hattie Williams is something of an exception in
the slums; many parents fail to show even the most minimal interest in their children's education. They do not support attendance
regulations, fail to return inquiries from teachers and principals
(sometimes because they are embarrassed by their illiteracy), and,
on occasion, actively conspire with their children to defeat the
efforts of the school. To them the teacher and the principal are
just two more agents of a society that is incomprehensible at best
and actively hostile at its worst. They have learned that good
schools, like good housing and good jobs, are for the white man.

But Negro apathy is just part of the problem. The major ob-
stacles remain downtown at the Board of Education, in the inertia of the powers-that-be, and in the immeasurable but very visible phenomenon known as "white backlash." When a Chicago
school administrator said that "race has nothing to do with teaching and learning. . . . It does not make any difference who sits
next to whom where learning is concerned" he was expressing
not only the official administration position, but was also speaking for a sizeable number of ordinary but frightened white parents who take a dim view of any racial adjustments. In the Bogan
High School area of southwest Chicago parents have picketed to
keep Negroes out of the school, and although they protest that
they are not racial bigots they have also expressed an obsessive

fear that the presence of Negroes will impair the standard of education and ruin the neighborhood. Many of them are middle and lower-middle class wage earners trying to scramble up, earning between $8000 and $10,000 annually; they own their homes, and they are, many of them, Catholics. Although some of them send their children to parochial schools, they are unalterably opposed to school integration at Bogan High and are among Benjamin Willis' strongest supporters in maintaining the principle of the neighborhood school. "We are very happy with Dr. Willis," one of them said. "We believe in the neighborhood school. When these kids come up here from Mississippi they're not ready for our program and so we're all for compensatory education. But we see the troubles other places are having with bussing. We're all for the superintendent." Did she like the education Chicago was providing? "We have one of our two children in parochial school and we like the phonics he's getting there. But we're willing to leave education to the educators."

The resistance of people in the Bogan area is part of a larger pattern of reaction and opposition to the concepts embodied in the Hauser and Havighurst reports and to school integration generally. Highly educated people on the North side who are not threatened by any imminent invasion of Negroes are becoming dissatisfied with the attention now being forced on predominantly Negro schools. "They can't spend all their time and money on this compensatory education," said a PTA officer from a northside Chicago elementary school. "What about us? We're taxpayers." Although such people are aware of the inadequacies of ghetto education, they are equally aware of the shortcomings of their own schools. "We need new buildings up here, too," she said. "When they talk about the slums—you ought to see the building my kids are in. It's one of the oldest schools in the city." Although she expressed nothing but contempt for Willis, feeling that his administration has generally disregarded the wishes of the community, and of parents in particular, she was indirectly reinforcing his position by emphasizing the educational, four-wall, problems of the system and by implying that the schools have more immediate concerns than the amelioration of racial and other social problems.

Nevertheless, pressure on the school board and the superin-

tendent to improve Negro education is likely to increase, whether
or not Willis remains in his job. In Chicago, as in other cities, the
civil rights organizations have pinned their hopes on the educational system, they have called attention to its deficiencies, and
they have begun to enlist the sympathy and support of some influential elements of the white community. "The people who
think like Willis are making a mistake in assessing power," Berry
said. "The old time power is held by a few men who can drink
whiskey at the Union League. But those are not the people who
can vote a bond issue through. That's going to take the people in
the street. And I think the business power structure is beginning
to see the light." In the summer of 1964 Berry succeeded in getting the signatures of 115 leading Chicago businessmen and community leaders on an advertisement stating:

> The time has come for this City . . . fully to recognize the un-
> precedented situation which confronts the public schools and
> to weigh the cost of improving education against the cost of
> not doing so.

So says the Hauser report—and it adds:

> Without the resolution of the problem of school integration
> and without improvement in the quality of education . . . the
> future of the City . . . will be seriously jeopardized.

We subscribe to these views.

The Board of Education stated that it, too, subscribed to the
principles of the report, but the objectives have not been implemented and time is running out.
*We ask all citizens to rise to this challenge. We urge the Board
of Education to get on with the job—and we promise our support.*

Among the signers of the ad were Joseph L. Block, chairman
and chief executive officer of Inland Steel Co., R. S. Engelman,
president of Spiegel, Inc., the mail-order house, Fairfax M. Cone
of Foote, Cone and Belding, Inc., advertising agency (and a
former member of the school board) and many other well-known
Chicagoans from the fields of business, education, and religion.
At the same time there have been strong expressions of concern
and criticism from the city newspapers, and especially from the

Daily News and the *Sun Times,* both of which are blessed with capable education writers, and from the influential Citizens School Committee. All of them asked for action on the various recommendations made by the study reports and for indications of good faith from the board and the superintendent. These recommendations cover more than the problem of Negro education and segregation, but it is with the problem of the ghetto schools that they are usually identified and with which Chicago, like most northern cities, is now most concerned. Until major steps are taken on that issue there will probably not be much progress on any other, for the future of education in the big city has been wedded to the future of education for the Negro. In that sense, at least, improved education and civil rights are a single problem.

III

Every large school system has its outstanding teachers and students, its academic deserts and its cases, and Chicago is no exception. The system, with 20,000 teachers, 500 schools, a junior college, a Teachers College, and a vast array of special services is a little universe in itself. Thus no generalization can be made without exceptions. There are great teachers in the ghetto, there is pedagogical deadwood on the affluent North side, and there are, presumably, students who could get a good education in any school. And yet, if one compares all the schools in the more affluent neighborhoods with all the schools of the slums the differences become immediately apparent. In Chicago they have been so well documented that few people still bother to deny them. All they quarrel about are the reasons and the solutions. To go from Du Sable to some of the white high schools on the North side or from the Negro elementary schools to some of their white counterparts is in some respects like traveling to another country. Here are the classes in honors English and advanced placement mathematics, the college-oriented students, and the stable teaching staffs. Here are the well-dressed, well-pressed kids, talking about the College Boards, the differences between the University of Chicago and Northwestern, or between Swarthmore and Oberlin. Here are teachers like Henrietta Miller and Sadie Engelstein asking relevant and exciting questions in their history classes, demanding inductive reasoning, and leading students to understand

the processes and limitations of their subject; and here, as a matter of common practice, are the assigned readings in modern fiction, the term papers, the open shelves of literature, and the
courses in calculus and analytic geometry. Here good education
usually takes place not despite, but because of, the school and the
environment.

There are differences among the white schools. Some, like
Mather High, are housed in bright new buildings resembling the
suburban schools a little farther out; others, like Senn, occupy
pretentious older structures surrounded by the single and double
family houses that once comprised the city's outer residential
ring. Some have high proportions of well-motivated middle-class
students; others are more mixed, and some are cosmopolitan
blends of students from every country on earth, and from Appalachia and Puerto Rico as well. When Mather was built, Senn lost
many of its Jewish students and some of its academic ambitions,
but it did not lose its outstanding teachers or its desire to maintain its reputation. Senn now has students from some forty foreign
countries—at one time it ran "Americanization classes"—as well
as a number of children from the mountains of Tennessee and
West Virginia and Kentucky, but it still sends 75 per cent of its
graduates to college. "That's not necessarily a good thing," said
Benedict Amar, the principal. "That's a halo effect from our
former student body which was really well motivated. But we
have maintained the same scholastic standards because our reputation persists. Our problem is now to impart the urgency of getting an education on the lower group." Senn has other problems,
too. Some of the students say that they don't get "enough of a
chance to talk about the things that really matter, like morals and
religion," that some of their teachers are dull and superficial—
"we never really get a chance to follow anything through"—and
that the school often rewards the conventional rather than the
original.

In some respects the white schools are wedded to the difficulties of the ghetto—are suffering from agonies that follow the civil
rights problem like a vacuum follows a truck. "It is true," said a
Chicagoan, "that compared to Du Sable Senn is heaven. But it is
also true that compared to the schools of some suburbs Senn itself,
a once great school, is wretched. It is its tragedy, not its glory, that

it still sends seventy per cent of its kids to college when both the community and the school are hanging on by their uppers. It is full of broken windows and teachers who have become broken records, as much a symbol of urban dry-rot as Du Sable if in a different and less dramatic and less contemporary way. It is suffering from the rigor mortis of bureaucracy in a system all of whose energies and most of whose resources are turned to the ghetto. The inability of the city to cope with the ghetto is already wrecking Senn."

Since the white high schools tend to have a relatively low turnover in staff, many teachers have been working with the same materials in the same classroom for many years, and since the system has not encouraged the discussion of controversial issues, academic discourse tends to stay on the safe side. Anthologies of literature are normally restricted to topics of irreproachable purity; sex education is banned, and the use of materials not on the approved list generally discouraged. In one Chicago school, according to the Havighurst report, an English teacher was forbidden by a nervous principal to assign Upton Sinclair's *The Jungle*; in another similar instance the prescribed book was *Exodus*. At the same time the city's relatively cumbersome machinery of curriculum revision makes it difficult for individual teachers to try new courses (there are notable exceptions), to encourage academic irreverence, and to break away from the formal requirements of the syllabus. Although the Curriculum Division is making efforts to get more teachers to summer institutes only a few are qualified to use the new programs in physics, chemistry and biology, and fewer still are really prepared to handle economics, anthropology or sociology. And even when the administration encourages the use of newer methods, as in foreign languages, many teachers continue to rely on their old ways. In a system as large and complicated as Chicago's inertia is as forceful as policy, and anxiety as important as progress.

And yet, despite these problems, the white schools seem to have more similarities than differences, and more in common with each other than with the schools of the ghetto. The Goudy School on the North side has a student population almost as culturally deprived as the ghetto Negroes, but it does not behave like a ghetto school. Winthrop Avenue, where Goudy is located, is lined with rotting automobiles bearing Tennessee and West Virginia plates, and down the street is the local office of the Council for the Southern Mountains. Here are the sons and daughters of mountaineers who have fled to the city, children named Morgan and Campbell and Combs, some of whom started their education in one-room schools and had never used a flush toilet until they got to the big city. And along with the Morgans and the Campbells there are children named Murakami, Nakata and Petrakos —Japanese and Chinese, Greeks, Turks and Hungarians—some of them highly motivated and intelligent, others so new to the city, the language and the country that it is hard to tell what kind of students they will eventually turn out to be. Half the student body is geographically stable; in the other half there is a turnover of 120 per cent each year. Despite these problems Goudy has become an unbelievably exciting enterprise. Under a principal named Helen B. Van Bramer and a staff of happy enthusiasts (including the cook, who manages to organize 120 meals daily in a space the size of a closet) Goudy has established working relationships with the neighborhood settlement houses, with the staff of the Council for the Southern Mountains (which sent some of Goudy's teachers to Berea, Kentucky for special training and a first-hand look at the situations from which the children come) and with other agencies. There are no vacancies on the Goudy staff, and although the building is overcrowded, no one seems in any hurry to transfer into a more comfortable situation. One of the most exciting classrooms in all Chicago is that of Myrna Parker, an attractive brunette who has taught the second grade at Goudy for about seven years. Trained at the National College of Education in Evanston, Myrna Parker is not frightened by questions or intimidated by confusion. She knows that both are an integral part of learning. "This is a progressive classroom," she said. After each period of instruction is finished "we have work periods when I let the kids who have finished their assignments go to various centers of interest in the room to develop and pursue their own projects." But for a visitor to her room such an introduction is hardly necessary. In one corner a little girl is helping a boy with some spelling words; in another a couple of children are shuffling through a pile of books. A few are drawing pictures, and several are completing required lessons in a workbook. On

he wall hangs a sheaf of fairy tales the children have composed
nd illustrated: tales about princes and fairies, about the queen
vho "painted the sun and gave the sun a face" and about everlast-
ng love. One is called *Kim, the Magic Ballerina* and it goes:

> The Magic Ballerina danced and danced, and she danced her
> way to the witch, and she danced into the pot and was never
> seen again, and the witch lived happily ever after.

And there is one about a bear who climbed a tree trying to
atch "6 worms." He fell out "and that was the end of him, and
he 6 worms lived happily ever after together."

Myrna Parker is proud of those stories and of the originality
hat went into them (most teachers wouldn't allow a child to let
he witch survive), and she is proud of the way the children are
aking advantage of the opportunities they have. "Some teachers
n our schools have globes, but they keep the covers on them," she
aid by way of example. "Now what's the point of having a globe
vith a cover on?" And so she runs her classroom. There is a con-
tant murmur during her "work" periods, and sometimes there is
nore than a murmur, but there is no anxiety, and no one is sitting
n his hands waiting until the others have finished the task of the
noment. Pencils are going, the record player is going, the books
re going. "We've developed an honor system and we elect our
wn class officers," Miss Parker said. "I can leave the room tempo-
arily and they'll run things themselves."

There are few teachers at Goudy who conduct progressive
lasses, and when Myrna Parker's children move on they have to
eadjust to more structured situations. But while this second
rade is different from most classes in the school, morale is uni-
ersally high. Children greet the visitor in the hall, and ask where
e's from, the teachers are enthusiastic, and no one is defensive.
The cultural conditions of the children are not regarded as blocks
o successful learning or as mitigating factors in despair. They are
imply taken as given, and education proceeds from there. Goudy
uns a social center two afternoons a week, and it conducts Ameri-
anization classes for the immigrant children. Meanwhile, the
eachers are constantly seeking better ways of doing the job.
We're not afraid to try anything," one of them said. Almost
very one of the fairy tales that Myrna Parker's children make up

in class ends with the hero living happily ever after. At Goudy School that expectation seems to come naturally.

There is good teaching in both white and Negro schools—and bad, too—and there are deprived children of all races. But there remains a basic difference in attitude and expectation among teachers and students that divides the city into two separate systems. The American school was invented for middle-class education; its teachers were trained to teach middle-class children with middle-class materials for a middle-class environment. They have been taught to associate success with decent clothes, bright faces, and clean teeth. They have been told (as in Chicago's primary language arts manual) that:

> The primary child exhibits a keen curiosity about things and situations in his own environment. To satisfy his native curiosity and extend his area of interest, the teacher provides . . . opportunities to relate pleasurable family occasions and to discuss various aspects of school life . . .
>
> Young children of all levels of intellectual abilities exhibit an avid interest in acquiring ever-increasing facility with the language.

Most teachers have never been prepared to handle children who do not fit the "normal" categories. The books they assign and the tests they give describe a world where people go to the family cottage, not one in which they chase rats and dodge bill collectors. Their whole system of values has been conditioned to expect more from whites than blacks, more from cooperative children than from difficult ones, more from conformity than rebellion.

Chicago, like New York and other cities, is now starting to train teachers for downtown classrooms. At the so-called Crane "campus" of Chicago Teachers College (a few rooms in a high school), Dean David H. Heller and a pick-up staff of part-time faculty members are concentrating on the training of teachers for inner-city schools, and especially for those of the West side which, many people feel, are even "tougher" than those of South Chicago. Because of its location in a declining area of Negroes, Poles, Italians, Mexican-Americans and Puerto Ricans, and because "we're on the make" Crane's programs are specifically oriented to the training of teachers for culturally deprived children, slow readers and pupils with other handicaps. There are courses in teaching reading to the disadvantaged, in human relations, and even in the manual sign language for the deaf. Of Crane's 1500 students all but 250 are enrolled in night classes; only a handful are full-time, and most are over thirty years old. There are mailmen and milkmen and truck drivers and housewives, all of them (since Crane offers only the last two years) with the equivalent of a Junior College background. Since the Crane operation is a stepchild of the other Teachers College campuses it has never been given proper facilities, decent quarters or even the recognition that it deserves. Begun with a few students in 1956, it now has close to 300 graduates, of whom 70 per cent are teaching in the inner-city schools (83 per cent are in the Chicago system and only 9 per cent are not teaching at all). "We have our students practice teach in difficult situations, although we try to put them in well-run schools," Heller said. "Since we have no minimum program —they can take as little as two hours a semester—we get all kinds, although most of them are not highly intellectual students. They're just people who want to do something; I've never seen a harder working group."

Heller and his staff have a Peace-Corps kind of enthusiasm about their work and a sympathetic understanding of the neighborhoods and children with which they deal. (Some of the most effective inner-city teaching, as at Cardozo High School in Washington, is being done by Peace Corps veterans.) But Crane has neither the library nor the space nor the materials the enterprise requires, and so this front-line command post is forever on the brink of annihilation for lack of logistical support. And even if the programs at Crane and the other Teachers Colleges are expanded it will be a long time before the city has an adequate corps of people willing to devote their lives to the slum schools. The rewards of the system, the objective facts of deprivation, the social biases of the staff and community, and the racial biases of the culture, and sometimes of individuals, all militate against the ghetto schools. Despite all the new ideas and special programs, education in the slums is still generally regarded as a losing battle, and as a low quality duplicate of education everywhere else. In general, the morale of teachers and administrators reflects that attitude.

IV

Two twenty-eight North La Salle Street, the building that houses the Chicago school administration, sometimes seems like a fortress of defensive people manning the last outpost of good sense. The city's continuing educational battles and the incessant demands of various interest groups have left many of the academic bureaucrats gun-shy and suspicious. "If you're going to quote me," one of the assistant superintendents said, "then we can call this interview off right now." Fiercely loyal to Willis, they feel that they have been unfairly treated by the press, the NAACP, the Urban League and by many other groups, and that a ten-year record of achievement has been ignored by elements who blame the schools for all social ills and who don't know themselves what they really want. They believe, moreover, that Chicago is a victim of discrimination in the allocation of state funds, in the selection of teachers for National Science Foundation Summer Institutes, and in a general failure to understand its major needs and achievements. The school system, they point out, has compiled an impressive record of accomplishment despite unprecedented growth, major shifts in the city's ethnic composition, and limited funds. They speak of new buildings, of the implementation of new courses, of a growing program of in-service training for teachers and of expanding cooperation with professors at the University of Chicago and Northwestern. They believe that they have not received adequate recognition for the work that has been done.

The greatest source of irritation, however, can only be assumed. The schools have suddenly been made responsible for the welfare of the entire city and have been indicted for failures that the whole community shares. Sargent Shriver, America's foremost anti-poverty crusader, was a member and president of the Chicago School Board at a time when the system was at least as inequitable as it is now; but that was in the middle and late fifties when no one had ever heard about de facto segregation, the culturally deprived child, the ghetto, or compensatory education. Now these things have become the central concern of the schools of the large cities. At the same time they are not exclusively the concern of the schools, and school people have not been trained to handle or even recognize them. Until recently, democratic education simply meant providing every child with the same resources no matter what his background, his neighborhood or his ability. Things like motivation were individual matters. A child who didn't want to learn didn't deserve to learn. It wasn't the school's job to reorient his home life and his neighborhood so that he might change his attitude. There have always been juvenile delinquents and teen-age hoods. Suddenly they were called dropouts.

The new social insights associated with the school desegregation decision of 1954 and with men like Kenneth B. Clark, Frank Riessman and Martin Deutsch demand a fundamental transformation of educational philosophy in the large cities. As Havighurst suggested, it will no longer be possible to demarcate education within a four-wall building or a six-hour day. The child's whole life, his family and his home are involved and must be considered. And the neighborhood must be considered because it affects the school and the school affects it. So far, however, no one has developed the institutions or trained the personnel to implement the new philosophy. The job has simply been handed to the teacher, the principal and the superintendent to deal with as best they could.

In Chicago most of them have declined the job, and it is that implied refusal that underlies most of the city's current controversies. People like Willis consider themselves professional educators, not social engineers, and they are unwilling to accept the responsibility for saving the city and ending cultural inequities because they know that they don't know how to do it. At the same time they have been too proud and defensive to admit their failures and ask for help. Willis' response to the demands of the Havighurst report and the civil rights organizations is to ask for more money, to propose the construction of new buildings and to speak of how Chicago is trying to "prepare kids for the rocket age with model-T facilities." But when he is asked, for example, why he doesn't use more volunteers from the community or why he doesn't cooperate more freely with the City Human Relations Commission he indicates by his answers that he doesn't want outsiders interfering with the schools, that the professionals must run things. For him the task is to find more money, get more staff, add new programs. Sometimes he behaves like a wily regent ruling on behalf of an idiot king, treating legitimate questions with an impatient disdain, and apparently enjoying a role that, in the theater, would be called "playing the heavy." Since a majority of the board of education has supported him (or is sufficiently bewildered and frightened not to interfere) no one has ever succeeded in forcing a full discussion of the city's educational problems or in working out a definition of the school's responsibilities in the urban situation. "The schools are a closed enterprise," said a Willis critic. "The people have nothing to say."

Why has Willis been able to stay on through five years of open criticism and controversy? No one has a satisfactory answer. Some people blame Daley for not using his influence as mayor, but he says he wants to keep education out of politics. Others believe that Willis has strong support from the downtown retailers, the realtors, the members of the Association of Commerce and Industry, and the bankers, who earn lucrative interest from the tax-anticipation warrants issued by the schools. Willis has the support of nervous white home owners fearful of the spreading ghetto, and of some white moderates who believe that he has been an effective educator and manager who handled the problems as well as anyone could, and who feel that Negro pressure tactics against the schools are just offensive as intimidation by right-wingers, the American Legion, or any other special interest group.

The board of education is split. A few of its eleven members are openly hostile. Warren H. Bacon, a bright young Negro insurance executive, feels that no progress will be made until Willis leaves, and Raymond W. Pasnick, a labor union official, has publicly urged the superintendent to resign. But the majority of the membership has consistently supported him. Frank M. Whiston, the board president and a big Chicago real estate operator, has been a loyal Willis man, and so has Thomas J. Murray, a Catholic (as in most cities, all ethnic groups must be represented) who spends at least a few moments at each meeting on a little speech of praise for Willis. Mrs. Wendell E. Green, a 76-year-old Negro from the colored upper class, has also been a champion of the administration. (Willis once said that she was the best member that the board has.) The two most recent appointees, James Clement, an attorney, and Mrs. Louis Malis, a housewife with a strong background of PTA work, have not committed themselves, but both have started to ask some pointed questions and have made the going a little more difficult for the administration. Whether their presence and the increasing pressure from the community will have any effect on school policy remains to be seen. Some members of the board already feel that a great deal of progress has been made: "You should have seen this place a year ago," one of them said. "There were boycotters and sit-ins in the halls, and the place was full of policemen. We've started some good programs for deprived children and for the emotionally handicapped and we're moving on other things." At the same time people like Bacon believe that Willis no longer has the kind of support he received in 1963 when he resigned and was asked to return. Clearly the demands of civil rights groups, the study reports and the boycotts have had their effect, although there is little agreement on what the effect has been. When asked about it, one member of the board not committed publicly to either side of the Willis controversy observed that "the board is moved by the community like running water moves a rock." "Too many people around here," a newspaper reporter concluded, "have equated the welfare of Willis with the welfare of the schools. That's our real trouble."

It is not the real trouble. Although Chicago's controversies have focussed on the personality and practices of the superintendent the city's problems are far more complex. Whoever has the job in the next five years will confront decisions that will make the last five seem relatively simple. Chicago's schools face ethnic, financial, political and cultural difficulties of unprecedented magnitude. The tax base has not kept pace with the mounting cost of school support, and increased federal and state financing is not likely to be sufficient in the next few years to close the gap even if it is not controlled by the politicians, as many people fear. At the same time the projected exodus of white families to the suburbs is continuing. Chicago has managed to stabilize a few neighborhoods on an integrated basis, and it has succeeded in establishing some successful middle-income housing projects but it has not arrested what Arthur Brazier called "creeping ghettoism," the almost irresistible spread of all-Negro neighborhoods. There were fewer than 300,000 Negroes in Chicago in 1940; there are now about 1,000,000. Most of them live in the slums.

But the demographic and financial conditions are merely the background of a far more acute problem, or series of problems. There are signs that the controversies over segregation and, indeed, the whole racial situation, are becoming not only more acute but will increasingly be regarded as direct contests for power in the city, and that the middle ground occupied by white liberals and Negro moderates will be narrowed. This seems to be part of the reason why the boycott and the demonstration, which were originally intended as appeals to the conscience of the community, have lost some of their attraction and why Negroes are turning to other techniques. And as the contest for power intensifies and the white exodus continues, the fate of the schools may become increasingly subject to the stresses of the political struggle and ever more alienated from the influence of a dedicated but politically disinterested community leadership. Without the moderation of goodwill such school politics will cripple effective education and ruin all hope for vital community life in the city.

So far, however, Chicago, with its influential Citizens School Committee—which helped rid the schools of corrupt practices in the 'thirties and 'forties—and with an active regional PTA, continues to enjoy the interest and dedication of people with no political stake in the system. Both these groups are now demanding changes along the general lines of the Havighurst report (Havighurst himself is a director of the Citizens Committee) and are asking for signs that the administration is acting in good faith to implement school integration where possible and to upgrade education across the board. If one projects their proposals it becomes apparent that in the next ten years urban education will have to undergo changes so fundamental that it will hardly fit today's definition of the term. Not only are there demands for more compensatory education and auxiliary services, but there will be mounting pressure to convert the school system itself into a new kind of social agency, a sort of localized welfare state involved in neighborhood planning, family counseling, recreation, health and nutrition, and in a full day program of education that serves children of three as well as adults of thirty. The separate elements of that agency are already in operation. The preschool programs of New York and Chicago, the job corps camps established under the federal anti-poverty act, compensatory education, the growing practice in New York of keeping schools open until late in the day so that children can play or study, voluntary tutoring projects, programs of parent education—all these things are already accepted as normal public responsibilities. To bring them together, however, in a planned program linked to a rationalized effort to achieve what Havighurst calls "social urban renewal" involves nothing less than the development of an entirely new kind of institution, a system of schools that comes close to monopolizing the lives of some children and that will require a wholly new attitude from parents and the community. It will demand collaboration between the school and local social agencies—meaning agencies created and operated by the neighborhood, not a group of welfare imperialists who have moved in from the outside; it will require a willingness on the part of professional educators to tolerate the inefficiency and frustration of working with citizen groups, long evening meetings, confusion and ignorance; it will require extra incentives for teachers in difficult schools, a departure from normal budgetary restrictions and from all the usual considerations of good management (so what if they steal a few books; it demonstrates that someone values them). Most important, perhaps, it means that the society must provide the possibility of decent employment, the promise that the community needs and values the services and dedication of all its people. "You either have jobs," said an Urban League official, "or you have the jungle."

The problems facing Chicago are problems confronting all metropolitan areas. They must stem the migration of whites to the suburbs and preserve whatever neighborhood stability they still have, and they must find the money and morale to upgrade an educational system constantly threatened by inadequate facilities, political controversy and collective despair. But the most crucial issue is to define the function of the educational system itself. Shall it be run on the basis of the older four-wall school and according to the precepts of democratic education developed a half century ago? Or must it become an entirely different kind of public institution involved in every facet of the life of the community? There isn't much reason to doubt the inadequacy of a school program that disregards the realities of the life and conditions that surround it. To perpetuate that disregard is not only to cripple education but to destroy all hope for the maintenance and restoration of the downtown city.

It may well be that the schools, burdened by old techniques and attitudes, will never be able to deal with these problems adequately. But American education has shown surprising adaptability in the three centuries since the people of the Bay Colony first instituted public education. The challenge for places like Chicago is to understand that this task is not peripheral but central, that cultural deprivation and Negro education are no longer minority problems, and that their effective solution requires more than auxiliary services and a scattering of "demonstration projects." And the problems don't end at the city limits. The highly regarded suburban school systems of Evanston and Winnetka—or Scarsdale and Bronxville, or Newton and Lexington—are creatures of the fleeing middle class. That middle class still depends on the inner city, earns its living there, uses its highways and subways, attends its concerts and theater, but rarely concerns itself with its education or its other social difficulties. As a consequence the high standards of education on the fringes are gained at the expense of education at the center. The concerned citizens, the PTA leaders, and the teachers move away, leaving the core at the mercy of the politicians and the jealous bureaucrats. But the children who are miseducated downtown will not disappear back into the old ghetto. Just as the last generation learned that it could not ignore *those* neighborhoods, so the present one will learn that it cannot ignore *those* cities. The suburbs and the loop, Westchester County and Harlem are not the separate worlds they once were. Urban violence, waste and ugliness—not to mention ruined lives—can no longer be restricted according to the convenience of a real estate dealer or with the precision of a line on the map. They are no longer subject to containment. Once the core rots the periphery will be hard to maintain.

3

Newton: University Pipeline

THE CITY OF NEWTON, a Boston suburb of 92,000 people, is a loose amalgam of ten postal addresses held together by prestige and an outstanding school system. Education is Newton's central topic of conversation, its basic industry and its most compelling reason for existence. A $30,000 house in neighboring Needham becomes a $36,000 house in Newton where the superintendent of schools earns half again as much as the mayor and where even the Taxpayers Association is reluctant to attack the educational budget.

Depending on the list consulted—and assuming such lists mean something—the Newton school system is either the best, the second best, or one of the top ten in the country. If you ask the seventeen-year old bellboy at the Charter House motel about the schools, he will quote you the most recent educational survey or the latest thinkpiece in *Time*. If you sit at the soda fountain of a drugstore at Newton Corner, the center of one of those postal districts, you will be told, without having asked, that the kid who served your coke has had a tough day in school, and that he will get the results of his College Board tests tomorrow. If you read James B. Conant, you will learn that Newton's schools "are said by many to be representative of the lighthouse schools that point the way to excellence in education."

There are about 18,000 children in the Newton system, a system that includes twenty-five elementary schools, five junior high schools, two comprehensive senior high schools, a technical high school and a junior college. What the junior college lacks in local prestige the rest of the system makes up in spades. Although Newton has a significant working-class minority, it ranks second among Massachusetts cities in the level of education attained by its adult population; it is wealthy, and it has been willing to commit some of its wealth to the great local enterprise. Newton's educational prestige has brought foundation grants which help support new programs and which, in turn, reinforce the prestige which helped secure the grants in the first place. Newton is one of the have-communities in education; here education is a religion, and almost everyone is a true believer.

The circuits of ideas, of attitudes, and of techniques which characterize the Newton system are more likely to originate at Harvard or M.I.T. or Tufts College than they are in the community, or even in the school committee. College professors work with teachers to develop curricula in history and the social sciences; materials such as those produced by the university-oriented Physical Science Study Committee, and the School Mathematics Study Group are being used in Newton classes; the high schools are divided into "houses," "research papers" begin in the seventh grade, paper-back books are on sale in the high school libraries, and academic consultants are brought in by the score to discuss special problems. The association between Newton and the nearby graduate schools of education is of such long standing that no one even bothers to mention it: Newton's first "joint" appointment with Harvard dates back some forty years.

The Harvard atmosphere is not restricted to the formal activities of the faculty. The school committee is generously endowed with eastern college graduates (Harvard, Princeton, Dartmouth, Mount Holyoke) and Charles E. Brown, the superintendent since 1960, an alumnus of Springfield College, holds master's and doctor's degrees from the Harvard School of Education. Even Newton's football teams and football bands are collegiate in the Ivy style. "The Wellesley band comes on in bright uniforms with epaulets and spangles and drum majorettes," said a Newton teacher. "Our kids wear blazers and gray flannels. . . . The Wellesley games are always away because nobody here cheers, and because we don't draw crowds at home. . . . By the time you get to high school in Newton you don't ride a bike, you don't go to school dances, and you don't swim in Crystal Lake, even though it's a fine place." Such attitudes have profound consequences for Newton—in and outside the schools.

Although the university style pervades much of the Newton

system there is no mania for modernity in the glass-wall-electron-ic-circuit sense (though Newton has some of that, too); the word *experiment* is so rarely used that it seems suspect, and decentralization of responsibility curbs the passion of any innovator who wants to reform the school program overnight. But the decentralization also makes it possible for individual teachers, principals, or groups of teachers to try new ideas and to function with a minimum of direction from headquarters. In this sense, also, Newton operates on the university model. Its teachers are faculty members, not "staff." Superintendent Brown, who began his Newton career as a teacher in 1954, said he tries "to create a climate to make improvement possible. We want to be open for ideas from any place, and to create a sense of dissatisfaction about what we're doing." The desire to be "open for ideas" illustrates Newton's passion to be relevant, to be "with it." The school committee does its homework, not only in studying the problems of the Newton system, but in keeping up with the latest critiques of American education and society. Committee members will quote you Conant or Riesman, or sections from *The American Melting Pot* by Daniel Moynihan and Nathan Glazer. A school principal talks about *The Child Centered Society* and *Education and the New America*, and experienced public librarians explain that Tom Swift and the Bobbsey Twins have been removed from the shelves because "nowadays there are better things to read."

Yet experiments and innovations, by whatever name, are still experiments and innovations, and Newton has them. Irving Schwartz, a young social studies teacher, is one of a team of five who are trying out a new tenth-grade course in a subject officially called "World History." The course was drawn with part-time help from Richard M. Douglas, a historian who is chairman of the Humanities Department at M.I.T. and who is—coincidentally—a neighbor of Charles Brown. The subject, in mid-January, is *Growing Up in New Guinea,* by Margaret Mead.

The class is drawn from Curriculum I—students who represent, in general, the upper third of the school (in academic ability), most of them bound for the best college that will admit them. There are about thirty of them—all of them neatly dressed; the girls in skirts and sweaters, wearing stockings and loafers; the boys in sport shirts and slacks or well-pressed khakis

—meeting in a room of the old High School (the second one, Newton South, was built in 1960). The room is decorated with nothing but a 48-star American flag; the white paint is peeling from the walls and radiators, and the blackboard still carries the outline of an earlier—and more conventional—class:

> Sectionalism 1848–56
> 1. Wilmot Proviso
> 2. Election of 1848
> 3. California Gold Rush
> 4. Compromise of 1850
> 5. Election of 1852
> 6. Railroads
> 7. Kansas-Nebraska Act

Schwartz talks fast, standing dead center in front of the room:

Schwartz: Now we're talking about how an anthropologist studies primitive people . . . this person is speculating, she is trying to draw conclusions. The question is how one can use his mind's vision—to draw up a hypothesis which is some kind of truth . . . Now the Manus adult, what's he like? [Several hands are up.]

A. They have a system—trading . . .

Schwartz: He's interested in business transactions . . . anything else?

A. He's interested in companionship.

Schwartz: Is that it?

A. No. They're interested in wealth and status . . .

Schwartz: Wealth and status. . . . All of his social relationships are based on his economic system, on wealth and status. Now how would you describe the adults' personalities? What are they like?

A. Always arguing . . .

A. Motivated by self interest.

Schwartz: Unfriendly, self centered?

A. They have strange attitudes toward marriage. Why should you stay with someone you don't like?

Schwartz: You're insisting that romantic love is an inalienable right. You know, the notion of choosing your own mate is a rather unusual one. . . .

Later in the class, the subject turns to the rearing of children in New Guinea, and comparisons are made with the class' previous conclusions about Navajo Indian culture.

Schwartz: What's the child's mind like? What kind of mentality does he have? [Three hands are up.]

A. They're by nature . . .

Schwartz: By nature—be careful. What's the nature of human nature? You remember we discussed that at great length without any visible consequences.

A. They're primitive. The parents let them run around until they're twelve or thirteen. . . .

Schwartz: They're nasty little rascals.

A. They have limited development. . . .

A. They're very unimaginative—very realistic. . . .

Schwartz: Why are they unimaginative?

A. They take everything as being materialistic.

Schwartz: Yes, they're very practical—but I'm trying to get you to say—what I want you to say . . .

A. They have no contact with older people. They're in a world of their own. They don't care about the outside world. . . .

Schwartz: Yes. There's a discontinuity from childhood to the adult world: Usually, Mead says, the child's imagination imitates the adult world. Because they're cut off from the adult world there's no adult pattern on which to draw. . . . Now remember the Navajo—he begins to learn from the earliest time. . . . How does the Manus child become like his father if childhood is discontinuous with adult life . . . ?

A. He has to pay for his wife; he has to borrow the money from his uncle. . . .

Schwartz: Yes. He becomes submissive . . . he sulks. How does he mature?

A. He has to pay his debt.

Schwartz: He marries for prestige . . . but until he's out of debt he has low status and this sort of shame socializes him. So he has to give up the carefree ways of boyhood. There's no way the characteristics of childhood can be carried on. Society has no use for this. Does he have free will?

A. No, he's sort of stuck . . .

A. I'd cut out . . .

The course Schwartz teaches—a course usually called "the Douglas stuff"—is divided into four units. The first consists of modern literary accounts of father-son relationships: Herbert Gold's story, "The Heart of the Artichoke," James Baldwin's narrative of his father in "Notes of a Native Son," George Orwell's essay about his days in boarding school, "Such, Such Were the Joys..." and several others. From this unit the students move on to a study of primitive cultures—the Navajos and the people of New Guinea—then to early cities of Mesopotamia, and finally to the beginnings of Western civilization as far as the Middle Ages. Their main concern is with tradition—and change—with the things that hold a society together, and with the developments which accumulate to become history.

The materials are mimeographed—often by teachers' wives —but they also include paper-back books, reprints from journals and newspaper articles. There is no text: the key to the course is a mimeographed introduction issued to each student in September:

> In what ways do you live in the same world today that you lived in yesterday? Why can you assume that you'll find it familiar tomorrow, after losing sight and touch with the world in sleep? To the astronomer and the geologist the passage of an average day makes little difference, despite the fact that the universe is older or that the earth itself—like its animal and vegetable cover—is never identical now to what it was yesterday. All these things have changed a little. They are older. Yet the basic structure persists. Strictly speaking, we know we cannot enter the same woods twice, or step again into the same river. In what ways then do we or don't we return to the same world in the morning that we left in sleep the night before? How are we also to explain whatever it is that holds a society together from one day to the next? "Custom" is one common-sense answer, like "habit," "law," "institutions," or "tradition." But what kind of words are these? What do these sounds stand for? Can you touch a tradition, or measure it? Even though your mood may change from bright to dark between Monday and Tuesday, you will still drive on the right, comb your hair, exchange green paper for goods, and expect the routine of home, city, and school to be repeated from one day to the next. We share these expectations, and read the papers for a record of yesterday's

exceptions to the rule—for "news" of breaks in the routine. But you don't get into the papers by getting to your first class on time or for combing your hair.

To put it in its simplest terms, then, the original question asks about both continuity and change—about what keeps a given human society intact, and about what it is that necessitates, permits or requires changes inside those patterns of consistency. Tolerance for change is itself a great curiosity. In America women's fashions are deliberately changed from season to season, from year to year. But in Puritan New England, traditional Japan, and most of the Middle East such practices would be unthinkable or unallowed. To the more reflective mind, very little is gained by explaining consistencies like these by one-word proclamations such as "habit" or "custom." These words merely beg questions about what the terms stand for, or how social habit is established, and why the patterns of customs vary so vastly from one society to the next, just as they beg questions about why the fabric of custom and habit can be steadily transformed through time to make history. Moreover, such words fail to explain such phenomena as revolution. Nor do they explain why, although the U.S. and U.S.S.R. share an almost identical technology, our ideas about its management and ownership can be so immensely different from theirs. . . .

For all the great historians, history is more than a record of the thoughts and deeds of the dead. It is a form of understanding, a way of seeing and knowing which goes beyond the isolation and narrow vision of those who live only in one corner of their own moment in time, like a child in his sandbox.

In many ways this course will be new and unfamiliar to you. For a while some of you will even wonder why it was ever called a history course at all, because for one thing it starts in present time and moves backward before it begins (though not until January) to proceed chronologically. Furthermore, it starts with short stories and parts of novels, completely disregarding war and politics and the usual subject matter of history. It starts with what might loosely be called the world of fathers and sons as reconstructed in imaginative literature, with the remembered response of adolescents to the structure of custom, habit, and tradition as the young discover it, in amusement or anger, through their own confrontation with the adult world. One index of historical change is the degree of difference between the old and the young in a given society. Literature can often be read as a measure of such differences. It will be up to you to determine how much history you can find in the literature of your assignments for the opening weeks of this course, where you will read not about civilizations but rather about individuals. And among other things you will be asked what you recognize in their lives, language, and point of view, and how you account for the variety of interpretation which you will meet.

The second part of the course makes an abrupt and sudden departure both from contemporary fiction and the relatively familiar setting of America and Europe in recent times. In the second unit you will turn to the description of adolescence and early adulthood in so-called pre-literate societies among peoples with the least experience of historical change. The purpose of this change of direction, for one thing, is to provide the advantage of contrast and comparison between your own culture, where the pace of change and innovation is intense and rapid, and cultures in which roughly the same technology, values, and customs have prevailed almost undisturbed for generations. . . . How are we to account for simplicity and small scale in the so-called "backward" or pre-literate societies? There has been no significant physiological change in the human species for 100,000 years. Why then the immense variety of cultures and societies maintained by members of the same species? Why can we casually say that Spaniards and Scots are "different"?

On the other hand, in even the simplest society we can identify elements of organization seemingly common to all human societies. Even in those remaining pockets of greatest cultural isolation we can identify a form of law and government, of custom and authority, of economic production and distribution, just as we can recognize a social system and a sacred system accounting for natural phenomena and human experience outside of human control. So too can we find shared agreements and values, which give a society its form and identity. Preliterate "cultures"—we will later try to define the word more rigorously—can be profitably studied to draw our own society into greater relief and perspective, and in order to refine our questions about the nature of human institutions and of historical change. You will be expected to look for evidence both of what seems to be universal in all human societies, and of those features which seem to be unique to any individual society. You may find that uniformity will appear at one moment, and uniqueness at another.

In the third part of the course we will move back to the earliest beginnings of civilization and thus to the earliest evidence of the city in the river valleys of the Ancient Near East. The city was an extraordinary human invention and actually a very recent one. If you were to place a dime on top of the Prudential Tower, the height of the building would still be too little to represent the duration of man's presence on earth, and the thickness of the coin too great to represent the brevity of time since the first cities appeared. And since the invention of writing came slightly after the invention of the earliest cities, our knowledge of the past derived from written accounts remains only a slight fragment of the human record. Although we will try to determine something about the origins of ancient cities some six or seven thousand years ago, we will be largely concerned in this unit with the variety of their structures and organization in Assyria, Egypt, Greece, and Rome. Before turning to more complex questions about historical change, we shall try to learn something about the traditions which held the ancient cities together, investigating their form and structure without going to the next step, which would be to examine their evolution, development, and decline.

Then, in mid-winter, we will start the fourth unit of this course and begin to look for the origins and formation of our own historical antecedents in Europe at the end of the Roman Empire. The balance of your study this year will be concerned with the formation of those institutions and ideas which are distinctly Western and European, and with the developing shape of Western society until the time of Columbus, Leonardo da Vinci and Martin Luther.

By the middle of the year you ought to be far more skillful in knowing what to look for and in understanding how social traditions function, than if you were suddenly to begin, in September, at the beginning of European history. We will ask you instead to start your explorations of human time with your own moment in the present, with the discovery and interpretation of tradition and traditions in the living world, in order to see something of the diversity of experience to which we have become so accustomed. The examination of pre-literate and ancient societies will confront you with material much less familiar in specific detail, but still recognizable as a different version of things you know. You will have to change your focus without changing the lens. Your vision ought to improve in the process,

your vision not only of things remote in time and space, but of
the environment you live in. Just as the observant traveler re-
turns to his own corner of the world to see it differently and
perhaps more clearly, so can we expect you to become a more
acute and a more knowledgeable observer by increasing the variety of what you study this year.

What strikes the eye in ordinary life are individual human
beings and simple events. What we see on the street are people
and objects. The eye does not directly see such abstractions as
"civilization," "society," "authority." But the mind's vision can
learn to see patterns in the behavior of individuals and the possibility of order in events which to the eye of the child are cha-
otic and disconnected. Your responsibility in this course is to
extend your own inner vision of human action, thought, and
feeling, while you increase your knowledge of history and of
the human record in some of its variety.

The young teachers of the course, and of the courses that will
follow, are academic cliff-hangers; in the middle of the first year
of trial (this was to be the first of a full three-year history program) they were still not exactly sure what they would be doing
with the same students in the eleventh grade. Often they sit up
until after midnight at someone's home discussing what they'll do
next, facing the vast collection of horrors that confront the conscientious in their field. The old certainties by which Western
man glorified his own culture are gone and the textbook has been
scrapped, physically *and* philosophically. George Washington
and the cherry tree are matters of anthropological curiosity, and
the conviction that every day we get better has vanished into an
atomic cloud; yet neither is there breast-beating about the fix
man has gotten himself into, or despair about the relativity of
everything in the universe. "Why the hell study history anyway?"
said one as the fatigue set in about 1 A.M. "To control the myths,"
someone replied, "to keep from being Goldwater." The intent
is to help the students understand where they are, and who they
are, knowing "that the historian must often face himself as the
rankest of amateurs and the least professional member of the
academy. . . . What we hope to get is a sense of the complexity
about the City of Man, together with a growing sense of confidence that it can be known, understood, and admired." The

City of Man—the heaven of a secular Augustine—and the hope
that perhaps it can be understood, echoing, not McGuffey or
Parson Weems or even John Dewey, but Einstein, Heisenberg
and Camus. In an essay called "The Value of Science," Richard
P. Feynman, a theoretical physicist, said:

> What, then, is the meaning of it all? What can we say to dis-
> pel the mystery of existence?
>
> If we take everything into account, not only what the ancients
> knew, but all of what we know today that they didn't know,
> then I think that we must frankly admit that *we do not know*.
>
> But in admitting this, we have probably found the open chan-
> nel.
>
> This is not a new idea; this is the idea of the age of reason.
> This is the philosophy that guided the men who made the de-
> mocracy we live under. The idea that no one really knew how
> to run a government led to the idea that we should arrange a
> system by which new ideas could be developed . . . a trial and
> error system. This method was a result of the fact that science
> was already showing itself to be a successful venture at the end
> of the 18th century. Even then it was clear to socially-minded
> people that the openness of the possibilities was an opportunity,
> and that doubt and discussion were essential to progress into
> the unknown. If we want to solve a problem . . . we must leave
> the door to the unknown ajar.

The Newton teachers are wrestling with substantial problems of belief and technique, and with the matter of finding an
effective means of discussing historical continuity and historical
change. But in doing so they function with certain clear advantages: the enthusiasm of those who feel that, despite the difficulties, they are on to something better than what they did before; a sense of their own command of the profession; and the
understanding that they have the help of professional university
historians and the support of their own school administration.
No interview with these teachers, however brief, leaves much
doubt about their enthusiasm or about their refusal to shut the
doors of perception and to cling to the certainties of an earlier
age. Allen Gartner, another member of the Curriculum I quin-
tet, feels that "this is the best thing that ever happened to the
mental health of the teachers. We've had some of the most excit-

ing moments of our lives . . ." But he is also willing to admit, in one of those dreary classrooms, in one of those brilliant sessions, that *he* doesn't have all the answers, but that the door to the unknown is ajar . . . is, indeed wide open, and that the excitement of education is in trying to look through it. What happens when Western culture—as in this morning's *Times*— hits a tribe of Australian aborigines? "What are the effects [as the bell rings] of the introduction of modern technology on primitive cultures? If they buy a western power plant, do they have to buy the jukebox too? Is it a package?"

Wayne Altree, the chairman of the Social Studies Department, is the presiding officer of change in his precinct. He teaches only one course, enjoys the confidence of Brown and of the department, and runs from school to school, and sometimes from college to college, hustling ideas and teachers, running meetings, and delivering the stacks of mimeographed readings, assignment sheets and instructions for his teachers. He pays the price of indulging ideas with his willingness to be a truck driver and delivery man on the side. "You know, this is all sort of shambling," Altree said. "Of course Red Wing shambles too [Red Wing is Altree's name for the typical high school]. The problem is how to get airborne so the teachers don't want to leave after every class and go down and smoke in the basement. The big difference here is that there is a vested interest in intellectual excellence. The department chairmen have enough power and independence to resist the administrators; the chairmen aren't transfixed with classroom work, and they have almost sole authority to hire teachers."

Despite their free-wheeling approach, their stacks of mimeographed materials, their reprints from *Scientific American* and their anthropologists (one mother complained about the word *penis* in a book), Altree and his teachers have succeeded in getting parents and the community to accept the new techniques. There are few complaints about the shambling and the abandonment of the conventional surveys—at least on the high school level. "The parents ask for extra copies of the materials," said one of the teachers. "I don't know whether they understand it; we had a meeting about it earlier in the year and they were all excited about it. Now and then somebody asks why we don't give the kids the conventional stuff—one damn thing after another with all the names and dates—but not often."

"People here love the schools," Altree explained. "It's the thing to do in Newton. It's really a love-hate relationship. Education is the universal solvent. Sometimes I think it's a pathological occupation—but there is also a genuine regard for education. They leave us alone." The hate side of the relationship is rarely expressed, but since the schools are powerful in influencing the careers of the children, many teachers assume that the hate exists. "Everybody is very nice to me," said one, "but I'm sure they feel that there's some kind of conspiracy here against their child."

The real hero of the social studies in Newton—in the grade schools and the high schools—is culture. If you walk from classroom to classroom at the Underwood (elementary) School, for example, you will move from Mexico to the Eskimo country to Africa. In David Martin's sixth-grade class, among the bottles and beakers for simple chemical experiments, are the displays:

AFRICA—BURGEONING INDEPENDENCE
African Vocabulary

Bantu	Katanga
Veldt	Tshombe
Congo	Apartheid
Adoula	

DIVERSE PEOPLES—CONFLICTING RELIGIONS

In the same school, in the first-grade room of Mrs. Carmella Nadeau, a brilliant teacher, stands a young lady who works for Educational Services, Inc., the organization which administers the "new" physics course (PSSC) and which now has a million dollars from the Ford Foundation to produce new grade and secondary school social studies materials. The young lady is observing, and getting familiar with the kids; soon they will be trying out anthropologically-oriented materials, working with the simple tools of primitive cultures in an effort to get—literally—the feel of prehistoric man.

On Chestnut Street, in an old red brick building, Wilson Colvin, the coordinator of junior high school education, is trying to stimulate curricular changes covering the first nine years. A committee of teachers and university professors has produced a manual of close to one hundred pages outlining a new program which is oriented to the study of cultural and historical "regions," but acceptance in the classroom is slow. Each primary school principal is virtually autonomous, and each runs his school in a different way. The people at the Division of Instruction on Chestnut Street—a place sometimes called the Nut Hut —have problems that Altree doesn't face. Altree already represents the teachers in his department; the Nut Hut represents no one. Its inhabitants must negotiate every change they make with the principals and teachers affected. "Just think of the poor female who majored in Phys. Ed. at Simmons," a teacher said. "The science people are telling her to get into the new math, the principal is on her back, and the guys at the Nut Hut want her to turn the social studies upside down." There is something unreal about the Nut Hut, the calm of a world that is being passed by. Nevertheless, Colvin continues to press his program. "We've had orientation meetings with the teachers; we're trying to involve them on an individual basis. We want to expose children to cultures with social problems so different from theirs that the problems jump right out. We have three master teachers working on social studies materials to implement the manual; and we've gotten the kids to ask better questions than the adults. There is a unit on Peru where we try to examine how words change their meanings as new cultures invade the old. The kids seem to understand faster than the adults." Colvin explained that so far integration—horizontally between disciplines, and vertically between the lower and the high schools—has not progressed very far: there is too much decentralization and diffusion of responsibility. Yet there is a remarkable similarity between Colvin's epistemology and Altree's and Douglas'. Among the basic premises of Colvin's manual is "an increasing regard for teaching the basic concepts and structures of the learned disciplines other than history, cultural anthropology in particular." The theme of Colvin's manual is culture and society; it is committed to "confidence in the capacity of the human intellect to comprehend change, to direct man's actions toward purposes, and to control his emotive tendencies in pursuit of rational ends . . . the societal problems man creates are amenable to human remedies." This social optimism is stressed wherever possible: the introduction of "controversial issues at an early age is a merit, not a defect; with only the provision that the controversial issues be handled so that they integrate rather than disintegrate the child's personality."

Colvin acknowledges that there have been protests from parents—indicating that here at least Altree's professionals fare better than the hypothetical kid from Simmons. "They'll accept the new math from a teacher because the parents haven't had it," Colvin said, "and they'll accept new things in science, but there are problems in English and social studies. They want a chronological study; they want American history to be taught the way they were taught it. You know, Americans are not deterministic about the future but we are about the past." The principal of one of the schools trying the Nut Hut material wrote that "I still find many parents and teachers concerned about children getting any chronological idea of how our civilization developed. Is it the best we can say that children will get it in a full 13-year program with many connecting links?" Colvin, who is worried about this himself, agrees that children should know some dates, and have some idea of how long it was from one to the next, and that they should have a body of general information. "But I can't see myself saying 'this is it, this is the information they should have,' and neither can anyone else. And if the pupils say that George Washington was a great man, they should know why."

Although there is little formal connection between Colvin's project and the various programs that Altree directs (to say nothing of the anthropological material that Educational Services, Inc. has introduced), all appear to be influenced by the same currents, and all have a similar quality.

While Red Wing worships at the temple of science and tips its hat to the platitudes of "understanding others" (funny, aren't they?) Newton has absorbed some of science's more obvious philosophical lessons and has learned that understanding others means very little until it has to do with an understanding of ourselves. In Newton, everyone has been hearing that kind of message.

II

As in most middle and upper-middle-class suburbs, the passion for education in Newton is fired by a good deal of parental ambition, especially regarding admission to the eastern colleges. But it is also tempered by other characteristics, characteristics that can be ascribed only to tradition, to a sense of something that does not exist in some of the newer neighborhoods. In Newton old-line Yankees like the wool merchants who used to live on West Newton Hill (sometimes called Pill Hill for the Boston physicians who later resided there) have supported a sound system of public education for over a century. Horace Mann moved his normal school there in 1848, and even before World War I Newton had established its first formal relationship with Harvard. No one in Newton can remember when local residents made it a general practice to send their children to boarding school (in 1964 about 250 kids of a school population of 20,000 attended prep schools, though many others are in parochial institutions). The city's major achievement, however, has come in the collaboration on educational matters of old Yankees and the thousands of recent middle-class Jewish arrivals, most of them from the city or the other Boston suburbs. Many of Newton's private clubs are closed to Jews, but the partnership in running and supporting the school system is firm. Jews now represent a growing third of the city's population, and they dominate some of its neighborhoods. The new Newton South High School is about seventy per cent Jewish, though local mythology sets the proportion even higher, and it is sometimes referred to as the Jewish High School. Of the remaining two-thirds of the community, about half are Protestants, half are Catholics, some of them working class Irish and Italians who once labored in the mills of Newton Upper Falls, where they still live. One local resident says you can divide the city between the Railroad Settlements (along the two lines of the Boston and Albany—the old resident commuters); the River Settlements (along the Charles where immigrant labor came to the textile mills) and the Prairie Dwellers (new suburbanites living in split-level houses—many of them Jewish). This description is oversimplified but it indicates that Newton is not simply a post World War II bedroom for undifferentiated middle-class families. The old traditions survive, and the new Jews with their historical commitment to learning have helped reinforce them, going into a tacit educational partnership with the Protestants. Since there are few Jews in the managerial hierarchy of the big corporations—which tend to move their personnel from place to place (the Jews in Newton are primarily professionals and small businessmen)—those that have moved to Newton usually stay to develop a stake in the community. Today three of the eight school committeemen are Jewish. One is a Catholic, and one, the most recently elected, is a Chinese.

Despite biennial elections, the Newton School Committee is a self-perpetuating organization. Incumbents do not lose elections and it is hard to find anyone who was ever elected against the wishes of the committee majority. "Newton may be the only place in New England," someone said, "where the sons of bitches always lose." School politics in Newton are clean and closed. They run on a model elaborated by Edmund Burke in the eighteenth century, a combination of *noblesse oblige,* high principles and something that can only be described as Class. This is not to say that the elections are not open to all comers—fifty signatures will put anyone on the ballot—or that the committee represents a tight local oligarchy. But the unpaid tasks of the committee do not attract many ambitious politicians, public campaigns are expensive, and the voters are happy. (Even if they were not, it would be comparatively difficult to mount an effective campaign against the existing establishment because Newton with its several neighborhoods and shopping areas has no daily newspaper of its own and no single downtown center, no drugstore or central square where gossip or opposition can be concentrated.) "The day the kids stop getting into college," a school administrator said, "that's the day when trouble will begin. In the meantime, everybody's for the schools." To be against the schools in Newton is like being against motherhood. The schools are to Newton what Du Pont is to Wilmington, Boeing to Seattle or government to Washington. What's good for the company is good for the town, and thus the school committee survives and thrives. Irene Thresher, a former member of the committee who later served in the state legislature, explained that when a school committee vacancy occurs "we go out and get a good man to run and we clear the way for him politically. Sometimes they call it a machine, but that's hardly correct. Good candidates are just not likely to run on their own." Usually the process of "nominating" a candidate takes place in the ward where the vacancy occurs (each member, though elected at-large, nominally represents one of the eight wards); the ward aldermen, church leaders, the retiring school committeeman and others are brought in. When their decision is made, they seek support throughout the city, usually with gratifying results. Rarely has such a nominee lost an election. "It's simple," a committee member said. "If you do nothing, then you'll probably get a boob." The elections proper are non-partisan, polite and free from the harsher elements of normal politics. In 1963, with several positions contested, not one candidate was openly critical of the committee, of the superintendent, or of the schools. Their campaign statements were circumscribed to the point of blandness, limiting voters who had no personal information to a choice between incumbents and challengers. The only unusual candidate, Donald A. Waite, a Baptist preacher who works for the John Birch Society, ran on a platform favoring the restoration of Bible reading in the schools. He was trounced by Francis P. Frazier, the incumbent Catholic.

The *quid-pro-quo* for the closed system is the committee's self-restraint. Committee members simply do not interfere with the school administration. "The Committee chooses a good superintendent, pays him a good salary and expects him to do his job," Mrs. Thresher said. "In Newton you don't call up the personnel department to say they have to hire so-and-so." Yet the committee is not an absentee board of directors. Although Massachusetts law gives school boards fiscal autonomy, the budget is kept conscientiously tight, making Newton's annual per-pupil expenditures—about $500—lower than those of many other suburban communities. The committee rarely splits on major issues, it never engages in public controversy, and it has no internal cliques or dissidents. It suggests, discusses and questions, and it keeps itself informed, but it lets Brown and his staff make the decisions. Haskell C. Freedman, the Harvard-educated Boston lawyer who heads the committee, describes this function: "The Newton Committee has never been a springboard for political office; it's just not done. If a member has a daughter who wants a job, she goes to teach in some other system. Some school superintendents in this country couldn't be head of the bookkeeping department and most communities get what they pay for. There are places where, as soon as they hire a teacher, a member of the school committee comes around to sell her insurance. That just couldn't happen here. We try to hire a good superintendent and let him do his job." Freedman, who was the committee's only Jewish member when he was elected in 1950, was first asked to run by an outgoing chairman who suggested that the "new people" ought to be represented. Freedman accepted because "we all have a commitment to democracy. My parents were immigrants and I know what this country means. In America everything depends on the public schools." And in Newton, he might have added, *noblesse oblige* and social responsibility are not the exclusive possessions of old-line patricians.

Yet the presence of the growing Jewish element is a source of concern, not so much to the old Yankees (some of whom are withdrawing from the city and its community life) but to the Jews themselves. In 1950 Newton had one synagogue; now it has six; one large segment of southern Newton is so solidly Jewish that it is called the Golden Ghetto, and there is a fear that social inbreeding and Jewish status seeking will become so blatant that the successful partnership with the Protestants will deteriorate. The counterman at one of the Newton delicatessen stores will tell you that many of his co-religionists are so deeply mortgaged for their houses on the hill, their Cadillacs and their cashmere sweaters, that they can't afford the difference between real delicatessen and the packaged stuff from the Star Market. And there is the story of a school administrator who received a letter from a new rabbi complaining that the schools ought to be closed on the High Holidays. The administrator replied by politely telling the rabbi to stop acting as if he still represented a minority group. Within the schools themselves, students are conscious of religious lines. At the Newton South High School a girl described her perspective of the social structure: "There are two Jewish crowds," she said, "and one Christian crowd. I guess there aren't enough kids who are not Jewish to make up more than one."

No one is certain about the ultimate consequences of the growth of the Jewish population; some fear that the Protestants will withdraw from the city altogether; others resent what they consider Jewish anti-semitism. Yet one consequence is clear: the school committee is quietly trying to hold the line. Many people feel that "everyone ought to be represented" and that, therefore, no one should be overrepresented. Francis Frazier alone hardly represents the full proportion of Newton Catholics, and no one on the committee comes from the resident working class (though the committee as a whole is supporting efforts to improve the education of their children); yet there is a tacit understanding to hold down the committee's proportion of Jews: Dr. Way Dong Woo, the Chinese-American from Ward 8 who was elected with the public endorsement of several committee members, represents the most solidly Jewish ward in the city.

III

If education is Newton's prime industry, it is also its greatest avocation. "A birthday party around here," someone said, "means a trip to the Science Museum." Wherever one goes, the conversation ultimately turns to education. A local hostess who wanted a change of pace invited the superintendent of schools to a party whose guest list had been purged of parents of Newton school children. Within minutes the conversation had turned to the usual topic.

The passion is evident everywhere. Not an issue of the weekly *Newton Graphic* passes without some story about the schools—the visits of college recruiters are faithfully listed—and of the 44,000 regular borrowers at the Newton public libraries 18,000 are children under 14, a figure that includes virtually every child in town. At the South High School, where the Curriculum I seniors reported a typical load of three to four hours homework nightly, a burden that prevents them from engaging in all but the most minimal extracurricular activities, no one had ever heard the word *grind* used as a pejorative student expression, and no one could think of any synonyms when it was defined.

Everywhere the thrust is up. "These kids," one of the branch librarians said, "are reading in junior high school what I read as a freshman in college." A normal high school course in Curriculum I is the equivalent in sophistication of a freshman college course, if not in the best institutions, then in the average ones. The best-selling paperbacks at Newton school libraries are George Orwell's *1984* and *Animal Farm,* Arthur Miller's *The*

Crucible, Aldous Huxley's *Brave New World* and Lorraine Hansberry's *A Raisin in the Sun.* In the study halls the current "texts" are likely to be Clinton Rossiter's *The American Presidency,* Lewis Mumford's *The City in History,* Sophocles' *Oedipus Rex,* Shakespeare, Aeschylus and Edith Wharton's *Ethan Frome.* Ordinary textbooks are covered with dust jackets which are as likely to say "Cornell," "Boston University" or "Michigan State" as "Newton South High School," although this particular practice seems more common among Curriculum II students, the average group (many of whom also aspire to college), than among those in Curriculum I. The dress in the schools is collegiate, the talk is collegiate. In recent years about seventy per cent have continued their formal education, and so Newton students share the usual middle-class anxieties about college admissions: the school paper lists the names of those accepted and a scoreboard of applications at the old high school keeps everyone informed. (The board, says Richard W. Mechem, the principal, was installed to encourage students to think of places other than the prestigious few in the East.) Students talk about "how kids get pushed by their parents," they can recite the grades of most of their classmates, and they confess that study rules out most weekday frivolity during the school year.

Yet the collegiate flavor in these schools transcends the admission panic, for the two Newton high schools are, in some measure, already like colleges themselves. There is less whoopee here than in almost any other secondary school in the country. Although most school dances are flops, the drama festivals are well attended, and while cheerleaders still enjoy a certain measure of prestige, the marching band is sick. A recent outside evaluation team took note of this situation and recommended that "ways of developing a larger and more effective band be found," a suggestion that says as much about the general culture of American schools as it does about Newton. High school bands have in some sense always represented the carefree days of American adolescence. The change in Newton thus may symbolize something more profound than a local lack of talent and enthusiasm; moreover, the suggestions of the evaluation team seem to reveal a wish about the seriousness of Newton's academic endeavor that is not indicated in other parts of the report. To

Brown this is not a matter of great concern—it is perhaps even a commendation. "The students here," he said, "are more interested in orchestra than in band." (Which may be precisely the problem. At sixteen, should they be?) The tone within the schools, upper and lower, tends to be intellectual, and this intellectuality dominates, and sometimes intimidates, the community. ("We've got a few Rickovers among the parents," said Henry Atkins, an elementary school principal. "They want to know why we don't have more homework and why we don't teach nuclear physics.") There is pressure for college admission, but it is far less shrill than in most suburbs; Newton, in many respects, is already one big campus.

Such an atmosphere usually leaves those not committed to intellectual enterprise outside the dominant culture, and Newton is no exception. Despite the presence of the Technical High School, those who are intellectually or culturally off the college track have few places to go; and since Newton includes not only an upper-middle-class majority whose children are interested in, and often qualified for, academic life, but also a working class (to say nothing of middle-class children with a limited learning ability), there exists a silent, excluded minority. A low-ranking Curriculum II student said he and his friends "don't think the same way as the others," but he lacks a hospitable place that provides sound alternatives to the rest of the local culture. At the age of fifteen he ran away from home; when he was found it was discovered that he had taken with him his ice skates and his school books. He simply had not learned to live any other way, and he wasn't doing well in the only style of life with which he was acquainted. . . . Does he *have* to go to college, as his father says . . . ? "Kids such as this," a teacher said, "go through the schools like a big undigested lump. For many years they were overlooked because they were neither disturbed nor disturbing. No one knows how many there are; my guess is that we have about 600 (15 per cent) in the two high schools." These 600, by and large, reflect the perennial correlation of class, motivation and measured intelligence. Children of working-class families dominate the lower Curriculum II and the Curriculum III courses while Jewish students make up a disproportionate share of Curriculum I. The Advanced Placement program is predominantly Jewish.

John Livingston, an energetic, perceptive history instructor, is trying to deal with some low Curriculum II tenth graders. The entire atmosphere in this room is different from that in the advanced classes. Several of the boys are over age—one is twenty-one years old; there are more signs of physical disability, more torn stockings on the girls, more evidence of decay. The intense faces are missing. Livingston shows them an *Encyclopaedia Britannica* film on the Renaissance; Michelangelo's statue of David appears in a sequence of Florentine art:

Livingston: Anybody know what that is?

A. It's Pope Paul . . .

Livingston: What, without any clothes?

[The film ends and Livingston, in his shirtsleeves, tries to organize a discussion.]

Livingston: What was the Renaissance? [Silence] . . . Well?

A. Civilization changed . . . the music . . .

Livingston: What about the music, what's different about it?

A. It was chant, the old kind . . .

Livingston: Gregorian chant. In Gregorian chant everybody sings together. The music was group music. Chris, if you'd lived in the Middle Ages your father would have been important only as a member of the group, important because he was a member of the saddlers' guild. People who didn't belong were—in the woods . . . with Robin Hood.

[Chris shrugs and smiles.]

Livingston: You remember the pictures of the church doors from the Middle Ages—you remember the saintly characters . . . (they were all alike, the same features, the same faces); Michelangelo didn't do things that way. . . . Now what causes changes like this?

A. There was a group of people who wanted to do something about it. . . .

"I'm living from day to day," Livingston said afterward. "You try to relate everything to their own experience. The thing that interests them most is religion; as kids they picked up a lot at home, and they'll fight if they feel that it's being challenged.

If you tell them that the doctrine of the virgin birth came out of the tenth century they'll fight: 'But the Virgin Mary, she's the mother of God.' . . . I don't know why some of them are in school at all. But there's nothing for them to do outside, so we think up academic leaf-raking projects. At least in here they won't burn up the unemployment statistics."

Livingston's concern for the so-called "terminal student" is not unique, and Newton is beginning to face up to the problems of this "undigestible lump." Although the parents of terminal students rarely make themselves heard—they do not appear at school functions, and they seldom complain—the professional staff has begun, partly on its own initiative, to seek means of engaging the disaffected minority, of trying to make their education more relevant. In the 1963 elections the League of Women Voters asked each candidate whether Newton was doing enough for the student who was not going to college, and although the answers were equivocal the question itself reflected the community's growing awareness of the problem. "In the last few years," said Brown, "we've had more questions about the marginal student than about anything else." Many people in the community feel that the Technical High School, which has about 325 students, is inadequate, and that vocational education is no longer an answer. (Since the Technical High School has entrance requirements, the two regular high schools must enroll the students who did not qualify for admission.) This inadequacy relates to Newton's special situation, that curious orientation in which childhood is regarded almost exclusively as a period of academic instruction. Newton has reversed the traditional order in which teachers and parents were in some sense the natural enemies of children, and in which being a child implied at least some form of good-humored hostility to the activities of the classroom. In Newton, parents, teachers, *and the majority of children* share a commitment to education and what it can do. They have also recognized that a college education is not suitable for everyone, but they do not yet fully understand the problems of those who are excluded. Is limited vocational training adequate preparation for modern life, or is it a device to get kids who are somehow difficult out of the way, where they won't interfere with the rest? Is the terminal student someone who has been sentenced to a life of drudgery, an apprentice tradesman who is capable of nothing better than evening after passive evening watching *Gunsmoke* and *Wagon Train*? Like most people, Newton parents would probably concede that being a terminal student is not the end of existence or a sign of moral inferiority, but few of them have any idea what it might mean on the positive side, and even fewer (in the middle-class majority) can visualize their children without a future in some college.

One of the professional responses to this problem was initiated in 1962 when Mrs. Miriam Goldstein, an English teacher, and Edward Martin, a history teacher, began to collaborate on what is essentially a combined course for terminal students. Both had been impatient with standard approaches—with such courses as "business English"—and both realized that the world had changed sufficiently so that no high school alone could provide adequate vocational preparation. "Some of these kids used to become accountants," Mrs. Goldstein said, "but no longer. What we thought of as vocational education was neither vocational nor education. What these kids need now is *real* education. We have to worry about teaching them to enjoy their leisure creatively, and about giving them a feeling of belonging, to find resources in themselves so they can keep from going berserk. . . . We want to open doors for them—not to lead them toward some middle-class utopia—but to show that we're behind them."

Martin and Mrs. Goldstein began their year of trial by discussing man as a creature of potential, by emphasizing the idea that "in contrast with other animals who always *are*, man can *become* something other than what he is." In a report on the year they said:

> Man's attempt to deal with his environment resulted in his invention of tools, language and myth. We "know" what man was like by applying inductive and deductive reasoning to whatever evidence is available. Modern myth and modern science are further evidence of the interaction between man's potential and his environment. . . . We want to get the student thinking about what it means to be human.

They spent several weeks on a unit devoted to the twin ideas of man as an inventor of tools and an inventor of language,

then began to discuss the relations of man and society, moving
generally from classical times to the modern age, yet never stray-
ing far from the students' own experiences. In one unit they
dealt with the concept of the lady and the gentleman. Using
some of Newton's Ford Foundation funds, they took their students to see *Pygmalion* so they could discuss the relations of
speech characteristics to social acceptability. "We don't try to
make them talk like Dr. Johnson," Mrs. Goldstein said. "We want
to build their confidence in their own dialect. But we also
want to show them that there's a handicap in being limited to
one dialect." Moving from Eliza Doolittle—who, the students
noticed, was more a lady than Higgins was a gentleman—the
students were exposed to medieval tales of chivalry, to accounts
of manorial life and feudal organization generally, and to a discussion of Chaucer's *The Pardoner's Tale* (from which Mrs.
Goldstein read in class). The students were asked whether it was
still possible to think of the lady and gentleman in medieval
terms and—setting off Chaucer against the rules of modern eti-
quette—whether the adolescent narrator of a contemporary short
story is a lady and the boy who keeps her waiting is
a gentleman. The students were taken to museums and shown
films, they read or heard excerpts from a great variety of literature and, after seeing slides of Florence, were taken to visit the
Boston redevelopment projects to see whether this, too, was a
renaissance. Throughout the year the teachers pressed questions
that probed beyond stereotypes, and they shunned drill work.
They spoke about the creation and flood myths of different civilizations to develop the idea that man is a hypothesizer, always
asking questions: why? what would happen if . . . ?

"There's nothing cheap about this," Mrs. Goldstein said.
"There are no short cuts. When we go to plays and films—next
week we're going to see *A Man for All Seasons*—the students get
in free, supported by [Ford] project money. You have to use the
most capable teachers, and Newton is willing to do this. The
people who are teaching in these courses also teach advanced
placement groups, people with rich backgrounds in different
areas; I had three years of college Greek, so I feel confident talking about classical myths and Greek heroes. We try to make the
kids feel that going to school is worth while. Last year we didn't

have one dropout, although we lost three students, all to the college prep course."

Martin and Mrs. Goldstein hope to make their program the core for a full course of study for terminal students involving teachers from other departments—art, mathematics, the languages, even physical education. "I hope," Mrs. Goldstein said, "that when the new high school is built (it is now in the planning stage) that there'll be a greenhouse. Right now the parents of some of our Italian youngsters work in the supermarkets and moonlight as gardeners. I think that should be reversed. I hope we can tie class work in with some real vocational objectives—a lot of the girls are interested in operating beauty shops, and I hope we can do something for boys in getting them interested in such things as the building trades. . . ."

The development of such interests, indeed the whole problem of the terminal student, has become a matter of high priority for Richard W. Mechem, the principal of Newton (old) High School. Outside his office, next to the scoreboard of college applications and the scholarship announcements from the Sloan Foundation, the General Motors Corporation and the National Merit Program, are posters headed: "CONSIDER THESE POSSIBILITIES . . . Service Station Salesman, Pharmacist, Travel Agent, Airline hostess . . ."

Mechem wants to link his high school with on-the-job training programs in the community, he wants to integrate the Technical School with the High School and, most important, he wants to attack what he considers the dishonesty of American society.

The high schools, he said, are expected to support values and practices which society sabotages behind a cover of lip-service. The school prohibits smoking but the world encourages it; the school is supposed to preach democratic equality while the world discriminates. Though he would probably not say it, Mechem has a sense that education is sometimes irrelevant because the school often functions as the community's liar—a fact that soon becomes plain to most students. In this respect, Mechem is a subversive. "Society has its myths," he said, "and it has always been the task of the school to shatter them. Kids are sheltered from reality until they are sixteen, then we have to lower the gate for the first time, to tell them that their opportunities aren't unlimited. The kids know that there are racial distinctions, that there are class differences, that you can't just go see the Mayor of Boston and get a polite hearing; when the teachers pretend the contrary, then the kids think the teachers are squares. . . ."

Right now, Mechem said, the world demands that a boy or girl be either entirely in school or entirely out; to him these are artificial alternatives and he wants to drop them, to make it possible for a student to be part in, part out, to stretch out his education and work at the same time, using whatever educational resources the community can muster. At the same time, he hopes to make the community face its own pretensions, and to re-examine its values. Since Newton is already one big campus, he proposes to use it as a classroom for social improvement and moral instruction, as well as for student development. And Mechem has plans.

In the summer of 1964 twenty terminal students from Newton—which has only a few hundred Negroes—and an equal number from Roxbury, which is predominantly Negro, were offered a pilot course officially called "civic education" and subtitled "what in hell really goes on around here." The course was planned in collaboration with the Lincoln Filene Center at Tufts College ("they have the resources, we've got the kids") to expose the students to each other and to the realities of Boston area politics and Boston sociology. It was about half legwork, half classroom discussion, all of it intended to examine the usual civics-course pieties against a first-hand view of the city in its seamy—as well as its glorious—aspects. Mechem innocently explains that "we're not trying to reshape the world." But if the program can be continued and expanded it will open an entirely new pipeline, connecting the schools with union halls, tenement houses and all of the sociological and economic phenomena that Dick and Jane and the friendly family physician are not. No summer program can reshape the world—many ultimately die from cultural shock—but if this one grows it is likely to make the classroom a place very different from what it is now. The hope, ultimately, is to expand the project to include every terminal student in town.

Mechem's major plan for the future, however, is one that is entitled "Newton High School—1970," a program that anticipates the construction of a new building partly replacing and partly supplementing the three dingy structures which now comprise the old high school. This plan assumes a much more flexible school organization (in this respect Newton is already less calcified than most schools), more student independence, a three-term year (18 weeks in the fall and spring, 8 weeks in the summer), and more ungraded programs. Students over sixteen, who are no longer covered by the Compulsory Education Law will not be subject to attendance regulations or to course requirements; all students will be free to come and go, provided they attend classes, to eat lunch (in a fully-automated cafeteria) whenever they choose, and to use library and open study areas throughout the school. This kind of flexibility will permit some students to work part time while continuing their education at their own pace, eliminating the in-out choice which Mechem finds so artificial; it will also permit far more individual instruction—as well as instruction in large groups—and it will free teachers from administrative and housekeeping chores. Mechem's hope, a hope that many others share, is to bring the schools entirely in phase with the community (and vice versa), to link classroom education with on-the-job vocational training where appropriate, and to integrate the Technical High School with the regular high schools. (With a $430,000 Ford grant awarded late in 1964, Newton is now starting to revise its program of vocational education in order to eliminate the necessity to make students choose the vocational track in the ninth grade and "thus at the age of fourteen to lock themselves into a forty-year working life in one of a limited number of occupations." What Brown plans is a core program in the junior and senior years of high school which will provide a base for specialization in the Junior College, thus tying the two levels together, postponing the choice of trade, and giving every student an educational foundation for later retraining, if necessary.) With such a start Mechem hopes to generate a realistic set of values that the schools and the community can share. This means a strong propaganda attack on the tyranny of white collar values, more support for the Goldsteins and the Martins, and a deferment of the choice between life at a filling station and life in a law firm. Mechem's 1970 is a time when the school and its culture will be relevant to every child in the community.

Such relevance is still a dream, and it will probably remain a dream well after the date has passed. "Our schools," Edgar Z. Friedenberg wrote in *The Vanishing Adolescent,* "are socially heterogeneous, and deeply riven by discontinuities of experience between the staff, the students, and those earlier individuals who wrote the major works and participated in the events with which the curriculum must deal. Between the high school staff and the street corner boy there is no common ground. Between the high school staff and Shakespeare there is not likely to be much common ground either. . . ." Newton provides far more common ground than most but so far it does not extend to many students in the lower tracks. And yet Newton has the advantage of its honesty and its interest. People like Mechem and Martin and Mrs. Goldstein will never get more freedom in a school system than they have where they are; and though they may encounter much of the usual inertia of the comfortable middle class they will probably be spared the community hostility that an assault on comfort usually generates. Newton has already established some genuine common ground between the teacher and the metaphorical Shakespeare: genuine because it usually rests not on the pretentions of semi-educated culture parrots trying to be "class" but on a genuine intellectual—*intellectual,* not status— interest. In this sense Newton is already ahead of the country, and it may be that on this score alone it will gain the respect of some of the boys on the street corner. In turning its interest, as in the summer program, to "what the hell goes on around here," using the realities of lower-class urban life as subject matter, it may gain the respect of others. If it fails to do more, it will not be for lack of effort.

IV

And yet Newton will always be a limited lighthouse. Its brilliance is internal. It can do what most other communities will never be able to do. Its ethnic composition and its educational tradition are so nearly unique so that even if others copy Newton's techniques, and some do, the adaptation, like Cinderella's slipper, will prove to be a bad fit. Newton has discarded techniques that many school teachers have not yet heard of. Where other suburbs listen dutifully and expectantly to the advice of university prophets (waiting, waiting, for the key to college admissions) Newton argues with the professors, takes what it can use, and discards the rest. Newton makes no attempt to have all the latest; while others try desperately to keep up with the Joneses of education—adopting whatever is currently fashionable, and with little attempt at evaluation—Newton competes with nothing except its own sense of inadequacy. Because it is decentralized Newton does not plunge; if anybody wants to team teach, he can, and if someone at the Hamilton School wants to try a new upgraded wrinkle, no one at the Nut Hut or in the superintendent's office will stand in the way. But this freedom applies equally to those who *don't* want to try it. Newton hires, and sometimes steals, the best teachers it can get, some at salaries exceeding $11,000, and then it tries to leave them alone. Its Midas' touch is freedom and self restraint.

This freedom is the blessing of an unusual community. While many suburban schools are intimidated by the ambitions of middle-management parents, transients on their way up at General Electric or I.B.M., Newton's college aspirations are tempered by some genuine respect for educational substance. Newton schools are known for their success in getting students into college but they are also respected locally for the substance that the getting represents. The young executives from Boston, the mobile managers of the split-level culture, few of whom are Jewish, tend to go to Wellesley and Lexington (which also have outstanding schools, but with problems that Newton never had) where their interest in the schools, though genuine, is likely to be transient. Newton is more stable; its population contains a high proportion of professional people and its "businessmen" are usually affiliated with small enterprises, not with national corporations. The people who move there usually move there for good, and if they do not, they behave as if they did. University professors who show no interest in the schools of Boston and Cambridge, and who sent their children to private schools while they lived there, work with Newton teachers in curricular development and talk enthusiastically about public education. In the Back Bay of Boston, in Chelsea and—until recently—in Cambridge, the schools were left in the hands of politicians who operated them like the street department and the water works, while people who, as Irene Thresher said, should have known better were just not willing to run or to fight for the election of others. The people who might take an interest in the schools of Boston move out. "Those who are left," Mrs. Thresher said, "are always the poor." Newton is thus the beneficiary of Boston's mess.

There are some people who hope, with Conant, that Newton will be a model, not only for other suburbs but even for downtown systems like Boston's. They say that the provision of such an example will be part compensation—at least in the guilt ledger—for the cities' loss of talented and interested people. But their hopes carry little conviction because they know—and will tell you—that Newton is unique, and that this unique quality was established at Boston's expense. Newton is populated by those who fled the city, and one cannot imagine a Newton school system without a Boston nearby. That is the dilemma, and Boston pays the price, a price in inferior education, in crowded classrooms, segregated schools and wholesale complacency. If Newton is getting what it wants—and it surely is—then is Boston also getting what *it* wants? There are a few people in Newton, just a few, who might tolerate limited educational planning on a regional basis (a kind of Metropolitan School District used for exchange of ideas and, perhaps, for some joint educational programs) but it is impossible to imagine Charles E. Brown, with all his ability, trying to cope with an undigestible lump so large that it clogs the community, or Haskell Freedman battling the politicians from South Boston who consider school jobs suitable rewards for the faithful. Neither they nor the universities from which they so constantly draw have yet installed ideological pipelines from Harvard to Chelsea, or from M.I.T. to the Irish of South Boston or the Negroes of Roxbury. Merely to state the proposition is enough to indicate the problems. Newton's success in putting its teachers and students in contact with the best thinking in the world is a remarkable achievement, and no one can complain that it wasn't more remarkable by blaming Newton for Boston's failures. But the fact remains that if Newton, at least some of it, is in touch with the historians and anthropologists of the universities, most schools are not, cannot be, and don't want to be. For them, most of wisdom still comes from below, making education no better than a compromise between academic competence and the wishes of Main Street; and sometimes it is far worse—a conscious attempt by Main Street to black out academic competence altogether. That Newton mastered this dilemma is probably its greatest achievement; and if Newton is in any sense a Conant-style lighthouse, it is so because it has hired competent professionals and has let them do their work. Like everyone else, Newton is getting what it wants.

4

The Isolated World of Appalachia

PERRY COUNTY, in eastern Kentucky, exports the best of its coal, its topsoil, and its manpower, and it receives little return for any of them. At night one can hear the engines of the Louisville and Nashville switching cars at the coal tipples, and the unemployed miners coughing on the street corners of the little towns. Where the strip mines have spared the hillsides there are places of incredible natural beauty, places where the folded green slopes wind in and out of the narrow river valleys, one beyond another, to the blue-green horizon. But in the old coal camps, inhabited by the ghosts of a once-hopeful humanity, the view often extends no farther than the abandoned railroad spur, the rusty washing machine on the next porch, and the pile of junk in the bed of the river.

Everything has eroded. The soil, loosened by generations of mismanagement and official disregard, turns the rivers into muddy creeks in the fall, and into raging black and brown torrents during the spring floods; the coal, now dug mechanically, is removed without control and with only the barest return to the public treasury while its waste pollutes the streams and defaces the land; and the men, victims of lung disease, crushed limbs, and beaten spirits, sit about aimlessly, waiting for the next check from "the welfare" or for something to "open up." Of the 35,000 people in Perry County—there were 46,000 in 1950—about seventeen per cent are unemployed, and over 9,000 are the beneficiaries of some kind of relief. The median family income is $2700 (meaning half are getting less); five of every six adult males have not completed high school, while a fourth of them never went beyond the fifth grade. It has been estimated that of the children who began school in 1948, about fifteen per cent graduated in 1960. There is no tradition of craftsmanship in the mountains as there is, for example, in the Alps, and when the mines were mechanized after World War II they left a large industrial, though rural, labor force with no resources and no income other than relief: 140,000 men now dig more coal than 750,000 could produce before the War.

The mountains are high in eastern Kentucky, most of the roads are poor, and little comes in from the outside: no money, no ideas, no hope. Here schools mean jobs for the politically faithful, for the friends and relatives of those who are elected to the school board, and education is a routine to be followed to meet state specifications—and collect state aid. To be a school superintendent like Marie Turner in neighboring Breathitt County is to have access to the largest payroll and, therefore, the greatest power in the county—power in politics, in local business, power even in the state house and in Washington. When President and Mrs. Johnson visited Appalachia in 1964, their hostess in Breathitt County was Mrs. Turner, a woman who, with her husband, has controlled school and county politics for forty years. Schools in Appalachia represent bank deposits, contracts for gas, oil and insurance and, most of all, steady employment. The miners whose children attend the schools are firmly committed to education, for they know what it means in getting jobs, and they want a better life for their children than they have had themselves. But they don't know, and no one has ever told them, that there are two kinds of education, good and bad, and that a diploma from Dilce Combs High School or the M. C. Napier High School is not enough. Their major complaint, if they have one, is that the school board hasn't been fair in passing out the jobs.

About 7000 children attend the Perry County schools—another 1500 go to the schools operated by the small county-seat city of Hazard. Every day they walk to little one- or two-room schools in the blind valleys—the hollows—that run into the hillsides, or they ride, some as far as thirty miles, to the consolidated schools that have been built since World War II. Some of their parents are subsistence farmers and small tradesmen—plumbers, carpenters, truck drivers, shopkeepers; or they are miners, many of them unemployed or partly employed, or they are simply welfare recipients, people so distant from their last full-time job that it cannot be said that they have a trade at all. The kids come from little shacks in the hollows, and from coal towns named in more hopeful days: Glomawr, Happy, Jeff, Vicco (the camp of the Virginia Iron and Coal Company), Blue Diamond. The predominant family names are Combs, Caudill, Napier, Brashear, Cornett, and since this is an area that has been ingrown and inbred for generations, every child has uncles and cousins and aunts all over eastern Kentucky. (Two of the seventeen pages in Hazard's phone directory are filled with listings for people named Combs.) Their relatives occupy seats on the school board, hold teaching positions, drive the school bus, and dish out the food in the lunchroom. Whenever a teacher calls a Combs in class, he must call him by his full name because there will be at least one other Combs in the same room. Like everyone else in the county, the kids are almost all natives of the place where they now live. Few of them have ever been anywhere outside the mountains, and many have never left their own county; they are strangers to department stores, apartment houses, flush toilets, telephones, and to the whole cultural structure that most of America takes for granted. About a fifth of them are living in a home that receives some kind of relief, and some know no other form of income. When a grade school teacher asked her students one day what they wanted to do when they grew up, several answered, "To get on the welfare."

Perry County runs twelve consolidated elementary schools, two dozen one-room grade schools, and four senior high schools. Of the high schools two are located at the extreme ends of the county, serving only a handful of students. The other two, Napier and Dilce Combs, have a combined enrollment of 1500 students. Although both were erected after World War II they look more like factories built in the 1930s. Neither school has a gymnasium or modern laboratory equipment and neither has been affected by any of the recent curricular developments that affect other parts of the country. Almost all their teachers are natives of Kentucky and graduates of its inadequate teachers' colleges, assuming they are college graduates at all, and nearly all are lifelong residents of the mountains. A good many are teaching in the same classrooms they occupied as students not many years before. They earn, on the average, about $3300 a year.

Perhaps most characteristic of these schools and of others in eastern Kentucky is their isolation, physical and ideological, and their irrelevance to much of contemporary life. They have neither modern laboratories nor libraries, except for the most paltry collections of cast-off books. They have large programs of interscholastic basketball but only the most minimal physical education, if any. Their teachers read from textbooks and ask students to parrot back the trite and the insignificant: "Before Rome could be a powerful nation what countries did she have to conquer around her?" [Pages rustle.] "How long did Hannibal fight?" [Pages rustle again.] "How long is the arm of the Statue of Liberty . . . ?" Their programs deal with the trivia of a world their students have never seen and don't understand, with formal (and sometimes necessary) structures—the features of the city manager plan, for example, or the rules of English grammar—and with the economic and social pieties of outdated textbooks. They are concerned with the development of a language that is often far removed from anything that actually exists, either in the experience of the mountain kids or, for that matter, in that of anyone else:

> Our economic system [says a required ninth grade book, *Civics for Americans*] is founded on these four basic principles: free private enterprise, competition, the profit motive, and private property. Businessmen and others must compete against one another in order to earn profits. These profits become their private property. This system is known as *capitalism*. By means of our capitalistic system we have built the most productive economy, bringing Americans the highest standard of living that the world has ever known.

The book says nothing about commodity stamps or aid-to-dependent-children; it does not deal with cultural isolation or the price ignorance pays to technological complexity. It describes things that no longer exist in Kentucky or anywhere else in America, except perhaps in the literature of the chamber of commerce.

Burdened with material like this, the schools of Perry County find themselves trying to act and talk as they think good schools should act and talk, playing a game of academic charades, victims of a formal rhetoric. Some of their teachers are persons of high dedication who watch their students fall farther behind each year, even as they try to remedy the failures of the past. A few are angry and frustrated ("I don't care if you leave the room," says the high school algebra teacher to a student, "as long as you never come back."); they hate their students, and sometimes fear them. But many are aware of their own deficiencies, of the inadequate equipment and the poor books, and some of them frankly confess that they don't know how they can make connections between what the students know, and what they should know.

"In case something goes wrong in the city government," says the civics teacher to his class at Dilce Combs, "people should write letters to the newspapers, to keep the elected officials on their toes."

A student interrupts: "My uncle says if the Democrats don't get in he'll lose his job." [There is some laughter.] The teacher resumes. "The citizen is responsible for the overall running of his community . . ." Then the student breaks in again.

"In Hazard they don't care; if they cared they'd fix it up," he says.

"It's not that bad," says the teacher.

"Well, it looks it. Hazard is just a mess of crumbling buildings."

"You just don't appreciate what we have," says the girl who sits next to him.

"That's because there's nothing to appreciate."

"You have to take into account the economic situation," says the teacher. "There's not much money."

"It all goes to the hifalutin big shots. You know the clothes they sent in after the flood. . . . The people that needed it, I didn't see them get it. They got a little bit so they could take pictures for the newspapers."

Such an exchange is a threat to the formal process of the classroom, and to the pieties of the community which that formal process serves to protect, and so the teacher quickly turns back to the classroom rhetoric, the discussion of the duties of the Good Citizen. He expresses regret to the visitor who asks why he did not take advantage of this rare outburst of civic irreverence. There is so little time, he says, and so much material to cover.

The social and moral issues that come closest to home are rarely discussed. "You'd get tarred and feathered," said an English teacher, "if you expressed an opinion that people don't agree with. It's not that I don't like them: I love these people, but they are narrow minded." So there is no sex education, even though school girls get pregnant each year; evolution is treated as a peripheral theory of questionable significance and the Bible is read aloud, but never as anything fit for discussion. "If I used the Bible as literature I'd have to interpret it," the same English teacher said. "We're encouraged by the school to ask the kids to read but not to discuss it." But such restrictions are rarely, if ever, regarded as serious handicaps, for most of the teachers share the attitudes of the community. "I believe in the Bible myself," said a young science teacher. "I talk about evolution, but I also tell them about Creation."

The irrelevance of the classroom is reflected in the number of students who leave school before they graduate, and in the tremendous efforts teachers and administrators make to keep them in. Paul Colwell, the principal at Napier, sometimes buys reconditioned shoes to bring to students who cannot attend school for lack of footwear; he visits homes to persuade parents to let their children continue in school, and he posts signs around his building emphasizing the value of a high school diploma. And on the second floor of the same dreary school a young and respected English teacher named Sharon Barnett drives her seniors to learn more grammar because "without it they'll never be able to read," and lectures her students about their illusions. "The boys that quit," she said, "they just want to get a job, a car and show off. I ask them: 'visualize yourself in ten years, what kind of a job and home will you have?' I tell them that the drunks on the street also had dreams once . . . These kids here have been protected by the mountains and by their parents, and the world has been shut out. . . . Their backgrounds are so poor; we could do so much more if they had the background. Next semester, after we get through with the grammar we're going to read *Macbeth*."

Although the campaign to keep kids in school has become a kind of national crusade—and nowhere is it more emphatic than in Appalachia, where one community, Whitesburg, Kentucky, has even erected a highway billboard to spread the word—more than half those who complete the eighth grade in Perry and neighboring counties never finish high school. Many of the girls get married, some because they have to. A few of the boys find jobs in the area, some drift north to look for work in Ohio and Indiana, and some do nothing at all. One can sometimes see them on the streets of the little towns, looking as if they knew that nothing important would ever happen to them again.

II

Goldie Bell, who teaches the upper five grades at the Scuddy School, probably has a disproportionate share of poor children. Her school is a two-room frame building located across a muddy creek from the unpaved road which represents the only access into the hollow. Down the road live the unemployed mine families who would qualify for the Scuddy PTA if the school had one.

In the adjacent room another woman teaches the three primary grades but, unlike Goldie Bell, she is waiting for the day when she and her husband, who is a teacher in another school, can move away from Kentucky altogether, following the now-familiar path to Ohio and Indiana. "If you eat your food you'll grow up so you can go to school," she says to the class, and then adds for the visitor, "but not this school. I want my kids to go to the best."

Mrs. Bell is a woman of about fifty who has been teaching for thirty years. If she continues her studies at Morehead College for the next three summers she will get her bachelor's degree, and then, unless she commits some political offense, she will be eligible to teach in one of the consolidated schools, assuming she wants to. In the meantime she must deal with a situation for which there is no formal teacher training. There are thirty-eight kids in the room, ranging in age from nine to fourteen, but some already look like old men and women, with sunken eyes and gray faces. One girl has no shoes, some kids have no socks, and many wear clothes that have been converted from something else: a boy's shirt from an old dress, trousers cut down from a larger size, a pair of boy's shoes two or three sizes too large for the girl who wears them. They sit on a miscellaneous collection of old furniture—desks, chairs and benches, working under four bare bulbs that hang from the ceiling. In the corner stands the coal-burning pot-bellied stove; since it is late September they are not yet using it. There are magazine and calendar pictures on the wall, and much of the blackboard is covered with social studies questions about Daniel Boone and the Kentucky scouts, a remembrance, perhaps, of a more glorious day, but also an ironic reminder of the things that now plague Kentucky. The men of the mountains served civilization, but they were never part of it, and now it has overwhelmed and destroyed them. (More than a century ago Cooper attempted to resolve this conflict in the fiction of Natty Bumppo and Leatherstocking, but he failed. Natty always retreated farther west. Now there is no place left to go.)

"I'm ready to work with the fourth grade now," Mrs. Bell says. There is nothing she can do to still the constant murmur in the room because most of the kids must work alone, the older assisting the younger. A seventh-grader named Mary Jean is helping a girl in the fifth grade with her reading, listening to her as she repeats the words in the book, and helping her with the difficult ones—trying to do it all as quietly as she can.

Goldie Bell continues.

Q. Who is it that's driving the big tractor in your story?
A. Jack.
Q. Why is he driving it?
A. 'Cause it's a man's job.
Q. What's the girl doing?
A. Washing dishes.
Q. They had one of those dishwashers didn't they? Not many of us are lucky enough to have one of those.

She goes to the blackboard and writes on it the words "Hit" and "It."

"I told you," she says to the class, "that *hit* was 'hit the ball'; and that *it* is for 'it is raining outside.' . . . Jack, don't follow with your fingers, you're too old. Watch those fingers and watch that *it*. When you get out of here and go to high school you have got to speak correct English." As Mrs. Bell continues a girl in the back is studying the *New Friends and Neighbors* Reader. The girl has no shoes.

> Jane and Spot were going up the street as fast as they could.
> So were Jack and Jim. [Jane is blond, and wears a blue dress.
> Spot is a cocker spaniel.]
> "Get out of the way," called the boy.
> But just then Jane stopped.
> The boys stopped, too.
> "Look boys," said Jane.
> "See what I have in my pocket."
> "Pennies!" said Jack.
> "What are you going to buy with them? Is it a toy for Spot?

Later in the story all the children go with their parents in the big blue family car to pick up the white and green cabin cruiser.

Goldie Bell is aware of the irrelevance of the readers, and she knows that there is something futile about many of the things she does. She has asked the school officials in Hazard to transfer the eighth graders to one of the high schools in the valley, to lighten the load a little, and to prepare them for high school work, but there was no room for them; she has asked for new supplies, for better books, but they are not available. The paints and crayons in her classroom were raised through the efforts of a local Presbyterian minister; if he had not provided them, the children would have no drawing materials.

Yet Goldie Bell offers no apologies for being in a one-room school or for doing what she does. She knows that, lacking a state certificate, she cannot get a job in a better school, and that even if she could, someone would still have to teach the kids at Scuddy. For although Perry County has closed many of its small schools in the two decades since World War II, about twenty remain, and most of them will continue to function for many years to come. Transportation out of the hollows is difficult, funds are provided grudgingly, and local pride and suspicion of the world outside generate resistance to every plan to "close down the school." The little sense of community that remains in the hollows rests largely on the schools; they are symbols, perhaps misleading ones, that life continues on its normal course—that things haven't changed, and that, for the children at least, better things are in store.

There is a continuity in these schools. At Town Mountain, southwest of Hazard, Mabel R. Jones, a Negro, has been working in the same one-room school for twenty years, teaching eight grades in a cinderblock building that replaces the frame structure in which she herself went to school thirty years before. The school she attended burned to the ground—wherever one goes in the mountains one hears about the time when "the old school burned down." (Here there is a magnificent view from the windows: the valley to the west, now in pastel fall colors of orange and yellow, is just beginning to appear through the rising morning mist.) Mrs. Jones has thirty-two pupils (she once had fifty-nine), most of them Negro, and though the number has declined, the job is still impossible. "If each of them can learn one thing in each subject each day," she said, "I feel that we're doing fine." Like Goldie Bell's program at Scuddy, Mrs. Jones' rests on improvisation, on student self-help, and on a sharing of effort. Her day begins with a prayer and a hymn sung by thirty-one sopranos and an eighth grader whose voice has just changed: "I took Jesus for my saviour, you take him too, hallelujah." Then the class breaks into separate groups; science for the sixth grade; workbooks for the second; United States history for the lone eighth grader, a "thinking game" for the first graders: "I have seven feet and four eyes, what am I?" says a little boy. The other five kids are mystified. "Grasshopper," the boy says. "A grasshopper doesn't have seven legs," says another, "he has six."

There is no tension in the room, only the normal self-help murmur characteristic of the one-room schools. Mrs. Jones is a calm, confident professional, going around from child to child, from grade to grade, trying to meet the most basic teaching problems; describing a camel to a child who has never seen even a picture of one, attempting to explain what a cell is, saying that a capital "B" has two stomachs while a small "b" has just one. She has almost no materials other than the meager collection of workbooks and readers. Her visual aids are cut from old magazines; there is no globe, no library, no encyclopedia. The parents of the middle-class children who attend the consolidated school near Hazard have organized a PTA and manage to raise some funds for library books, but Town Mountain enjoys no such advantage. Its greatest—and only—luxury is Mabel Jones.

Most of the children who attend the one-room schools have been sitting in the same room with the same teacher since they began their formal learning. By the time they finish the eighth grade they will be at least a year behind the kids from the consolidated schools, and so the high schools group them by ability in the freshman year (though not beyond), hoping to remedy in a year the deprivation of a lifetime. When they come out of the hollows they have seen and done almost nothing beyond the most elemental, and unless they have been fortunate enough to attend class with someone like Goldie Bell or Mabel Jones they have probably learned to despise education, for the one-room schools tend to be places of rejection and exile, places to which the system assigns the uncertified and the incompetent, the misfits, the sadists and the political outcasts. If a child attends one of these schools there is no hope of rescue next year, when he moves to another class with another teacher. He will be there until he finishes the eighth grade, if he ever does.

III

The political system that controls education in Perry County operates almost flawlessly to achieve the objectives for which it was designed. It functions to maintain the power of those in office, to keep taxes to an absolute minimum, to provide jobs for the faithful and contracts for local business. It serves to drive out the most ambitious, to keep outsiders away, and to keep the poor and the unfit in their place. It thrives on local suspicion of the outside world, on fear of "agitators" and on the smugness of the county-seat burghers who do well on low interest rates, minimum wages, surplus labor, and a denial that there is such a thing as poverty.

"We Like Hazard," says the sign on Highway 15 just outside the city. Another proclaims "We Like Perry County." And while the sponsor of these signs, the People's Bank—which pays one per cent interest on savings accounts—professes its delight, most of the county does not. The ambitious students want to leave as fast as they can get out—what is there to do here? they ask—while the unemployed shuttle from their rickety porches to the welfare office filling out applications for benefits (if they can write) and waiting for their checks and their food stamps. There is a mixture of fear in the despair, fear of change among those who hold power, fear of reprisal among those who are its victims. From time to time bands of angry, frustrated men attempt to strike back at the system which has destroyed them, falling back on a strain of violence that has been part of mountain life ever since the frontiersmen learned their first lessons from the Indians. "Strikes" are organized by the unemployed to block nonunion miners from entering the pits, bridges are blown up, and trains are derailed. At the Louisville and Nashville depot in Hazard signs are posted offering rewards for the arrest of those who engaged in some recent unauthorized dynamite work at nearby railroad trestles while, downtown, people profess sympathy for the miners' plight but this . . . this is too much! A few hundred unemployed miners have joined the Appalachian Committee for Full Employment, an organization supported by some outside union funds and staffed locally by a group of idealistic but untrained college students. The committee has attacked the schools and the school politicians, the police, the sheriff, the mine companies and the power structure in general, thus feeding local suspicions and local fears (the visitor to Hazard is asked cautiously and incessantly whether he is "one of them"). There is fear of violence, or that one will be told of the conditions on which violence thrives, fear of news from the world outside—always a potential reminder that the mountains are being left behind—and fear of the system itself. There is the former high school teacher, now a clerk in a county office, speaking furtively behind closed doors about his exile to a one-room school forty miles from home after he had been identified with a man who ran against an incumbent school board member. There is Bud Luttrell, the police chief in Hazard, a genial, smiling, honest man, who is worried about the communists moving into Perry County, and convinced that the college students who are trying to help the miners represent the vanguard of a red attack. "They're in every town in the county," he says. "I know what's going on. They indoctrinate our people, then they win a school board election and bring in these (college) kids from Madison, Wisconsin. Next thing, who knows what they'll be teaching. . . . They're indoctrinating our most simple people, trying to stir them up." And there is the weekly *Hazard Herald*, a paper that has reported some of the abuses in local school politics, but which is also fearful about "outside agitators." And there is the Superintendent of Schools, Dennis C. Wooton, who deplores the presence of "those professional troublemakers. They're not good Americans." Wooton, who is considered a good superintendent in Perry County, insists that no teacher has ever been sent up a hollow for a political offense, although he conceded that the most frequent complaints he gets come from people who want lunchroom jobs and positions as bus drivers. "We try to spread the jobs around," he said.

The school board in Perry County, as in other parts of eastern Kentucky, is elected from districts within the county, and each member looks after his own district. Since the area is so inbred, nepotism is inevitable: it would be almost impossible to hire anyone from the county who is not related to somebody on the board, and since the schools almost never hire from outside every board member "has people on whom he can't vote," a formality which has no practical effect on the board's course of action. Wives and children of board members work in the system as teachers, janitors and secretaries; the board buys property from the relatives of its own members, and makes contracts with them. Wooton's son-in-law, Curtiss Spicer, is principal of the new Dennis C. Wooton Elementary School (the school, of course, is named for the superintendent; in Kentucky, said someone "we don't wait till they die") and Wooton's daughter, Spicer's wife, teaches the fifth grade.

Such nepotism inevitably has political consequences, and most of the mountaineers take them for granted. After a recent election a woman wrote the *Herald* wondering "why our new board member doesn't have the same power our former board member had about hiring teachers or school personnel in our district." Teachers, janitors, and other employees get drawn into the campaigns; sometimes superiors solicit funds for election expenses, or pass out literature for distribution, but usually the employees need no such reminders. They know that they have jobs now, and that almost anyone can drive a bus and, if necessary, teach a class. Although Kentucky law gives teachers tenure after three years on the job it does not protect them against re-assignment to another school many miles from home, or against pressure to support the incumbent board. Some years ago efforts were made to pass an educational Hatch Act in Kentucky to pro-hibit teachers and other school employees from participating in school board politics, but they failed, and so teachers remain in the political arena. In 1962, for example, a teacher named Combs was sent from a high school to a hollow after he became identified with a candidate named Combs who was running against an in-cumbent named Combs. In the same campaign two advertise-ments appeared in the *Herald*; the first was signed "Teachers of Dennis C. Wooton Elementary School" (of which Wooton's son-in-law was already principal):

> We, the faculty members of the Dennis Wooton Elementary School . . . feel that the school system is being operated better financially, educationally, cooperatively, morally and spiritual-ly than ever before in the history of the school system. We feel that as long as we do our jobs we'll have nothing to fear [a can-didate had charged intimidation]. We believe Mr. Wooton and his present Board are for education at its best and think that they should stay in the positions they now hold.

The other advertisement, which appeared the following week, was signed "a group of interested teachers" and said:

> We wish to express our opinion that to take a member from the present Board would be unwise at the present time (SINCE PROGRESS IS BEING EXPERIENCED). To do so would most likely dis-rupt our program and certainly slow down our progress.

The advertisement then pointed out that "we have our pro-fession—under the leadership of present administration [*sic!*]—to the place where most of the public respects us and are inclined to believe us . . . we can now once again face businessmen and ask for credit."

Most teachers are not willing to talk about the intimidation, and many who were exiled to one-room schools have quit their jobs to find employment somewhere else. The majority of those who remain are underpaid, undereducated and unrespected, and they have neither the ability nor the interest to propose reforms. Many do not respect themselves, although some have a genuine feeling for the children they teach, and for the plight of the community. Yet their chances of altering the situation, of bringing in new ideas, of getting more money for education, and of eliminating the subtle fear in the community are small. (Wooton, who has been superintendent since 1958, has achieved certain improvements in his schools. Buildings have been repainted, outdoor privies cleaned up, and school grounds improved. The percentage of noncertified teachers has declined, largely through state pressure, and a few new consolidated schools have been erected. But Wooton has not changed the basic structure under which the schools function, nor has he materially affected their standards.)

There is a kind of internal perfection, a logical consistency, in the social and educational structure; it is not dominated by evil men, but by ignorance, poverty and isolation, by feelings of kinship and by a strong sense of place. There are those who thrive on it—merchants who can pay their clerks and counter girls $21 a week; storekeepers who could never compete against the national chains that prosperity would bring; and small dealers in coal and gas and other supplies who survive on friendly contacts rather than competitive prices. But for the most part the system maintains itself through inertia and isolation. People from the outside are almost never hired. A clergyman who has worked in Perry County for some fifteen years said that "they want people who will be docile. Even if an outsider wanted a job here he couldn't get it. They look with suspicion on outsiders. The way to get hired is for someone to go to a board member and say 'poor old so-and-so needs work!' When they're hired that way they'll cooperate. Those that don't get sent up a hollow." The school officials defend the system by saying that "outsiders wouldn't be happy here," implying that someone from the outside might want to change things, or introduce a new idea. (Few would be interested in applying: Perry County's top salary for teachers—after ten years, and with a master's degree—is the state minimum, $4960). But outsiders are not merely a threat to the men who control the schools, they are also resented by the community for taking jobs away from local people. When a high school band director was brought in from another state the school board was immediately on the defensive. No local men were available for this vital job. "Band directors," someone explained, "are scarce as hen's teeth."

There are almost no critics of the school system or of the standards of education. Those who suffer most from them, the children and their parents, are usually not aware of what is happening until it is too late. "The mountaineers are not worried about the schools," Wooton said, "just about getting something into their stomachs." Since most of them have little education themselves they don't know how to judge what their children are getting, even if they were interested enough to care. (The school board itself is handicapped. Most of its members never went beyond the eighth grade, and it is said that one quietly secured a special elementary school certificate from a teacher who taught him many years before so that he could meet state requirements for school board membership.) Although a small number of Perry County high school graduates continue their education—most of them at Cumberland, Eastern Kentucky, and other state colleges—there is a growing, confused resentment against the rising admission standards of the University of Kentucky, which has begun to look like Harvard from Hazard. Many applicants, said a Perry County school principal, are "being frozen out," but neither he nor anyone else in the area has a clear understanding of what the freeze means for the region's schools. Most of the business and professional men of the little towns—some of them U. of K. graduates—remain smugly indifferent; many of them are suppliers to the schools, friends of board members or relatives of school employees; their taxes are low (about $150 on a $15,000 house), and as one of them said, "everybody here is good friends." On Saturday afternoons they listen to broadcasts of the university football games, and proudly proclaim their team's victories, but they miss the more important message: half of the school districts in their region produce mean scores of under 80 on the High School Senior Achievement Test (100 is the national average); nine tenths have scores under 100. But they are not worried. Bud Luttrell, the Hazard police chief, summarized local feeling when he said "I think the schools are doing a fine job. I can't see anything wrong with them."

The small towns in the mountains—Whitesburg, Hazard, Jackson, Hyden, Manchester—are, in their own way, as isolated as the hills and hollows that surround them. They seem to share a refusal to believe that anything is seriously wrong, even though poverty is visible on the main streets, and the State Employment Security Office is usually the busiest place in town. Most of them were centers of the local coal industry, ugly little places jammed into narrow valleys, their unpainted houses clinging to the hill-sides. Some are now trying to attract new business—a small cabinet factory, a wood-processing plant, or a resort hotel for the top of a nearby mountain—and these efforts have generated a certain amount of community concern and collaboration. In Hazard, which has been a leader in this regard, a group of businessmen got together after a devastating flood in 1957 to initiate a program of community planning that yielded some slum clearance and urban renewal, a new sewage treatment plant that eliminated part of the stench of the North Fork of the Kentucky River, a city park, and other improvements, many of them financed with federal funds. (Its little school system is run honestly and provides education that is a notch, though not much more, above that of the county.) But even in Hazard there are people who deny that there is poverty anywhere around them or that Appalachia faces serious problems other than flood control, and who feel that they were libeled by national press descriptions of mountain conditions. Stories are told of people in the county seats who had never heard about chronic unemployment until they saw something about it on the national television networks. (In Whitesburg, a group of church ladies was incensed to learn that some of the clothes they had contributed to a national drive for the poor had been returned to their own county.) Even those who concede that problems exist are reluctant to ask for new taxes because—as usual—"taxes will discourage business from coming in."

The most consistent criticism of the Perry County schools has come from the *Herald* and from the woman who directs its editorial policy, Mrs. W. P. Nolan. Mrs. Nolan, who is the wife of the *Herald*'s publisher, and a young reporter named Gurney Norman have written conscientiously about deals between the school board and the relatives of its members, and about teachers who have been exiled to one-room schools under doubtful circumstances, and they have attacked the narrowness of the board's outlook:

> Perry is the cheapest County in Kentucky when it comes to spending money [said one editorial]. It spends a mere $174 [per child] a year and ranks 120th among 120 counties.

"Somebody should talk about shortchanging the kids," Mrs. Nolan tells the visitor. "If we'd had good education around here fifty years ago we wouldn't be embarrassed now in the state or the nation. We don't need a lot of help. Much of that federal money goes down the drain. We need help on just three things: flood control, highways, and education. If we get that we'll be all right."

But the *Herald* is an isolated voice, and a weak one at that. The paper's attacks are rarely directed at the full structure of power, at the smugness of the local citizens, at the whole network of pettiness that keeps education impoverished. Like most others in the community, Mrs. Nolan is suspicious of "outside agitators" and outside assistance, and there exists a gulf between the paper and those who most need help: miners with no resources, families with too many children, kids without shoes or the money to buy books or lunch. Despite the periodic clothing collections, and the other charitable work that the paper helps sponsor, there remains a crippling shortage of people concerned with the poverty of the old mining camps, with the ugliness and narrowness of the towns, with the continuing plunder of natural resources, with the despair, and with the cycle of economic and educational futility that renews itself in each generation.

IV

The Appalachians have, by now, attracted the attention of a vast collection of national organizations: the Ford Foundation, the churches, the federal government, the television networks. For a while the mountains were so full of cameramen that one motel owner began to specialize in the television trade, running safaris by jeep to places which, he promised, "ain't been worked yet." But long before the press arrived, before the Appalachia Bill or the Economic Opportunity Act or the Manpower Development and Training Act, local and regional organizations worked quietly to improve the lot of the mountaineers and their children. Institutions such as Berea College and little Alice Lloyd College have been providing educational opportunities for kids who have no financial resources. The Council for the Southern Mountains has tried to foster regional planning and development, and the Eastern Kentucky Resource Development Project has been functioning like a broad scale extension service and social welfare agency, teaching handicrafts such as woodcarving, rug weaving, and the art of making furniture; trying to help build a tourist industry and training people to operate it; counseling young men and women, and promoting everything from better schools to the elimination of roadside junkyards. The State of Kentucky has committed increasing resources into the area and has forced schools slowly to upgrade their standards, to hire certified (though not necessarily qualified) teachers—thus making nepotism a little more difficult—and to provide minimum offerings in certain subjects. As a result the mountain counties have consolidated many of their one-room schools (although there are still seven hundred left) and have increased the percentage of teachers who are college graduates. They are also working hard to reduce dropouts and school absences because state aid, which is absolutely essential, depends on average daily attendance; in some mountain counties, and Perry is one of them, *nine-tenths* of the school budget comes from the state.

For the kids in Perry County, the most promising educational program is that offered by the Hazard Area Vocational School, a state supported institution which trains high school juniors and seniors and adults in auto-mechanics, heavy equipment operation, carpentry, practical nursing, television and radio repair and other trades. Students from the two larger high schools are bussed to the vocational school for three hours of training each day; completion of the program is not tantamount to competence in any of the trades offered, but it represents a start. About one hundred Perry County high school students are enrolled in the vocational program each year, and with the added resources and publicity that the federal government has begun to provide, the scope and attractiveness of the program are bound to increase. Walter Prater, the director of the vocational school, believes that every person properly trained in any of the trades he offers will find employment, not necessarily at home, but in Michigan, Indiana, and other midwestern states.

Whether or not he is right—whether today's training is to-morrow's obsolescence—is still a matter of debate. What is certain is that there are few jobs in eastern Kentucky for unskilled workers or semi-skilled workers (and even for skilled workers), that despite the national attention and the local bootstrapping Appalachia is now growing its third welfare generation, and that for many dependency has become a way of life rather than a temporary exception. In this sense almost every skill is obsolete in the mountains, a fact that is clear to many young men and women: "Most of the kids—I mean the good ones—want to leave," says the high school senior. "They know there's not much to do here." And there is the girl who hopes to become a nurse: "If you spend three or four years in training you don't want to come back here. You earn twice as much in Louisville or Lexington—people don't mind if you tell them you want to leave. They don't care. Things around here aren't all peaches and cream."

Appalachia has become an area of declining population. In the past decade Perry County lost nearly one-fourth of its people: the ambitious and the able leave, and sometimes the shiftless and the incompetent leave as well. Every weekend the winding mountain roads are crowded with cars bearing Ohio and Indiana plates carrying people who are coming home for a visit and each week a few more buy an old junker that may or may not make it to the state line, and head north, taking their problems to the cities of the midwest. "That's what the schools should do," a clergyman said, "train them up so away they can go. Let's get the young out, and let the old people die off."

But the young don't all leave and the old don't all die, and what remains is increasingly the "vast paleface reservation" that Harry M. Caudill, the Whitesburg attorney and author of *Night Comes to the Cumberlands,* has described. Caudill is surely the most eloquent spokesman the mountains have produced; he speaks with a mixture of love and anger, with an amusement born of frustration, and with a passion rooted in personal experience.

When the stranded miner had exhausted his unemployment insurance benefits and his savings [Caudill wrote in *The Atlantic*], when he had come to the ragged edge of starvation, was cloaked in bewilderment and frustration, government came to his rescue with the dole. It arranged to give him a bag of cheese, rice, cornmeal, beef, butter and dried milk solids at intervals, and in most instances to send him a small check. Having thus contrived to keep the miner and his family alive, the government lost interest in him. Appropriations were made from time to time for his sustenance, but little thought was given to his spirit, his character, his manhood. He was left to dry-rot in the vast paleface reservation created for his perpetuation in his native hills.

Caudill tells the visitor that "you have to understand the culture if you want to understand education," and he goes on to describe the mountaineer as the most American of Americans, a man who has become an alien in his own country. The mountaineer still displays a residue of his frontier traits, dumping trash into river beds as he once laid waste to the forests of his hillsides, a man who never learned the style of life demanded by the more European, more cosmopolitan civilization which now dominates his nation. At the same time he has become dependent on the dole and on the county and state politicians who dispense it. He wants education for his children but does not know what it is or how to get it, and he is too much at the mercy of those in power to initiate changes, even if he knew what he wanted to achieve. Unlike most of the other poor in America, he generally does not own a television set, rarely sees a newspaper headline and almost never goes to church. People from the hollows are suspicious of the "fancy" town congregations. When they go at all they attend little Freewill Baptist churches in the hollows or on the roadside, riding there in old station wagons marked CHURCH BUS and, as often as not, JESUS IS COMING SOON. Most of them are women; the men, said a Baptist minister, "feel it isn't manly." But even those who go rarely hear anything that might stimulate them to better their economic or cultural outlook because the churches are concerned almost exclusively with the Ten Commandments and the hereafter.

The national poverty program, the federal vocational training measures, the Appalachia Bill and the federal aid-to-education act of 1965 may ultimately have their effect in eastern Kentucky and elsewhere in the mountains. New highways may bring not only tourists but also ideas, and new funds may stimulate educational improvements. And yet, as the county school systems are now constituted, and as the political structure now functions, most of this money may be used simply to strengthen the local machines, to increase dependency, and to keep the local tax rate low. Caudill feels that only a federally administered program of public works will break the hold of the political machines and improve conditions in the mountains: he proposes putting the jobless miners to work reforesting the hills, building consolidated schoolhouses and new roads and decent housing to replace the shacks that litter the hills; he suggests a Southern Mountain power project similar to TVA to produce cheap electricity and control the natural and human devastation of the hills, and an educational Peace Corps "to break the old cycle of poor schools, poor job preparation, poor pay and poor people."

Whether any such projects will be initiated on a sufficiently large scale remains to be decided. But the history of federal and state programs in the mountains and elsewhere suggests that little is ever done against the wishes of the local politicians. If that pattern continues, if the local politicians maintain control, then any program, of whatever magnitude, will probably fail.

It is a long way from Scuddy Hollow to Chicago or Cincinnati, but ignorance and incompetence are not perishable, and they survive the trip. While education is alleged to be a local concern, miseducation crosses state lines without regard for the strictures of constitutional purists. There are schools in Chicago which conduct "urbanization classes" for new arrivals from the southern mountains, hoping to acquaint them with the ways of the city, and almost every metropolis in the northeast can compile a roster of social atrocities committed by people who have never learned what to do with garbage or toilet seats. Even the best graduates of the Appalachian schools can't compete with the average product of the northern cities—to say nothing, of course, about the suburbs. They have never heard a note of good music, seen a play or learned a line of serious poetry. Their highest mathematical achievements are elementary algebra and plane geometry, and their comprehension of science is antediluvian. They have never learned to ask a significant question or distinguish the intellectually relevant from the trivial. Caudill tells of an unemployed miner who saw to it that his son finished high school only to discover that when the boy sought a job with a company in California:

> They said a high school diploma from Kentucky, Arkansas, and Mississippi just showed a man had done about the same as ten years in school in any other state [Caudill quoting the miner in *Night Comes to the Cumberlands*]. But they agreed to give the boy a test to see how much he knowed and he failed it flatter than a flitter. They turned him down and he got a job workin' in a laundry. . . .

> Me and my wife ain't got nothin' and don't know nothin' hardly. We've spent everything we've got to try to learn our young-'uns something so they would have a better chance in the world, and now they don't know nothin' either!

The Perry County schools spend on four children what the suburbs spend on one; the son of a commuter earning $30,000 a year gets his books free, while the children of jobless mountaineers must buy theirs. The urban and suburban schools double their allocations for science equipment with federal funds but Perry County doubles nothing (a senior at Napier High School reported that in his biology course "we got to look through a microscope once or twice"), demonstrating again that the law operates impartially by prohibiting all, rich and poor, from sleeping under the bridge.

Appalachia is the big paleface reservation, with one exception. The Indians—some of them—have the remains of a culture to preserve; they have a language, a religion, a heritage, and thus the white man's education is a risk; but the mountaineer has nothing but his dependency and his isolation. His music comes in canned from New York and Nashville, along with the play-by-play of the Cincinnati Reds. There is little about him that is still original or even quaint. He is often a man with a great deal of dignity and intelligence, far greater than one might expect under the circumstances, and often even his children show a fierce pride, sometimes refusing the free lunch that represents the only decent meal of the day, but there is little left in the way of cultural diversity, no pluralism left to destroy, only problems to solve. The people of the mountains are displaying some of the classic symptoms of institutional adjustment—the kind of adjustment that once-curable mental patients make to hospitals, and that some criminals make to prisons. They have adjusted in the same way that southern Negroes learned to adjust to discrimination and deprivation and (in the same way that many Jews adjusted to Nazi concentration camps), often coming to the aid of their own oppressors.

The problem in breaking the cycle of "poor schools, poor pay and poor people" is to break into this adjustment, to provide the Southern Mountain TVA, the housing, and the roads, *and* to create maladjustment, to offer some hope. Caudill's idea of an educational Peace Corps is already being tried on a private volunteer basis, despite the suspicions of local politicians. But such an effort cannot succeed unless it ultimately develops into a new and revolutionary form of county-agentry, a program which sends talented and trained young men and women into the hills and hollows for the purpose of informing the mountaineers of the basics of decent education and how to get it, a program of voter education and registration designed to achieve objectives very similar to those of the deep South. Since there are significant psychological parallels between the southern Negro and the Kentucky mountaineer, the experiences of dealing with the problems of one might well be applied to the problems of the other. Unless such measures are taken—and this may mean upsetting political machines that have the tacit support of politicians all the way to Washington—the schools of the mountains will remain in a deep sleep, stirred only occasionally by a particularly odious instance of political malfeasance. And unless they are roused from this sleep they will continue to export their ignorance, continue to breed misery and frustration, and continue to do the worst when they should be doing the very best.

5

Main Street in Dixie

U.S. HIGHWAY 80 is Main Street in the deep South. It is called Commerce Street in Dallas, Madison Avenue in Montgomery, and College Street in Macon. Running from Savannah to San Diego, it spans Georgia, Alabama, Mississippi, Louisiana, Texas, New Mexico, Arizona and California; it crosses cotton fields and deserts, it passes sharecroppers' cabins and modern department stores, state capitols and little county courthouses, and billboards inscribed "Christ Is the Answer" and " Fight Communism Through the John Birch Society."

Through part of its eastern third, U.S. 80 is the only visible sign of the federal presence—of the fact that the counties it crosses are part of a larger country, a nation officially committed to certain political and legal attitudes which the region does not share. Here is Montgomery, the one-time capital of the Confederacy; and Vicksburg where Grant won his first major battle, and Savannah, General Sherman's Christmas gift to the American people in 1864; and here also is Selma, the home of the Alabama Citizens Council, and now become a byword for the brutality of southern bigots and the courage of southern Negroes; and Meridian, Mississippi, where the confession of an alleged participant was not enough evidence to hold men accused of the murder of civil rights workers. This is Faulkner country, but it is also a land of new electronics plants and textile mills, of good manners and pride in being soft spoken, and of suburbs that look just like Darien, Connecticut, or any of a hundred other places. For some citizens the Confederate flag remains the prime symbol; race, sexual guilt and rural fundamentalism unify the social fabric, and sentimentality, often called tradition, is the hallmark of the intellectual outlook.

The states joined by the eastern third of U.S. 80 are among the poorest in the nation. All of them are still heavily dependent on row crop farming, despite recent in-migrations of northern industry; all of them are hampered by low levels of education and by lack of a strong tradition of popular support for public schools, and all of them still manifest their old frontier instincts of violence. Moxie, Dr. Pepper, and Coca Cola are staples of the diet, along with pork and hominy; the school zone sign has a soft drink advertisement on the back, and the Baptists run the churches. In rural areas the sheriff is still the law and the Negro—along with the Bible—remains the central figure of the culture.

Race, religion, and political conservatism. These elements —bonded and blended—structure life in the deep South, and underlie its problems. The Negro's subservience in the social order, especially in the rural areas, has given him a kind of freedom from the white man's conventions. No one expected him to behave morally, to support his wife or to educate his children. When he got drunk he behaved as expected, and when he lied he was simply acting according to his nature. Until recently he was an indispensable part of the economy, but mechanization of the cotton plantations is beginning to change that; now his prime function is to sustain the status of the bigot, to prove that the white is somebody, no matter what he does or whom he controls. In the towns and larger cities where civil rights groups have been active the Negro has become someone to deal with, either in negotiations, in the courts or with a shotgun. But in the small towns and on the plantations he continues to be regarded as he always was, a funny, unreliable, dishonest fool. His historical presence has produced the peculiar combination of social and sexual guilt that W. J. Cash described in *The Mind of the South,* for the white man—because of the necessity to keep the race pure—made demands of his women that he frequently disregarded himself, and thus every light-skinned black is a reminder of the young men who, in days past, made nocturnal visits to the slave cabins. This guilt makes the maintenance of segregation all the more important just as it makes the idea of miscegenation unthinkable, and, at the same time, darkly attractive.

And along with the presence of the Negro there is the tradition of political conservatism—the particularism of John Calhoun and John Taylor of Caroline—and the fundamentalism, religious and moral, of the revivalist, the camp meeting and the neon cross. "We've discussed the race question in class," said a teacher—obviously a liberal—in a southern school. "But I've never dared say that God didn't create the earth in six days." The church is a major institution in the southern community; it is well attended, it is constantly running prayer meetings, suppers and revivals, and it is—with certain exceptions—thoroughly conservative.

But now the props that have sustained the culture of the South are crumbling. The newly militant Negro, supported in part by the force of the federal government, is beginning to make demands of his southern masters, and even Highway 80 is no longer solid. The intelligent businessman of Atlanta or Macon has no more sympathy for the sheriff with the cattle prod than does his counterpart in New York, and there are people all over Georgia—and a few even in Alabama—who know the world is changing. There is a new technology, new systems of communication and a vast but, in some places, little understood shift from biblical and moral simplicity to ambiguity and complexity. These changes have generated economic and social adjustments everywhere in this country, but in the South they threaten the psychological composition of the entire society. Where they have been felt, the reaction has often been violent.

Highway 80 is at the center of the southern defense system against the modern world. George C. Wallace lives there as governor of Alabama, and Paul B. Johnson as governor of Mississippi (and so did Martin Luther King, Jr. when he organized the Montgomery bus boycott); its communities have led in the legal and physical resistance to integration, and its schools are political and ideological battle stations in furtherance of the southern cause. (In May 1964, ten years after the decision in *Brown* v. *Board of Education*, 2000 of the 1,218,000 Negro school children in Georgia, Alabama, Mississippi, and Louisiana were actually going to school with whites.) School buildings have been bombed, elaborate pupil transfer plans invented, state tuition programs adopted, revised, and readopted; teachers have been intimidated and fired, textbooks have been altered, and state-wide programs of indoctrination instituted to convince students and teachers that integration and communism are equally dangerous and, most likely, originate at the same source.

The schools of the South have been part of a closed and often repressive society committed not only to segregation but also to a fundamentalist and authoritarian attitude which regards "character" as the prime virtue and independent thought as a major defect. Even in the larger cities they often still operate with rural and small town assumptions: the Bible; the evil of cities; the horror of sex; the fun of games, bands and military parades; spare the rod and spoil the child—and they remain hostile to modern social attitudes in general, and to racial equality in particular. In many places they still engage in sentimentality about the Old South, about the days when the region was prosperous and when great plantations were worked by capricious but lovable darkies. The official Alabama history textbook for the ninth grade points out that:

> With all the drawbacks of slavery, it should be noted that slavery was the earliest form of social security in the United States. The master was responsible for looking after his overaged slaves. It is true that the average ages to which slaves lived were less than those of whites. But this difference was not great, and a similar difference between the races exists today.

Through their partial veto over all standard textbooks, the southern states have been able to impose their attitudes on national publishers who find it difficult to get books adopted if they include pictures of whites and Negroes working or playing together or candid references to racial discrimination. Although some publishers have started producing separate editions for North and South many texts still reflect the pressure of the southern censors. "We're cautious," said a former member of the Alabama Textbook Committee (which is composed of teachers whose choices are subject to review by a politically appointed state board). "There's always fear of the United Daughters of the Confederacy, the DAR and other groups. Books that include anything outspoken are simply not adopted." Southerners say they want only "fair treatment." In choosing a book, said a Georgia curriculum supervisor, "we look for balance in authorship, to see if all sections are represented. . . . Now here's a chapter headed 'The South Strikes First'—that's offensive to us. . . . You know it's become fashionable in some places to muckrake. We still like to have a prayer and sing the Star Spangled Banner." Books acceptable to southern schools have accounts of "the war between the states," never the civil war; they stress the horror of Reconstruction, and the malevolence of carpetbaggers and scalawags, they exclude references to Jim Crow laws and lynching, they patronize Negroes, they romanticize the Old South, and they point out that when Negroes voted and held office after the Civil War, government in the South was a shambles of gold spittoons, debauchery and corruption. One of the most commonly used history texts is a book called *The Making of Modern America* by Leon H. Canfield and Howard B. Wilder (Houghton Mifflin): "How were slaves treated?" the authors ask. And they answer the question:

> No doubt there were individual plantation owners and overseers who were as cruel as Simon Legree in *Uncle Tom's Cabin,* but such cases were unusual. Many relationships between members of the two races were as happy as the one produced by Joel Chandler Harris in his stories about Uncle Remus and the little white lad who listened entranced to the tales of "Brer Rabbit."
> On the whole, the slaves of the South received fairly good treatment. In fact, it was against an owner's best interests to abuse the slaves for they were valuable property . . . they were adequately fed in most cases and given the proper care. Most of them submitted to their lot without protest. They probably worked no harder than the nothern "hired man" and at least they had fewer worries about unemployment and old age.

Combined with such sentimentality is the absence of any forthright classroom discussion of the problems of civil rights, of the significance of recent court decisions, or of the social and cultural changes that integration will ultimately demand. Instead, the southern schools have erected a battery of political and ideological defenses designed to assuage guilt, to affirm the validity of the going moral and political biases, and to drive away the specter of modernity and change. Some of these defenses are local and futile: in Bastrop, Louisiana, for example, the Morehouse Parish School Board voted not to buy textbooks which include illustrations of Negroes and whites together, and in Mississippi the Citizens Educational Association is at work inspecting textbooks for signs of "socialism, race amalgamation and one-worldism." In other instances the defense machinery is state wide and officially enforced. Both Alabama and Louisiana have established mandatory evils-of-communism courses in their high schools that link social welfare programs and civil rights agitation with the Communists. In Louisiana the course is designed to instill in future citizens a belief in

> ... decentralized government, representative democracy, free competitive capitalism, separation of powers in government, private ownership of property and the means of production, reasonable and limited taxation [and] the reserved powers of the states.

The unit points out that Communists deliberately stir up racial conflict, that "socialism and the 'welfare state' are way stations on the road to communism" and that "well-meaning but impractical 'do-gooders' and disgruntled intellectuals are often duped into spreading the party line."

In Alabama the legislature directed the schools to "emphasize the free-enterprise-competitive economy of the United States as the one which produces higher wages, higher standards of living, greater personal freedom and liberty than any other system of economics on earth," and declared that "the successful exploitation and manipulation of youth and student groups throughout the world today are a major challenge which free world forces must meet and defeat."

Such ideological bastions are reinforced through careful selection of textbooks at the state level, through subtle pressures on teachers, and through the many intangible ways that small communities teach their children accepted behavior and beliefs; when an Alabama second grader announces to his teacher that it must have been a nigger who stole his father's farm tools, he is not challenged or questioned—the teacher simply accepts the statement—and when a group of high school juniors in the same community ask their teacher if they can discuss civil rights she declines because "they're all on the same side anyway, and they'll just get hot under the collar, so what's the use talking about it?" Her job is not to question established ways, or even to put students into a frame of mind that might lead them one day to do it by themselves. On Highway 80 most of the important questions have answers; the task of the schools is to reveal them.

II

The Lanier High School for Boys in Macon is one of six high schools serving a community of 125,000 that is cordial and at the same time politically conservative, socially rigid, and proud both of its traditions and its industrial growth. The city has tried to combine what the Chamber of Commerce calls "Old South charm" with "new South progress," benefiting from the huge Warner Robins Air Force Base seventeen miles away, and from a number of growing brick, textile and container manufacturing plants. Two colleges, Mercer University and Wesleyan College for women, and a little theater give the community a touch of the cosmopolitan, there are new suburbs and a new commercial prosperity, while the old residences on Vineville Avenue remain as decaying reminders of a past that the community is reluctantly giving up. The local slogan is "Macon on the move," but the motion is relaxed. Nevertheless, Macon is probably one of the most liberal towns between Savannah and Shreveport.

The Macon schools are controlled by the Bibb County Board of Public Education, a legally self-perpetuating body chartered in the last days of Reconstruction which has functioned in paternal grandeur ever since 1872. The board operates 50 elementary and secondary schools for 20,000 white students and 13,000 Negroes, levying taxes which are theoretically open to review by the county commissioners, but which have never been challenged by that body. The taxes are low; Bibb County spends $231 per year (1961–62) to educate each child, a little less than the Georgia average and about half the figure for a typical large northern city. Some Maconites have begun to grumble about the political inaccessibility of their educational patriarchs, but most of them are pleased by the stability the board provides—especially in the first stages of integration—and by the performance of the schools generally. "This is the best goddam school system in the state," said a Macon businessman. "We've got not only the best white schools but the finest colored schools. The new Negro high school is even air conditioned."

Macon's junior and senior high schools are segregated three ways: white boys, white girls, and Negroes (token integration began in 1964), a pattern that is rare even for the South, but which also indicates the region's double standard for moral and sexual

behavior. Although there once was criticism of sexual segregation, that criticism subsided when the possibility of racial integration began to appear a decade ago. If Negroes were to be
forced into the white schools, it would certainly be unwise to mix
the sexes. "I'm sure glad that this is just a boys' school now," said
a Lanier senior. "You know, I wouldn't want a girl I liked sitting
next to one of *them*."

Lanier and neighboring A. L. Miller High School for Girls
are the city's oldest high schools (since World War II two new
ones have been built for whites and one for Negroes), and wherever one goes one hears references to "the Lanier tradition," an
intangible quality that eludes outsiders and that most natives
can't fully define. For many years Lanier—named for the poet, a
Macon native—was an athletic power in Georgia, and its alumni
enjoyed successful careers in the various state colleges. (One of
them was John Birch, who went on to Mercer where he inspired
one of the few religious heresy trials of the twentieth century: the
Mercer Baptists were not orthodox enough for him.) Many Maconites are graduates of Lanier, and most of them will tell the
visitor that Lanier was, and is, one of the best high schools in the
state.

Lanier's principal, a former football coach named Thomas
J. Porter, reflected the community's pride. (Mr. Porter died early
in 1965.) He was pleased by the good behavior and grooming of
his students—enforced by a system of citizenship grades and, occasionally, by a paddle—and he especially enjoyed the activities
of the Lanier junior ROTC unit, to which every boy must belong.
"This is the biggest ROTC unit in the country," he said, "and we
like to think it's one of the best." Every Monday, Tuesday and
Wednesday all Lanier students attend school in uniform—they
have Thursday and Friday to get their outfits washed—and each
day they spend an hour on the elements of military science and
drill. The Army, which operates the unit, gives junior ROTC
graduates no credit for their high school training, no advance leg
on a commission, and no other advantages when they enter military service, but the community does not question the "military"
at Lanier. When the school board learned that Congress had
voted to expand the junior ROTC program (over the objections of
the Pentagon, which sees no military value in it), it promptly

decided to investigate the possibility of getting a unit for the other boys' high school. "We're like the old Prussians," said an amused member of the school board when he was asked about it, "we just love uniforms and parades."

Competition for promotion within the ROTC unit is intense; to become a cadet captain or colonel in the senior year is to achieve high status, and since such rank is determined not only by performance in military activities, but also through points gained in extracurricular activities, high grades and "citizenship," the ROTC becomes part of a general system of rewards and punishments. Students say they will not challenge teachers because they may incur demerits and therefore jeopardize their chances for an ROTC promotion. "They can hurt you," one of them said. "It's that personal data stuff: Take the football coach —he finds out everything. If you say something, he'll find out and it'll go on your citizenship record—or if you're on the team and quit football." But the students, most of them, don't object to the military; they enjoy the attention it gets them and they share the community's pride in their good behavior and appearance. "You won't find many long haircuts around here," one of them said. "Anybody can wear a clean shirt and have his hair cut neat."

Lanier's ROTC, its "tradition," and its conservatism are all part of a set of attitudes which explain the reasons for the school's outstanding local reputation: Lanier was never intended to produce aggressive, intellectually daring individuals. For forty years it has functioned to develop soft-spoken, well-mannered young men who knew their responsibilities in a rather slow-moving, polite and well-structured society. No one ever attempted to produce brilliant original thinkers. In the pre-war South there wasn't much demand for them.

Now, although the South is slowly changing, Lanier has fallen behind. "We've got some 1928 textbooks," a student said, and some 1928 teachers." Most courses are run conservatively; "there is a minimum of student discussion, little questioning of established ways, and faithful adherence to the textbook. The football schedule is posted in every room, but there are few signs that intellectual activity is promoted with equal vigor. The work tables in the physics laboratory, which is also headquarters for the Pep Club, are cluttered with paper streamers, posters and decora-

tions, while the teaching equipment is scattered in various corners of the room. Although attempts are being made to modern-
ize instruction in such fields as mathematics, Lanier is still committed to its honored traditions: most students, said a teacher,
don't even carry their books home with them, and they read nothing that is not assigned. Lanier has no effective departmental organization, no physical education outside of ROTC (and, therefore,
the coaches must teach academic subjects), no instruction in
music other than band, and a staff of teachers who, though they
earn above the average for the state, are underpaid and prone to
moonlighting. ("I earn more at Reserve meetings," said a Macon
teacher, "than I'd get from the pay raise from a master's degree,
so why should I bother? I'd love to study, but I can't afford it.")
Lanier's students are well-mannered; they have learned to stay in
line, and not to be too vocal or inquisitive. Even when they are
asked to debate something they are often unable to do it.

In a history class eleventh grade students were to discuss limiting the powers of the Supreme Court:

"There's got to be a final say-so in these things," says a boy
who has been asked to defend the Court. "If there wasn't we'd
always be arguin' and not accomplishin' nothing."

"We need a Supreme Court," says a member of the opposition. "But I don't see where they need nine men. We need maybe
five or four."

"All of us need prayer in our schools," says another critic of
the Court. "If we have proper respect for each other's religions I
can't see why we can't have prayer and daily Bible reading. . . .
Since the Court ruled out prayer and Bible reading we're less
close to God." (Macon, like many southern communities, has ignored the Court on Bible reading and school prayers.)

"How could you have four men on the Court," someone
asked. "They'd always have ties."

"Okay, make it five then."

"What they should have is a law to make the judges hold office only until the other party gets into office. Then the new President could appoint the judges."

A number of Lanier's teachers have been making efforts to
promote more inquiry and independence among their students,
despite the fact that too much free thought is likely to bring pro-

tests from parents. ("The other day," said the teacher who conducted the discussion on the Supreme Court, "a kid's father blew
off because his son had been asked to defend the Court.") Some
teachers at Lanier, and several at the other Macon high schools
have encouraged an increasing amount of student discussion, but
only rarely will they express their own opinions, even when students drift into the irrelevant or the absurd; for the most part,
they ask only those questions that can be answered by looking in
the textbook.

A few blocks from Lanier, at A. L. Miller High School for
Girls, Clara Nell Hargrove is trying to infuse new vitality into
another institution overgrown with status. Miss Hargrove has
been principal for about two years, and she has succeeded in at-
tracting and stimulating a number of new teachers and in alien-
ating some teachers and students used to older and more traditional ways. "School spirit is way down," said a girl in the hall.
"When we play a game now [i.e. when Lanier plays] they don't
come out and cheer any more. Sure, a lot of the kids go to the
games, but it's not like it used to be. There's so much homework."

Miss Hargrove is trying to find instructors who will initiate
things, and she has found some. In a small, improvised room
above the library, Nancy B. Anderson, a young Wellesley graduate from Connecticut (married to a Macon attorney) is getting
girls to read Carl Becker and Charles Beard, and even Cash's
Mind of the South, and John Dollard's *Caste and Class in a Southern Town.* She brings *The New York Times* to class—common
in northern cities, but extraordinary in many parts of the South,
where the *Times* is considered dangerous—she asks searching
questions, and constantly forces her students to examine their
ideas: when a girl complains about the size of the national debt,
Nancy Anderson asks if the girl knows to whom the government
owes it; she wants to know why the nation is concerned with
economic growth—"Why not," she asks, "let it go on as it is?"—
and she asks if anyone knows *why* it is good to have a balanced
national budget. "I try to make them face questions, I try to push
them without telling them where I stand, though I think some of
them know."

Nancy Anderson is part of a minor renaissance that Miss

Hargrove is trying to fan into a full revival. She hopes to add some advanced placement work and greater flexibility for students at both ends of the ability scale; she is trying to rejuvenate or eliminate weak courses, and to replace their retiring instructors with people "who'll start things." (A recent evaluation of the school recommended "more emphasis on the creative and the challenging," more flexibility for students who wish to go into vocational programs, and more use of community resources.) In doing this, Miss Hargrove faces not only the normal difficulties of energizing the faculty, but also in countering long-established attitudes in the community. She must deal with parents who, according to the evaluation, have difficulty in considering "anything other than college for their daughters," and with a complex network of social expectations, for Miller, like Lanier and the other white high schools, is heavily affected by the social interests of the community and its students. "People in Macon," said a member of the Miller staff, "are very conscious of where you live. There are teachers here who want to know who a girl's mother was and there are certain students that some teachers would be reluctant to fail. . . . We have students who are overprivileged as well as underprivileged." Old college fraternity and sorority affiliations affect business and personal relationships in Macon, and failure to belong to the right one, or to live in the right place is sometimes sufficient ground for exclusion. Officers in the high school ROTC, said a Lanier teacher, "used to all come from the right side of town, and even now there's still some people who'd be anxious about flunking the children of board members. Here you're either on the right side of the tracks or you're not."

The preoccupation with social identity is reflected in high school fraternities and sororities which run elaborate parties and dances, some costing thousands of dollars. Although the board of education has ruled not to "recognize" these organizations, they dominate student social life. "Some have more status than others," said a teacher at Miller, "and so the girls begin to worry in the ninth grade about what sorority they'll join." The parties and dances, held at private homes or in downtown hotels, are financed through membership dues and parent contributions, and from the receipts of various student projects (car washing, for example). Every Tuesday night the sororities and fraternities have meetings. "They sit around drinking cokes and plan their parties; it's a way of getting out of the house," a Lanier teacher said. "Then some of them go to the Pig'n Whistle and drink more cokes. Nothing much happens because if a girl gets into a boy's car she's hurt her reputation, and reputation around here means a lot."

The students imitate their parents' social life, and they are constantly reminded that they are important people. The newspapers carry full descriptions of high school activities. Each Sunday the *Macon Telegraph and News* runs a page called "T'ween Teens" that reports on club elections, popular songs, and the family and church affiliations of student officers:

> It must run in the family—Howard Miller, a junior at Lanier is succeeding his older brother, George, as president of Beta Honorary Club.
>
> Both brothers have been very active participants in the events at Lanier, and deserve the honor their classmates showed by voting them into this important office. Sons of Dr. and Mrs. Sidney Miller, they reside at 735 Woodridge Drive and attend Ingleside Baptist Church.
>
> Howard is vice president elect of two other clubs: French Club and Chess Club. He is a corporal in ROTC and a member of the crack squad. Outside school he is a member of Alpha Kappa Omega fraternity. . . .

Articles of this kind, the tone of school administrators, and the emphasis on club activities and fraternity affiliations are constant reminders of the things that the community holds in esteem. "Reputation," good hair cuts, social identity, "character" (meaning conformity and obedience) and promotion in a military organization that has no military significance set the tone in the schools. Although teachers are rarely intimidated for expressing unpopular opinions, few have any inclination to try. Most of them are southerners—some from Alabama and Mississippi where pay is lower and attitudes far more illiberal—and they share local attitudes. Those who do not sometimes encounter a cloud of confusion and indifference, for in trying to generate intellectual curiosity and independent inquiry they tend to run against the grain.

The two newer high schools, Willingham and McEvoy, completed in the late 'fifties, are beginning to challenge the older schools; when they were built many people expected them to be poor relations to Lanier and Miller, but they have defied the predictions and are beginning to enjoy a respect that rivals Lanier's. But so far there has been no public comparison. Most Maconites are convinced that the white high schools are doing an evenly good job ("the board," said a Macon newspaper man, "has created a good image") and that they are successful in placing their graduates in good colleges (Emory, Mercer, Georgia Tech). Although a few of these graduates have complained about the preparation they received, especially when they go to eastern colleges, their complaints have never been vociferous enough to cause concern. The white high schools are doing what is expected of them, and doing it well.

III

The Ballard Hudson High School, one of Macon's two Negro high schools, is a sprawling one-story "campus style" establishment erected in 1949 and now so overcrowded that its high dropout rate is almost an educational necessity. Ballard Hudson is directed by a principal named R. J. Martin who has sometimes been called the Czar of Negro education in Macon. Martin, often addressed as Professor Martin, was, until recently, one of the two Negroes who were in touch with the board of education and the superintendent of schools (the other was the supervisor of Negro elementary schools), and he is said to have run not only his, but all of Macon's Negro schools, as he saw fit. "He had a veto power over who should teach, and who shouldn't," said William Randall, the head of Macon's chapter of the NAACP. "He wouldn't let some teachers teach in their field, and he spent more time on contests, on raising funds to buy band uniforms and things, than he did on education. . . . The board of education had no communication with the Negro community, and they let him run the show. Now there's a committee from our group that keeps the board informed." Negro administrators have been accused of setting financial quotas for teachers—sums they were required to raise in their classes to support school activities—of sending Negro school children into the streets during school hours to sell raffle tickets, and of discouraging Negro transfer applications when integration was ordered in 1964. Because Negro students lack funds, and because Ballard Hudson's cafeteria is inadequate, most of them eat no lunch; instead they are encouraged to buy cookies and Coca-Cola from a battery of huge vending machines, thus helping to support the various school fund drives, and, indirectly, taking pressure off the school board and the tax rate. The funds so raised help offset shortages of supplies and equipment; in the white schools affluent students and parents help buy equipment that the financially conservative board won't provide. But in the Negro schools it is often levied as a hidden tax on the education and the nutrition of the students.

Despite these inadequacies, and despite the criticisms—and, perhaps, partly because of them—Macon is often said to have one of the best Negro school systems in the deep South. "The board is a millionaires' club composed of old antebellum types," Randall said, "but they've done a good job administering the schools. Sure the Negro schools aren't up to the white schools; they're more overcrowded and the Negro teachers carry a greater load but the board is trying to correct the situation." The morale of Negro students is fairly high, despite the dropout rate, the teaching staff is being upgraded (Macon's Negro teachers typically earn more money than its white teachers because they have more advanced degrees, of whatever worth) and the threat of integration is helping convince the community of the necessity to maintain good Negro schools. Nevertheless they are not up to the white schools, and whenever one talks about integrating the teaching staffs the white administrators concede the argument by objecting that such integration would lower standards, and by insisting that the handful of Negro students who transferred into the white high schools—at the twelfth grade—have experienced academic difficulties.

Ballard Hudson and Peter G. Appling, the other Negro high school (erected in 1958), are coeducational institutions serving a Negro population of 42,000 that is relatively stable and almost fully employed. (Although most Macon Negroes still occupy menial positions as laborers, dishwashers and domestics, many are also employed at Warner Robins Air Base, and thus have aspirations set in terms other than those of the Old South.) The schools themselves are on the edge of several vast social transformations and thus contain examples of almost every stage of Negro development. There is the respectful department chairman, representative of the old Uncle Tom who came to the back door, hat in hand, to solicit for a worthy Negro project; there are the almost-militant students reading *Black Like Me* and *The Fire Next Time,* so interested in the new Negro writers that the Ballard Hudson librarian must keep them on a special reserve shelf; and there is the undereducated teacher from Fort Valley State College reading from the textbooks, and asking her students to recite paragraphs back to her. In one room there is a teacher of history, not certain of himself or his world, saying to the visitor "we tell them that segregation is wrong, but we can't go too fast. We answer their questions the best we can." And in a room down the hall there is the bright young man with a master's degree from Columbia University, teaching modern mathematics, hoping he will have time for some calculus and analytic geometry. And a few doors from him there is a teacher of sociology named A. C. Kellem, Jr., speaking about things that he couldn't discuss if he were at Lanier, taking advantage of the double standard, using words like *incest,* encouraging students to tear apart the mythology of romantic love, even encouraging discussion of the unmentionable subject of miscegenation. There is more maturity in this classroom than there is in all of Lanier.

"Should there be uniform marriage and divorce laws throughout the country?" Kellem asks. Many hands are up.

"People mature at different ages and in different ways," a girl says. "If a person doesn't want to stay with a person, then he should be allowed to get a divorce."

"Suppose there's some children involved?" Kellem says.

"You can hurt children too."

"But the marriage counselors try to keep homes from breaking up," Kellem says. "A lot of juvenile delinquency begins in broken homes."

"It sure doesn't help to keep homes from breaking up if the parents are always fighting," another student says; the girl who spoke first interrupts.

"You have to love the children," she says. "If you're with someone you hate there's so much hate you can't show the children any love. If you hate one another, the children are going to see right through that. You can't pretend."

"If there's true love and loyalty then there'd be no divorce," says the boy.

"You are now speaking on the utopian side," Kellem says, and then he adds, "All those myths: if I can only unite with her, then my troubles will be over; I can't be in love unless I've fallen in love; or that one about beauty. So many people have father and mother fixations. They start out thinking they're playing house, with a game of let's pretend, and then they learn better. . . ."

Since Negroes often are exempt from moral, and social repressions that the white community imposes on itself Negro teachers are freer to discuss what they want, provided that they don't upset the class and political structure. And since the Negro high schools—by virtue of the same double standard—are coeducational, they enjoy a kind of maturity denied the white schools. At the same time, the Negro schools often make desperate attempts to be like the white schools, to have the bands, the activities, and the college preparatory courses that the white schools have. "They want ROTC over there," said a white administrator, "and if we had torture chambers they'd want those too." What Macon's vocal Negroes want most at Ballard Hudson is a better vocational program. Many of the school's seniors hope to go to college—most of them at Negro institutions in the South—and for them a college preparatory program makes sense. But the seniors represent only a third of their eighth grade class; the rest have dropped out because the college preparation was irrelevant and the vocational training unattractive. Negroes at Ballard Hudson can learn to alter clothes with a sewing machine, but they are not offered courses (as are whites) in plumbing, electrical work and other more highly paid and challenging trades. Thus there are increasing demands for upgrading the vocational program and for an end to the double standard. "Jobs are opening in the South for anyone who possesses the necessary skills," said Randall. "There are so many plants with defense contracts; the government says don't discriminate or lose your contract. They'll hire 'em, but most Negroes don't have the skills. The schools are behind."

The most pressing problem for Macon's Negro schools is not overcrowding—new buildings are going up—or even in finding better teachers, but rather in deciding what kind of world they are preparing their students for, and what kind of schools they are going to be. They lack a model, for surely they can never be like Lanier or Miller, although they sometimes seem tempted to try.

There will be more integration in the years to come, but it will be a long time before Macon has genuinely bi-racial schools. When integration was ordered by a federal court in 1964 the board of education responded by quietly enlisting the cooperation of the community; there were no demonstrations, no newspaper photographers at the school gates, no scare headlines, and sixteen Negroes were enrolled in three white high schools without audible protest. (The Negro girls at Miller have generally been accepted by fellow students. The boys at Lanier have been isolated and disregarded by their anxious classmates, leading one administrator to comment that "we've got the most segregated integrated niggers in the country.") Since the board of education is almost immune from political pressure, and since its members are respected and often able men, continued integration will probably be achieved without violent protest, despite the fact that Macon, like many southern communities cannot rely on de facto housing segregation. There are Negro neighborhoods, but in many parts of town Negroes live on back streets and alleys and in old servants' quarters immediately adjacent to the white middle class. Nevertheless, it is not likely that there will be full integration in the near future. Even now school construction plans are being drawn on the assumption that there will be continued separation of races. Therefore, people like Martin and other Negro school administrators, and the board itself, are confronted with a problem that has hardly been faced, and which they alone cannot be expected to solve: what kind of life will the Negro have in the South twenty years from now? What kind of jobs will be open to him? What part will he play in the community, and what kind of attitudes will he have about himself? ("You try to act as if you're equal," said a senior at Ballard Hudson.) Since Macon is moderate by Highway 80 standards, and since there is increasing communication between the races, it will probably be Macon and cities like it that set the pattern for the region. Ultimately the challenge is not only to act as if you're equal, but in knowing what you want to be equal to.

IV

Although Macon is used to deliberate rather than precipitate motion, it finds itself moving at a gradually accelerating pace. The Bibb Manufacturing Co., which once dominated the city with proprietary affection, is starting to sell its textiles overseas and is thus discovering certain advantages in international trade, foreign aid and a broader perspective; the Air Force, the two Macon colleges—and especially Mercer, whose divinity faculty has been a strong liberal influence—and other organizations are importing personnel from the outland, people with varied, and often more worldly attitudes. Intelligent and moderate editorial voices at the *Macon News* and *Telegraph* (which publish a combined Sunday edition), and active leadership in the Chamber of Commerce and other community groups are promoting governmental reform and civic improvements, and acclimating the city to expansion, growth and change.

This motion reflects itself in the schools, and especially in the vocational and elementary schools which are relatively free from the social aspirations and restrictions, and from the rigidity which affect the old high schools. The Dudley Hughes Vocational School, which is white by day and integrated at night, has burst beyond its walls to accommodate new programs and trades; it runs classes in printing—including color offset printing—business, cosmetology, barbering and woodshop in its main building; electrical shop, television and radio repair in another; auto mechanics in a converted garage, and welding and machine shop in an old prison outside of town. And there are other signs of motion and of energy. Spanish is being taught in most of the grade schools, using television, tapes, and, occasionally, a Cuban refugee; modern mathematics is being tried in several; teacher aides are working at several others to free regular teachers of clerical chores, and, most important, there is a feeling of dissatisfaction with old ways and routine work. At the Hall School, where the entrance is decorated with displays of mineral samples and plastic models of the heads of primitive *homo sapiens* (Lanier displays athletic trophies, and pictures of Lee and Stonewall Jackson), the principal, Mrs. Lillian D. Mahone, seems to know every one of her 619 pupils personally—and their families as well. Mrs. Mahone has made the school, located in a new white collar neighborhood, a kind of community center, and she has enlisted close to a hundred mothers as teacher aides to work in the library and relieve teachers of lunchroom chores and clerical duties. ("You know," Mrs. Mahone said, "when a teacher has to spend all that time keeping records or putting on bandaids you're telling the children that teaching isn't so important after all. Now the teacher is a little more free to teach, and even to have a cigarette and a coffee break.")

At the Whittle School, one of the oldest buildings in the system, a veteran teacher who adopted the "new math" materials of the School Mathematics Study Group has thirty-five sixth graders crackling with activity as they work with sets, congruences and the meaning of rational numbers. And downtown, at the board of education offices, Edith Grimsley, a young elementary school supervisor, pushes and prods teachers and principals to try new techniques and new ideas. "Our schools aren't all that fine," Mrs. Grimsley said, "but if some schools do well they'll make the others take notice. We have to bring in new ideas; if somebody wants to try a new program, the parents will support it."

Macon's motion and its inertia are making it something of a weathervane for the "new" deep South. There are new voices and attitudes coming into the community, and some of them have even found representation on the board of education (where a bright and highly successful young businessman named William P. Simmons led an unsuccessful effort to begin voluntary desegregation well before it was ordered by the Court). But they still have difficulty in being heard. In 1963, when right wingers attacked the Foreign Policy Association Great Decisions Program in Macon, the schools quietly severed their connection with it, never explaining why, or even announcing the decision, and when the Supreme Court declared prayers and Bible reading unconstitutional, the teachers were told that "this won't affect us," and instructed to continue their daily classroom devotions. There was no protest about either decision.

And yet, Macon has come to tolerate attitudes and positions that many southern communities do not. Negro teachers can belong to the NAACP without jeopardizing their jobs, and all teachers can express themselves on public issues outside the classroom. There is reluctance to accelerate desegregation, but there is no die-hard resistance, and local Negro leaders feel that they will have increasing access to, and influence on, the established community leadership. As the city grows and new people continue to move in, the old voices, the established traditions, and the social rigidity will be replaced by a newer element and by other considerations. Demands have already been made for greater diversity on the board of education, and even for some kind of interest-group representation. Although those demands subsided when the segregation issue came to a head, they will undoubtedly be made again. The paternal structure and behavior of the board protected the schools when conflicts over integration could have torn them apart. But once that threat subsides, the schools will have to be responsive to the new and let the old be history.

V

The Beauregard School and the Sanford School are located about four miles apart near the center of Lee County, Alabama, a rural rectangle that runs from the Chattahoochee River on the east to a point about fifty crow miles from Montgomery on the west. The county includes two small cities, Auburn, where the university is situated, and Opelika, a textile town and county seat, which has recently become the location of a U.S. Royal Tire Co. plant. (Because it is a university town, and because of an unusually liberal weekly newspaper, the *Lee County Bulletin*, Auburn is one of the most moderate and enlightened towns in the region.) Since both Auburn and Opelika maintain their own school systems, the Lee County schools are almost totally rural, educating 3600 students, half of them Negroes. Beauregard, named after the Civil War general, is a twelve-grade school for about 450 whites; Sanford, named after a local Negro family, is a twelve-grade school for 600 Negroes. Each is located in an open field; neither is near anything except the other.

From his window at Beauregard, the principal, J. W. Harris can see the small frame building that houses the class for "exceptional," i.e. retarded, children. Beyond it is a cotton field, the white bolls visible through the brown stalks, the rows running out of sight to the east. "No," he says in answer to a question, "the school hasn't changed much. We try to keep up but we haven't made any big changes. . . . The county is changing. Many people

now work in town at the tire plant or at one of the mills in Opelika. They're weekend farmers; there aren't too many real dirt
farmers around here now."

Recent changes in the local economy, the mechanization of
the cotton plantations, and the appearance of the tire plant have
had only a marginal effect on the Lee County schools. Although
salaries have been raised considerably over the past decade (beginning pay for a teacher with a bachelor's degree is now $3700)
and although almost all the one-room schools have been consolidated, the educational program has changed little, and the system
remains completely segregated. In adjacent Macon County, where
Tuskegee Institute is situated, a school was burned down after
integration was ordered in 1963; the Tuskegee High School was
closed and, after it was ordered reopened by a federal court, was
boycotted by white pupils. Although Tuskegee Institute stands
like a beacon for Alabama Negroes with educational ambition, its
proximity to Lee County has generated little civil rights activity
there.

Like other systems in Alabama, the Lee County schools are
financially impoverished, and so hamstrung by legal restrictions
that they must obtain state-wide approval of a constitutional
amendment each time they want to increase the local tax rate.
Local property taxes are minimal—there are people who pay
$100 or less on $20,000 houses—and local interest in the schools
(excepting academic communities like Auburn) is not much
higher. In effect, the schools are almost totally dependent on the
state, on the bounties of the governor and the legislature, and on
whatever academic initiative the politically appointed State
Board of Education is willing to provide. About eighty-five per
cent of the school budget now comes from the state, most of it
raised through a sales tax intended, according to several people,
to "keep the niggers in their place."

The most important consequence of the new technology is
the fact that more Negro students attend school; the typical daily
absence rate during the cotton-chopping and picking months
(September, October, November, March, April and May) is now
down to twenty-five per cent. Before mechanization it had been so
high in some schools that the teachers padded attendance rolls for
fear that corresponding state-aid reductions would lead to the

elimination of their jobs. "We were told to mark them present," a former Negro teacher said. "Even on days when there weren't but maybe two kids in the room." Although the school system has a truant officer he paid little attention to Negro absences, and still doesn't. "I used to go out and speak in Negro schools and churches," said Martin C. Whitten, who has been superintendent of schools for almost thirty years. "I begged and pleaded for them to keep their kids in school, but they said they had to be in the fields. We've gradually moved up on the number of months they stay in school. Of course, the teachers were pitiful. Before the war they got $28 a month for four months' work—$112 a year for teaching."

Although Beauregard and Sanford are only five minutes' drive from each other they are completely separate. Each is served by its own buses—driven by high school students—each has its own principal, its own little library, and its own incomplete collection of laboratory materials. Neither offers any foreign languages, any art or music other than band, and since each is so small (17 students graduated from Beauregard in 1964) the teachers must be prepared to conduct classes in at least two and sometimes as many as four subjects: a typical day's schedule at Beauregard might be eighth grade social studies, eleventh grade health and physical education; ninth grade Alabama history; eighth grade health and physical education; study hall, and ninth grade physical education. At Sanford the science teacher offers chemistry and physics in alternate years, in addition to algebra, advanced general science and general mathematics. No Lee County school can afford a full program of vocational education; the Sanford School has none at all. "The Negroes should have some vocational type of training, and I hope we can build some shops," Whitten said. "They don't really have what it takes to do the other kind of work; they can't help what nature gives them."

Despite the system's limitations—and despite the fact that some Negro teachers sense a desperate need for a more diversified program—there is little vocal criticism of the Lee System. Since Auburn and Opelika operate their own schools, most of the county's educated people concentrate their attention on them. A few Auburn education students practice-teach in Lee County, and some of the county's Negro teachers commute from Tuskegee, but they exercise only a minimal influence on curriculum, and none on the financial structure. Whitten senses the inadequacies, but he has neither the staff nor the funds to do much about them.

The schools are physically isolated, and this physical isolation is symbolic of their academic difficulties. Their students have never been exposed to any thought or experience not indigenous to Lee County. Before they come to school they have learned that the races are different, and in what way, and after they get there they are taught that they live in a confederation of sovereign states, all of them separate and distinct, and that they lost the war between the states because, according to their textbooks, "the North had a more convincing propaganda line than the South. The abolition crusade against slavery fired the Northerners against the Southerners. In waging war convincing propaganda is useful." Their little library at Beauregard contains Thomas Hardy and *War and Peace,* a long shelf of romances, Walter Scott, *Southern Belle* and *Gone With the Wind*; a promotion magazine lauding George Wallace (next to a copy of *Scientific American*), but not a liberal newspaper or magazine other than *The Atlantic*. The reserve shelf contains the only available reading on the subject of communism: J. Edgar Hoover's *Masters of Deceit,* and *Cliches of Socialism,* published by the right-wing Foundation for Economic Education. Many of the students are unable to read a newspaper without stumbling over the words. "If I can teach them to write a paragraph I feel I've been successful," said Jean Flanagan, a Beauregard English teacher—who, as the wife of an Auburn student, represents only a temporary injection of worldliness. "When they go to college from around here (about twenty-five per cent do) many of them start by failing freshman English. They're very unsophisticated. The world has never been brought to them. They've never learned to think, have never been made to think. They want to be given answers. They don't read newspapers or magazines and they never talk to anyone whose ideas are different from their own." Besides teaching grammar and composition, Jean Flanagan tries to make her students test their prejudices (high on her classroom wall, along with the Norman Rockwell paintings and the electric clock advertising Dr. Pepper, the students have pasted a huge photograph of Barry Goldwater) but she is one of the few teachers in the school, or in the system who does. Down the hall the senior class is making current events reports in a government course, reading from little newspaper clippings about the supernatural, the problems of fire insurance, and the slaying of Negro Major Lemuel Penn and the subsequent acquittal of four members of the Ku Klux Klan who were charged with the crime (no discussion). "They have their minds so firmly fixed," says the teacher after the class, though she considers them the best group she's ever had. "They refuse to see things any other way; but if they learn what's in the book they can pass their college course in government." She does not understand that the recitation of miscellaneous pieces of information is worthless, and that mindless regurgitation of facts reinforces their stubborn prejudices and their frustrations with the tricks that the world plays on them; that her job is not necessarily to change their minds, but to bring them a little of the mysterious ways of the universe, and to ask them to examine the way in which they made up their minds in the first place.

Four miles away at the Sanford School for Negroes, the seniors are studying communism in a government class, as required by Alabama law. It is a dry sunny day; 213 of the 604 Sanford students are absent, most of them presumably working in the cotton fields, but this is a better attendance record than Sanford used to have. The twenty-five students in the government class, children of tenant farmers and sharecroppers, are the survivors of what was, five years ago, a class of about eighty. The rest have disappeared.

The blackboard in the classroom is covered with the teacher's writing; she is still writing as the students come in, completing two parallel columns, one headed *Democracy*, the other *Communism*. Under *Communism*:

> Class conflict taken for granted.
>> Proof: "From each according to his ability, to each according to his need."
>>> "The idea of equality is not an unshakeable eternal truth."

> The value of the individual is in proportion to his usefulness to the state. His private interest must always be subordinate to those of the regime in power.

Under *Democracy:*
> Basic equality taken for granted.
>> Proof: "We hold these truths to be self evident, that all men are created equal . . ."
>> The 13th Amendment
>> The 14th Amendment
>> The 15th Amendment
>
> Respect for the individual
>
> Equal rights before the law, and equal opportunity to vote and hold office, hold a job and be promoted.
> The right to buy a home and to participate in the activities of the community.

Since the books for this unit have not yet arrived (the students must buy all their texts after the fifth grade) the teacher works from her own notes, and from "reports" the students have prepared from the school encyclopedia.

"Under the capitalist system in the United States do we find the poor becoming poorer and the rich richer?" she asks. A student vaguely shakes his head and says no.

"When Marx said the rich become richer and the poor poorer he didn't take into account production, or minimum wage and hour laws. How does the income tax disprove Marx?"

"You get your money back," a student says.

"When? How?"

"You get it back when you retire."

"Who was Lenin, did anybody read about Lenin?" she asks.

"Lenin was one of Marx's helpers in writing the Communist Manifesto," says another student.

"What was the Communist Manifesto? Who would like to take that for a report?" There is some momentary confusion while assignments are made. Then the class proceeds.

"Life, liberty and the pursuit of happiness—that's what we have where?" she asks.

"In the United States," the class replies in unison.

"In a democracy the people govern themselves," she says. "How does the government represent you?"

"In the Senate and House of Representatives."

"Yes, and you vote for whom you want," the teacher says.

She goes to the board. "And under Communism," she says pointing to the words, "the value of the individual is proportional to his usefulness in the state. . . . Class, what does the Declaration of Independence guarantee us?"

"Life, liberty and the pursuit of happiness," they reply.

The teacher discusses her two lists, point by point, cliché by cliché, asking questions that the students answer by reciting the blackboard liturgy, never quite sure what it means, or why it is there in the first place. The American economy is superior because in this country it takes fewer man hours to produce a loaf of bread or a dress, and, therefore, it takes less pay to buy them. (How many classes does an Alabama student miss to earn a loaf of bread?) Karl Marx was wrong because the poor are not getting poorer; in America we all have the opportunity to vote. . . . Before the bell rings the visitor asks how many of them have someone at home who has ever voted in a state or national election. Two of the twenty-five raise their hands, and even they don't seem quite sure. Then what do all the words on the board mean? What does it mean to say "equal rights before the law and equal opportunity to vote and hold office?" At first they don't understand the question, and it is explained to them. Finally a student answers. "We have the opportunity to vote," he says, "but sometimes they won't let us."

An apathy born of oppression infects the Sanford School; some of its students have accepted the white man's estimation of themselves, in some instances consciously exchanging their self respect for the moral and social irresponsibility to which Negro subservience is entitled. They sit in class almost lifelessly, reading textbook paragraphs and stumbling over words when they are called on, listening dully while a teacher explains the plot of an absurdly simple story. Some are obviously tired ("We can't assign much this time of the year," said a teacher, "because they work in the fields"), and most are bored. Their most pressing ambition is to get out of the South: in the northern cities, they say, there will be jobs and equal opportunity. "Many of these kids are afraid to speak up," said a teacher from Tuskegee who is considered something of a rebel. "They live on white-owned property and they've learned to yassuh and nossuh at the back door. *I'm* talking to my students. I've told them to push for their rights. They've got to be enlightened about what's being offered them and what's holding them back. The white man will respect you if you've got something to respect. I told the superintendent I'd try anything to stimulate them." In a class on Alabama history she tells the students, "The Indians didn't work out as slaves. They slipped away, they were always shrewd. . . . The Negro was brought into America as a slave to do hard work, to do the work that the white man didn't want to do. . . . The indentured servants worked until their debts were paid off (this isn't in your book) and they had the easier jobs. . . . Why do you think so many Negroes died on the slave ships?"

But this teacher is an exception. She began college after her oldest child was in high school, and somehow she learned that education, self respect and ambition are intimately related to civil rights and racial justice. Moreover she has the intelligence and energy to question the local folkways. Many teachers are not as fortunate. They have gone to the rural schools—and later to Negro Alabama State College—and they have never known another way of life. Although most of them have a great deal of sympathy for their students, their problems overwhelm them: what and how do you teach a student who is in school only four months every year? How do you provide relevant education in a school that has no shops, and where only one graduate of twenty goes to college? What do you say to a child who is hungry and does not now, and never will, have the money to buy lunch, or even the cookies and coke from the vending machine? And how do you train students from little huts without running water or electricity (let alone books or television) *all of whom* want to leave the South for the northern cities as soon as they are able? What can you do to prepare them for *that*? More important, the teachers themselves are committed to the system that employs them. They are dependent on it: many of them, despite their college degrees, lack the training to compete against whites in a genuinely integrated system. Teaching is a good job for a Negro, and some of the strongest opponents of school integration are Negro teachers, men and women who have been beneficiaries as well as victims of the inefficiency and inadequacy that segregation creates. Many lost their jobs in the border states after integration was achieved, sometimes because the jobs were abolished when schools were merged, sometimes because white parents didn't want their children taught by Negroes, and often because they could not compete with the whites from across town. "I adjust to almost anything," says a Negro principal in eastern Lee County. "Most of this civil rights thing is a lot of bunk. I don't go to my own church, so why should I want to sit in at someone else's? There's always been injustice in the world and there always will be. My biggest problem is to teach these first and second graders to use flush toilets, which they've never seen before, and to keep the building clean." (As he speaks he turns to a little girl in oversized shoes and an undersized sweater who, lying as only a child can, says she brought money for a coke—her lunch—but that she lost it, and he gives her a nickel.)

And the irony: that southern rural whites are being educated for the South, while many southern rural Negroes move to the northern cities, fractionally educated, often illiterate men and women, and boys and girls, going directly from Mississippi to southside Chicago, to the Fillmore District in San Francisco and to Harlem. These are the newly independent colonials, the American Congolese, many of whom know oppression and subservience and violence (or soon will know it) but who have never learned a third alternative. They represent one of the South's most significant exports and its cruelest joke on the nation.

VI

"The southern white man," said a Georgia Negro, "can be rational on everything but race," and it is this side of him that is impeding his own efforts to improve his schools and his society. For the sake of race the southerner endures almost unbelievable inefficiencies and complications; for the sake of race, and partly for the sake of fundamentalist religion and politics, he has denied himself and his children access to the outside world, saddled himself with a regressive tax structure that won't adequately support public services, and with politicians, especially in Mississippi and Alabama, who have constantly talked him out of social services he desperately needs. He has taxed himself to support a propaganda campaign that appeals to fear and frustration while he himself lacked the funds to buy textbooks for his children. In some instances, he has abolished public education and other services rather than share them with Negroes.

Despite these restraints, despite the tortuous path the southerner has chosen since World War II, he has managed to make changes, or at least to tolerate them. "I can't believe," said a southern college professor, "that the South is being dragged screaming into the twentieth century. It rather likes it." Voices of moderation have not been stilled, though it sometimes suits northern convenience to say that they have. The southern economy is growing and becoming more diversified: even Alabama is now more an industrial than an agricultural state. The South has achieved a measure of token integration: not only Macon, but even Jackson, Mississippi, and Bullock County, Alabama, accepted at least the legal principle without violence or friction. Leaky one-room grade schools have been closed, hundreds of new buildings have been erected, and a gradually increasing amount of money has been allocated for public education. Even his political critics sometimes concede that George C. Wallace is "the strongest educational governor" Alabama has had. Since he took office he has helped provide funds for increases in teachers' salaries averaging about $700 per year, raised the allotment for state-supplied textbooks, and launched an ambitious plan for the development of junior and community colleges. There was even talk in 1964 of supplying free textbooks up to the twelfth grade, a beneficence many Alabamans oppose because "everything about state texts smells of politics." Changes are taking place faster in cities than they are in rural areas, and faster where modern industry is bringing in outside personnel. In one community professional employees at a new plant were so concerned about the local schools that management was persuaded to ask the authorities for a tax increase to finance improvements; almost everywhere the "new people" are reported dissatisfied with the education their children are getting.

And yet, the states of the deep South are still at the bottom in almost every quantitative measure of education. By George Wallace's own figures, Alabama ranks 44th among the 50 states in teachers' pay (1963 figures), the average salary running about $4615 per year (the Georgia average is $4740, and the national average is close to $6000). Alabama's politically appointed State Board of Education still has a veto power over the decisions of the State Textbook Committee, which is composed of teachers, and it uses it. Competent teachers continue to flee the state, and in many cases the South, southern graduates still rank among the lowest in standardized national tests and, most important, the climate of uncertainty and often of fear continues to dominate southern schools. Few teachers are willing to criticize a man like Wallace even in a private conversation or to challenge the more cherished myths of the local culture. (In some departments at Auburn, when a new faculty member is hired, he is presented a framed picture of the governor "that you might like for your desk.") "We have a tenure system," said an Alabama school principal, " but if we want to get rid of 'em we can do it." Teachers have been fired for belonging to the NAACP, for taking part in civil rights activity, or even for being married or related to someone who did, and books are still selected to conform with regional biases (generally known as "objectivity from the southern point of view") and fundamentalist dogma. Two of the best and most widely used American history texts are not approved in Alabama, nor are the materials of the new evolution-oriented Biological Sciences Curriculum Study (both are approved in Georgia).

To the extent that the South's sense of itself—its regional and social consciousness—continues to be tied to racial and religious fundamentalism, its schools will remain restrictive and provincial, for these considerations affect every corner of southern thought and almost every subject of the school curriculum: history, government, sociology, economics, literature, biology. They affect the way the South looks at its "traditions," they underlie its sentimentality, its Victorian morals, its repression.

> The Supreme Court [said Louisiana's State Superintendent of Schools in 1960] cannot nullify the laws of biology. Eminent anthropologists and sociologists—who have probed deeper than the left-wing sociologists who fabricated the rationale of the Court decision—deny the validity of the contention that segregation has had an adverse psychological effect on children. People who take the time to contemplate the wonders of God's creation must observe that God has created differences for a purpose. Racial differences are certainly of Divine origin.

This is the biology, the theology, and the psychology (not to mention the politics) that still shape the view of the world in the southern classroom. It is not merely the view of vicious conspirators or willful politicians—or for that matter of all southerners, or of southerners alone—and it does not simply deprive the Negro of *his* rights and self respect. It is, rather, a part of a lingering American tragedy, almost, one might say, a curse, that in some measure affects every American, black or white. It has conditioned the mind of the southern Negro as well as everyone else—and therefore the southern Negro *is* a problem, not only in the mind of the South, but in everyday life. He has been taught irresponsibility and subservience, to be, as they say on Highway 80, a "grinnin' nigger," a fellow who is childlike, foolish and unambitious, and it is surprising that more Negroes don't act the part. But it also paralyzes the southern white. It poisons the schools, cripples social relations, and deforms the moral life of the community. It makes cowards of teachers, apologists of administrators and criminals of public officials.

At the same time, it has loosened a flood of moral righteousness from outsiders who have sometimes put the spokesmen of deep South decency and moderation on the defensive. Northern students with a psychic need for sanctification by a policeman's club have occasionally generated as much useless embarrassment and contempt as positive integration—despite the great and positive contributions of SNCC and CORE. The South does have its share of fat-bellied cracker sheriffs who stick Negroes with cattle prods, its quota of frightened and hateful men, but it is no longer solid, even along the uneven course of Highway 80. Macon does not identify with Selma and Meridian, and its moderation requires support as much as Bull Connor of Birmingham needs opposition.

The cosmology of the southern classroom provides ample proof of the constraints the South has imposed on itself. It is a place where the lens of race makes the whole world appear distorted: children of both races are miseducated. But it also indicates what the white man can gain if he frees himself from his fear, and it suggests that, when the Supreme Court declared racially separate schools inherently unequal it spoke, ultimately, not only for the deprived Negro, but for the white as well.

6

The Good Life in California

DREAMS ARE MADE to order while you wait. You can vote for and
against something on the same ballot at the same time; or back
your swimming pool to an oil well; or ride your surfboard on a
November morning while you listen to Beethoven; or live forever under Endowed Perpetual Care in the Garden of Memory;
or BEAT THE BIRCHERS on election day, or join them any day. You
can see Olivia de Havilland *in person* at the Movieland Wax
Museum, the house of the future at Disneyland, and the Old
West at Walter Knott's Berry Farm. You can love Chinese and
hate Negroes in the same breath; hear Thelonius Monk and Joan
Sutherland on the same evening; or drive for two hours without
seeing anything other than the bumper sticker on the car ahead.
It says "Goldwater for Halloween."

It is a place of unmatched beauty and excitement—the tow-
ers of the Golden Gate, half visible in the fog, the skyline of San
Francisco from the Bay Bridge on a clear day, the elegance of the
Carmel peninsula—the grandeur of the Coast Range rising from
the Pacific below Big Sur—and it is a place of endless boredom
—Castroville, the artichoke capital of the world, the desert west
of Yuma, the sandhill developments in Orange County, and the
trail of neon on its Harbor Boulevard.

Everything is available, and most of it is, one way or another, a bet on the future: plates from Dr. Beauchamp, the credit
dentist; furnished town houses, $1300 down, where the manage-
ment provides baby-sitters, a nursery, a study hall staffed by
teachers for adolescents and golf carts for shopping; body development, body exercise, body care; education for anyone in
any subject on any terms; and real estate at any price. It is a place
of believers, fervent believers, living the dreams that won't ger-

minate in the cold winters of Wisconsin or the worn soil of Oklahoma; believers in Cinderella, the good fairy and the witch; believers in the cyclotron, the computer and the contraceptive; and believers in belief, and in nonbelief; a supermarket of aspirations, a magic mountain one thousand miles long, in which anyone can become anything—queen for a day, rich quick, happy forever. "If you stay here for three weeks," they say, "you'll never want to go back." Those who resist shudder that they've seen the future in freeways, traffic jams and sprawl; and those who stay impatiently wait for it.

California is all things and all places. It is two states, or perhaps three or four. Its huge area and climatic differences produce such great variations that almost any description is inadequate and almost any suggestion a possibility. A few thousand signatures will put even the silliest proposition on the ballot—a legacy of the progressive politics of Hiram Johnson—and that included, in the 1964 election, everything from prohibition of pay television to the elimination of railroad featherbedding. Herb Caen, the columnist of the *San Francisco Chronicle*—yet more than a columnist, rather an institution, like an educated milkman—quoted a suggestion that the state be split across the middle: half would be "us" (the Bay Area) and the rest would be called Disneyland. The northern half has water and the southern half is perennially trying to get it; the northern half tends to be relatively stable; the southern half is restless, growing and, frequently, adolescent. San Francisco thrives on its reputation for being cosmopolitan, liberal, and highly sophisticated, the West Egg for America's intellectual Gatsbys, while the southern half is always said to be a playground for reactionaries, sunworshippers, faddists and other kooks. But southern California is also a place of oil wells, aircraft factories, and savings-and-loan associations, where private enterprise has erected its own welfare state and profit-making institutions provide enough security to make Lord Beveridge archaic; where almost everything is an open question; and where the spectrum of belief and opinion and tolerance of behavior is as great as it is anywhere in America.

Although southern California is known as Birch country—and in many places it is; and although San Francisco is supposed to be liberal—and in ways *it* is, the distinction clouds the complexities of both. San Francisco conservatism sometimes rivals London's, and its provincialism often matches Boston's. Some San Franciscans see America as composed of only three parts— San Francisco, the East Bay and the East—and they regard residents of Oakland as New Yorkers regard the denizens of Newark and Jersey City—barbarians who live on slag heaps behind factories; and most of them, though they take pride in their good relations with Orientals, are only dimly aware that the 4000 Negroes of prewar days now number close to 100,000 and that nearly all of them live in ghettos. Yet they tolerate almost everything, including intolerance and southern California. Unlike Los Angeles, San Francisco is a community in which all neighborhoods have not yet been homogenized, in which it is still possible to go places without a car, and in which one can be any kind of brow, high, middle or low, without feeling too defensive. Its citizens do battle to protect Golden Gate Park from the freeways and the cable cars from efficiency and destruction. They know they inhabit one of the world's most beautiful cities, and they derive their conservatism from a feeling that most changes are ultimately for the worse. They have, many of them, a genuine sense of place, and thus have earned a right to their provincialism.

By contrast Southern California is . . . almost everything it has ever been called. The place where they pulled up the orange trees and planted people. Forty suburbs in search of a city. Couch canyon. The factory of dreams. It is a place where the land has been settled and the social and political problems have not, and where almost every public campaign seems somehow to rest on the belief that utopia is just around the corner, blocked only by the intransigence of Communists or Birchers, or even phonics and personality tests. Los Angeles is at the heart of it, but Los Angeles itself is just part of a cluster of places that stretch a hundred miles along the coast—Santa Monica, and Beverly Hills, and Seal Beach, and Huntington Beach, and Newport Beach, and Santa Ana and Balboa—each year creeping closer to San Diego and the Mexican border on the south, and to Santa Barbara on the north; a place of cars, oil derricks, three-par golf courses, electronics plants, housing developments and self-service drugstores all mixed together like toys that weren't sorted after

they came from the box; a place where you can plan your picnic
a week or a month or a year ahead, knowing that if the smog
allows the sun will shine, and all of it so new that everything
seems possible, yet so old that a few families trace their land holdings to royal patents from Spain.

More than anything else, California is a state of mind, a magnet that attracts thousands of immigrants each day from the Middle West and, to a lesser degree, from the East—students from
Illinois, pensioners from Missouri, teachers from Nebraska, engineers from Ohio all sharing a belief in the American cornu-
copia, refusing to admit that life is brutish and short, denying
the tragic, and affirming that the good life is imminent. If reality
fails the image, they try to remake it, keeping the vision more or
less intact. Thus they have established the most universal system
of public education in the world—a system that comes closer to
accommodating every person of whatever talent, interests or
means than any other ever created; thus they have also become
enmeshed in the greatest number of fringe organizations and
utopian movements; and thus their penchant for confusing one
with the other.

But education remains at the heart of much of it: education
not merely for a job, or to get into college—for in California almost everyone can get in—but education for the Good Life, for
weekends on the beach and in the pool, for identity in a society
that provides little, education for morals, patriotism and religion,
education to be charming, handsome and successful. California
leads the country in the salaries paid school teachers (an average
of $7375 in 1962), in the percentage of kids who graduate from
high school, and in almost every other quantitative measure of
educational performance available. Its junior college system, despite great weaknesses, has become a model for other states; its
state university graduate schools are considered among the best,
if not the best, in the country, and its undergraduate colleges,
public and private, sustain the possibility that a college degree—
in marketing or physical education or television or recreation administration or forestry or classical philosophy—is available to
anyone.

The base of this huge educational pyramid is composed of
a jumble of school districts in which critics have found the best

and the worst and almost everything in between. Many of them serve no particular community, but simply an area, a territory carved out of the map; two or three elementary districts feed two or three high school districts with which they are not necessarily contiguous, all of them constantly negotiating with each other and with state education officials about reorganization, acting under the stimulus of a recent act of the legislature which contains both a carrot and a stick to make order of the jumble. These negotiations include so many variables that even the administrators are confused: state and federal aid, bonded indebtedness, tax base, number of classrooms, and pupil population. Frequently one district will negotiate simultaneously with four or five others on two or three different plans of reorganization, all of them somehow inadequate because there are no communities, no logical boundaries, no civic cohesion and, often, no clear educational philosophy. Adjacent elementary school districts feeding the same high school sometimes operate from different assumptions: life adjustment in one, a rigid academic program in the other; even within the same system, or the same school, different tracks and programs are likely to be vastly different. (The public address system interrupts a mathematics class with the morning announcements—yesterday's interscholastic water polo scores, the time of the next football pep rally, the officers of the German Club, and the list of National Merit Semi-finalists.)

Everything is fluid—subject to change by next week, or even tomorrow morning. A liberal school board is recalled and replaced by a conservative one; a superintendent is fired; parents march in to see the principal, clutching a list supplied by the DAR of unpatriotic books, or a statement about the teaching of sex, or something they heard about personality tests; a kid sneaks a tape recorder to class to catch a teacher's subversive remarks; hearings are held; policies revised and then re-revised; charges are published in the newspapers; people are called Communists and Birchers, and occasionally a teacher is fired. And while this goes on in one district people in adjacent areas become nervous and look around to see if the controversy will spill on them. They know that it doesn't happen very often, that most districts are stable, and that most school boards are composed of people strong or conservative enough to resist pressure from all extremes, but they also know that it can happen.

Max Rafferty, the State Superintendent of Instruction, reflects this academic insecurity. Rafferty, who had been a small city superintendent, was elected to his post in 1962 on a platform of educational fundamentalism and political conservatism, combining an appeal for higher academic standards with a pitch to the Right. "We have been so busy educating for 'life adjustment,'" he once wrote, "that we have forgotten to educate for survival." The schools should teach patriotism and "the grand old songs," he urged; they should return to hero worship and abandon trivia. American prisoners in Korea were brainwashed because they had never been taught the words of Nathan Hale, and had never learned to love their country; the schools were responsible for "the phony sophisticates who clutter up our colleges and agitate against ROTC and parade in support of Fidel Castro." But Rafferty appealed not only to political orthodoxy but also to those who felt that the schools were academic featherbeds—to parents who were sick of Jane and Dick and the friendly policeman, impatient with fun-and-games, who had heard Robert Hutchins say that the high school is the place where the band practices, and who interpreted Sputnik as an indictment of the educational system. Rafferty made a "return tó fundamentals" mean two things: patriotism, morality and religion on the one hand; stiffer academic courses on the other. "Education during the past three decades," he said, "has deliberately debunked the hero. The quest of the Golden Fleece has been crowded out of our textbooks by the visit of Tom and Susan to the zoo. The sterile culture of the Pueblo Indian looms large in our curriculum, but the knightly Crusaders and the deeds of the heroes before Troy are now passed, and so is the deathless ride of Paul Revere. . . . Today too many schools—especially on the elementary level —are teaching trivia."

Once in office, Rafferty began to issue statements on every conceivable aspect of school policy. He asked the schools to do something about "youthful, leather jacketed, cold-eyed mobsters on motorcycles," to teach children that "in this life the decent get the brass rings"; to teach phonics, more moral and spiritual

values, ("there is a very positive and important place for God in
the schools," he said), and to present evolution as "an important
scientific theory or hypothesis," not as "a permanent unchanging
truth." He stumped his own and other states discussing religion
and patriotism, opposing "the recent trend toward divorcing education and religion in the public schools," asking for an end to
"life adjustment" and pleading the case for "fundamentals." At
the same time he became engaged in a continuing public controversy with the president of the appointed State Board of Education, Thomas W. Braden, who, Rafferty said, was a "political
hatchet man" lacking in patriotism. Braden, an Oceanside newspaper publisher who once worked for the Central Intelligence
Agency, and who has the support of Governor Edmund G.
Brown, replied by calling Rafferty a red-baiter, and by asking
him to spend more time at his desk and less making speeches.

Since Braden and the ten-man board set educational policy,
and since Rafferty must work through the civil service bureaucracy of the State Department of Education which resists him, his
effect *within the system* has been minor. Dorman Commons, a liberal member of the board, called it "miniscule." "But," he said,
"you can't deny that Rafferty has made an impact because he has
given heart to certain local groups." Organizations calling themselves Parents for Prayer, Parents for Rafferty and other names
have descended on local school officials to see if the Rafferty program was being implemented; they applaud his public statements, his attacks on progressives and Communists and on Tom
Braden, cheering their hero as they cheer the Angels, the Dodgers
and the Rams. They have carried petitions to the state board,
investigated textbooks, attacked personality tests (a Red plot)
and have learned to regard phonics as they regarded Moise
Tshombe, Barry Goldwater and General Walker. But their most
immediate objective has been the scalp of Braden himself. Headed by a state senator from San Diego named Jack Schrade, a
group of legislators demanded that Governor Brown remove
Braden who, Schrade said, has "consistently identified himself
with leftist and antipatriotic viewpoints." The people of California, he added, had elected Rafferty, not the state board. "If
Braden were to run for public office he couldn't beat an asthmatic
turtle across the tennis court, yet he has the gall and audacity to

launch a personal statewide vendetta against Dr. Rafferty." Organizations in Orange County threatened to oppose school bond issues if Braden stayed on, and the controversy became hot enough to bring in Brown who replied by attacking "extreme right groups that believe the public schools are socialistic" and by saying that he had no power to fire Braden even if he wanted to. (Some Californians think Rafferty himself hopes to run as a conservative Republican in the 1966 gubernatorial campaign.)

Although the polemics of the Braden-Rafferty feud have little directly to do with educational policy—involving, rather, things like Rafferty's refusal to judge a Bill of Rights essay contest which, he implied, was tainted by some leftist sponsors—it symbolizes California's divided allegiance, its split sensibilities about where it wants to go and what it expects of its schools. Rafferty and Braden are both more symbols than instruments of policy. Each has his own cheering section, and each has some people wondering whether the donnybrook is worth it, either in political or educational achievement. But even if both were to retire from the scene the issues would remain and the battle—with other champions—would continue. At bottom it is more than a contest in epithets and personalities: it reflects the deep split between Southern California and San Francisco, between the right, center and left, between the establishment and the freewheeling newcomers, and between California's respectable conservatism and its rootless insecurity.

II

La Habra flows into Fullerton, and Fullerton into Anaheim, and Anaheim into Garden Grove, and Garden Grove into Westminster and Fountain Valley and Huntington Beach, and all of it is called Orange County. Before World War II Fullerton's population stood at 10,000 people, and the county's at 140,000. In 1963 Fullerton reached 70,000 and the county passed 1,000,000 and earned itself the designation "standard metropolitan statistical area." While oil companies sank new holes in the boondocks, developers dug up the orange trees and the sand hills and replaced them with curved streets named Los Ranchos, San Lorenzo, Rosarita and Vista del Mar (from which one sees nothing but more houses); they planted shopping centers and palm trees and redwood fences; they advertised ranch houses five per cent down and forever to pay—all guaranteed by the government —and they watched as the people came, and came, and came. Commuters from Los Angeles, employees of Hughes Aircraft, Hunt Foods and Beckman Instruments, pensioners protecting their savings against taxes and inflation, they settled in the old clusters, and the clusters spread and flowed together, and when the freeways were constructed, the clusters spread and flowed some more, like butter in the California sun. They built swimming pools and churches and schools, and every weekend they went, and still go, to the beach, surfboards strapped to the roof rack, waiting for the next raise and the next promotion when they can move closer to the water or farther up the hill. Missiles came, and so did electronics, and along with them came engineers and technicians, and a corps of doctors and dentists and teachers and TV repairmen and garage mechanics. Disneyland began to draw tourists into Anaheim, and local residents too, and Walter Knott of Buena Park, who once sold berries by the side of the road, prospered, enlarged his restaurant, erected a re-creation of an old California ghost town and other attractions, and became official Orange County greeter for the gentlemen of the Right. Barry Goldwater came there to rest and talk campaign strategy, and John Rousselot, the ex-congressman, set up shop nearby as official publicist of the John Birch Society.

Fullerton, near the northern end of the county, is one of its most established communities; people lived there before World War II, and a few even before World War I. Old families like the Chapmans operated ranches and grew oranges and, after the people began to come, converted their holdings into ranch houses and oil leases. But even Fullerton is almost altogether new: whether you count water meters or telephones or sewer connections, Fullerton is as new as the electronics plants and the freeways that nourish it. In 1893 it built its first high school; its second was opened in 1954, its third in 1956, its fourth in 1959, its fifth in 1961, and its sixth in 1964. The high schools were built for the county and the people who came to it, campus-style buildings with no corridors: when students change classes at Lowell or Sunny Hills High they do it outdoors, and when they come to school they travel, most of them, in their own automobiles.

Each building is flanked—almost surrounded—by asphalt parking lots, by tennis courts and archery ranges and playing fields, and, usually, by an outdoor swimming pool. And as the people kept coming—most of them from other parts of the West and the Middle West—and as the children came, new teachers were hired to meet the increases, special services were added, and the tax rate climbed. New courses were initiated in mathematics and science, the language program expanded, and team teaching began in some subjects at some schools. But the expansion and modernization took place in schools which serve no real community. ("Four or five years ago," said Donald H. Kennedy, the principal at Lowell, "this was a bean field.") The Fullerton District draws its 11,000 students (1964) from La Habra and Buena Park, from Lowell and Yorba Linda as well as from Fullerton, and all of these places suffer the newness, the fragmentation and insecurity of subdivisions that have no focus, no traditions, and which are populated by people of so many backgrounds that a consensus would be hard to get on anything. In coming to California, many of their inhabitants expected more than they found. They did not escape rising taxes or urban complexity or moral ambiguity, and often they found that they had exchanged the security of the small town for the anonymity of the suburb. Most of them demanded, and still demand, much of the schools—expected them to be the gates to the good life—but a few were also frightened as they looked in, seeing only more complexity and ambiguity and change: courses that bore only a vague, if any, resemblance to the old patriotic history, arithmetic full of strange new symbols, and a whole battery of services that seemed unnecessary at best, and perhaps even dangerous. Like all immigrants they saw their kids initiated into a world they did not understand, but *unlike* other immigrants, they had been given to understand that this was their country and their culture.

Trouble began in 1960. A Fullerton High School guidance counselor named Joel Dvorman had been elected to the board of education of the Magnolia School District in neighboring Anaheim, home of Disneyland, and a place which was growing even more wildly than the developments of Lowell and Fullerton. Dvorman, it was whispered, was a Communist. He was a member of a certain group known as the American Civil Liberties

Union, an "extremist organization" which was against religion
and in favor of policies advocated by the Russians. Dvorman
held ACLU meetings at his home; he voted against the distribution
of Bibles in the schools; and he was suspected of having associated with Communists and with communist-front organizations.
In 1947, as a college student, he had been a member of American
Youth for Democracy, a group that was later (after he was no
longer a member) listed as subversive by the Attorney General.
Dvorman, moreover, had held a meeting at his home which was
attended by a person who had pleaded the First Amendment before the United States House Un-American Activities Committee.

In the fall of 1960, while a campaign was launched in Anaheim to recall Dvorman from the Magnolia board (California
law permits recall at almost all levels of government), parents
began to attend meetings of the Fullerton board to demand Dvorman's dismissal from his high school job. And then everything
began to happen at once. Fred Schwarz's Christian Anti-Communist Crusade held a four day "Anti-Communist School" in Orange County, and parents succeeded in getting the Fullerton
board to excuse students who wished to attend it; a high school
girl walked off with an examination from her sex-education unit
(against her teacher's instructions) and started a new furor; the
parents of another student objected to the use of an anthology
called *Adventures in Reading* edited by J. M. Ross and others
because it included selections by authors alleged to be communist sympathizers, and because the book was said to have been
blacklisted by the DAR; another group of parents began to attack
personality tests as communist devices (one of them told an elementary school guidance counselor that all the test results were
forwarded to Paris where they were placed in a secret file); a
teacher at Fullerton Junior College, which is operated by the
same board as the high schools, was attacked for using an ACLU
questionnaire in his classes; two known Birchers pressured one of
the Junior College publications to use right wing material (when
the editors refused, the publication was attacked in some of the
area newspapers); a proposal for an increased tax ceiling for the
Fullerton high schools was defeated, and, in April 1961, the fol-

lowing month, Dvorman was recalled from the Magnolia board
by a vote of almost three to one. Despite this barrage of attacks
and the continuing pressure from parents and certain area newspapers—though not all of them (plus a number of people who
called themselves parents but, apparently, lived elsewhere) the
Fullerton board refused to fire Dvorman. Dvorman had failed to
tell the superintendent, Ernest G. Lake, that he had belonged to
American Youth for Democracy—Dvorman simply did not consider it worth mentioning until the reactionaries confronted the
board with it—and that, Lake says now, made it hard for the
board to protect him. (Lake told a public meeting at the time that
Dvorman had shown poor judgment, and the board concurred.)
Nevertheless, Dvorman remained in his post as counselor until
the end of the 1961 spring term and, the board informed an investigating committee of the National Education Association, he
was scheduled to return to it in the fall.

Dvorman did return to the high school, but not to his former
job of guidance counselor. When classes opened in September—
his friends say it was by mutual agreement—he was teaching remedial arithmetic. In January 1962, while he was still a young
man, he died of a heart attack.

No one knows who started the "Dvorman incident" or how
the various campaigns were controlled and financed, but Dvorman's death did not end it. When Dvorman was recalled, the
right-wing of Anaheim gained control of the Magnolia District,
initiated an "Americanism Program" and, in the spring of 1963,
hired a superintendent named Charles Wilson who replaced the
old balanced reading program with a system of phonics that was
so rigid that even the publisher of the materials Wilson adopted
suggested it be used only for remedial work. ("Congratulations
for your fine work in bringing parents and phonics together for
the advancement of reading among the children of your district,"
Rafferty wired him.) Wilson also initiated a series of publications
called "The Magnolia Way" which were sent home with the children; one proclaimed America as a "God Centered Nation," another asserted that American patriotism was "ESSENTIAL FOR THE
SURVIVAL OF ALL MANKIND, not just the children of the Magnolia
School District," and, in December 1963, Wilson issued one headed "Our Traditional Christmas Must be Preserved."

There is ONE belief that has defied change (it said in part) . . .
It has remained because it is an ETERNAL TRUTH, defying the
powers of man to pervert or time to diminish its message.

"For unto you is born this day in the city of David a Saviour,
which is Christ the Lord." Nineteen hundred and sixty-three
years later this is still the symbol, the significance, the very soul
of Christmas . . . although an attempt has been made in the past
years in the United States to bring about a "changed" celebra-
tion of Christmas.

. . . *Be we Christians or not,* Christmas is a vital part of *our
American culture, our American way of life.* . . .

And what is a Christian Christmas?

It is the second chance for the people of the world. It is the
eternal hope for peace on earth, good will to men!

In the spring of 1963—after the old superintendent had
been fired—a parents' committee started a campaign to recall
the district's right-wing majority, but it failed by fifty votes. A
second attempt, supported by a majority of the Magnolia District
teachers, was made in April 1964, after all the principals in the
district had resigned in protest of Wilson's policies. The recall
organization was called "Save Our Schools" and it was headed by
four mothers in the district. "Somebody was taking pictures of
the people who came to our house," said Jane Oseid, one of the
sos leaders. "We got anonymous phone calls and were called
nasty names. But after the first try we had some experience
and got some professional help." The defenders of the Magnolia board majority brought out the old Dvorman issues;
in a full page statement in the *Anaheim Bulletin,* published by
Raymond Hoiles, an individual who believes that both the post
office and the schools should be run by private enterprise, they
again called the ACLU an extremist organization "whose recent
programs have included an effort to remove the words 'under
God' from our Pledge of Allegiance" and lauded the district's
"Americanism Program." The sos campaign, on the other hand,
stressed the low morale of the schools (ninety-five per cent of the
teachers said in a poll that they would not recommend Magnolia
as a good place to teach), the failures of the phonics program, and
administrative inefficiency.

> Why is it [said an sos circular] that the three board members
> —through anonymous handbills, whispering campaigns and
> editorials in the *Anaheim Bulletin*—have implied that the prin-
> cipals, teachers, citizens, County Superintendent of Schools,
> County Counsel and State Board of Education either are part
> of a Communist conspiracy or are simply dishonest? . . .
>
> Why is it that *extremists* from throughout Southern Califor-
> nia are being *recruited* to come to Magnolia School District and
> help "get out the vote" for Allen, Downs and Milligan [the
> three Board members]?

Although sos charged that the board was "indoctrinating"
children, it never attacked the Americanism program directly,
and it never identified the imported extremists (although everyone was certain that some of the Magnolia defenders were Birchers). On April 28, 1964 the three majority members of the board
were recalled and replaced.

Back in Fullerton, meanwhile, a new skirmish had taken
place. While the parents' group in the Magnolia District was
fighting and losing its first recall campaign, right wingers challenged two incumbent board members in a regular election in
Fullerton, charging "mandatory socialism taught as free enterprise," demanding an end to sex education, and asking that students be taught "patriotism and pride in our free enterprise system." Dorman Commons, vice-president of an oil company and
now a member of the state board, headed a group of businessmen
and other persons who rallied behind the incumbents and helped
defeat the challengers. In retrospect that campaign now seems
placid, but with Fullerton's tempestuous history and the battle in
adjacent Anaheim, still going on, the election was regarded as
critical. "The board," Commons said, "was composed of good solid people, some of them from old Fullerton families. When they
were called communist dupes some people became conscious for
the first time of the tactics of the extreme Right. Magnolia didn't
even exist ten years ago and it has never really congealed. Here
there was leadership and more of a community. The Birchers are
more likely to disrupt new communities; they appeal to people
who believe the world is black and white—many of them people
from the Middle West who ran into things that frightened them.

Right now [October 1964] they're busy campaigning for Goldwater. But they're still around; they haven't quit."

Nevertheless Commons and the small establishment in Fullerton have won their campaign, Jane Oseid and her ladies have
won theirs—at least for the time being—and the mood of the
schools in northern Orange County has relaxed. "We've had our
battle," Lake said, and he may well be right, although the memory of it still lingers. Alan Elliott, the principal of the Acacia
Elementary School in Fullerton said "it was a little tough for
someone who had been cleared for secret work by the Navy to be
accused of trying to poison the minds of children," while Don
Oseid, the husband of the woman who helped lead the Magnolia
campaign—himself one of the most exciting teachers in Fullerton—recalls how "the kids from the Birch families would sit
there, never smiling. We knew which ones they were: they'd look
at you and ask 'what did you say?' as if they were taking it all
down for somebody else." Another teacher speaks of the student
who came with a tape recorder: "a pathetic kid, he was a dupe
for his parents, and they were dupes for a Birch doctor; they
came with the DAR list. They'd never read the books themselves."
But Don Oseid, like Lake and the other teachers, feels that the
climate has changed, that it changed even before Fullerton's
1963 election. "We were nervous—everybody was nervous, but
that's not true any more. The Birch kids are isolated now—they
get kidded by other students—it all feeds their paranoia. You feel
sorry for them." People like the Oseids now speak with the confidence of veterans who have been through the toughest battles
of the war and have discovered that the resources of the enemy,
while substantial, weren't as formidable as they had feared. In
winning their campaigns they developed a certain pride in the
outfit and in the community for which they won them. As for
their opponents, four years of adverse publicity, nationally and
locally, has made the label *Bircher* more and more of an evil
word. Although Orange County is represented in the California State Senate by an avowed member of the society, individuals locally identified as having Birch sympathies are constantly
on the defensive, a position which is, of course, derived from
their view of the world (everybody, after all, is part of the Conspiracy) but which has been increasingly reinforced by public

criticism, by defeat in local elections, and by Goldwater's big defeat in 1964. "I don't know why everyone who believes in morality and free enterprise is called a Bircher," said a professional man in Fullerton who was identified as one—and probably is one. "You don't have to be a Bircher to know there's a communist conspiracy going on." And this suggests one of the reasons they lose. When the national Birch organization announced its intention to use communist tactics by setting up front organizations the whole right wing became tainted with its name: it is sometimes as hard to be a genuine conservative without being called a Bircher as to be a liberal without being called a Communist. It also suggests why the John Birch Society *as an organization* sometimes appears so threatening. (Is a school election campaign that includes some known Birchers any more affected by their presence than a civil rights drive is affected by the presence of some communists?) Most of the parents who jammed the school board meetings, who carried the DAR lists, who searched the textbooks, who considered compulsory school gymnasium showers a Red plot—it is, after all, a form of collectivism —most of these people have never belonged to any political organization and wouldn't know a genuine conspiracy if one fell on them. Many are simply disillusioned by the conditions of their lives, not convinced that their houses or their automobiles are really theirs—were ever really earned—and that they won't disappear as easily as they came; they are frustrated by the moral complexities of their surroundings, by the anonymity of their station, and by the loss of the certainties that sustained them in some other place at some other time. They have come a long way from home.

And *they* are all around—unhappy people who tried to cast out the devil and failed, but who, in failing, may also have succeeded in making the schools a little more cautious and—insofar as these things can ever be measured—in moving them a notch to the right. Several teachers said they have remained uneasy ever since 1960 when the attacks began, and one superintendent confided he was constantly reminded of "latent extremism. People see me at club meetings or at church and ask 'why are you against phonics?' and I still hear objections to references in textbooks to the Army of the United Nations in the Korean War and to mention of the UN generally." A professor at California State College at Fullerton said the schools are "sticking to safe courses" using standard texts, and that student teachers are often advised to avoid controversial subjects. At the same time school districts like Fullerton's have worked out statements and procedures defending the teaching of "controversial issues"—defined as anything about which "there is a significant difference of opinion among a substantial number of citizens" (and that, obviously, covers a lot of topics). The Dvorman incident, said a high school social studies department chairman, had "a sobering effect on all of us. You have to be on your guard a little more and if you go to bat for something be sure you're well equipped. But we haven't given up on controversial issues." There are constant reminders that the potential for trouble is still there: In 1964 every graduating senior was sent—no one knows by whom—a copy of the right-wing tract *None Dare Call It Treason* and the Goldwater diatribe, *A Choice Not An Echo*; high school textbooks are still being attacked as socialistic, despite the fact that most of them are as bland as last year's whitewash. Some Fullerton teachers continue to rely on books like *The Rise of the American Nation* by Lewis Paul Todd and Merle Curti, the latter one of the most respected American historians, which performs a characteristic balancing act on Joe McCarthy:

> Congressional Committees were sometimes charged with handling individuals accused of subversion without proper regard for judicial practices. Among the most controversial of these was the one headed by Senator Joseph R. McCarthy of Wisconsin . . . Senator McCarthy carried on extensive investigations of possible Communist influence in government. He brought charges against leading Americans no longer in government service, against the Department of State, and against the Army. Many Americans applauded McCarthy for his efforts, but others criticized him for what they called his recklessness and his disregard for constitutional rights. In 1954 McCarthy's influence declined. . . .

And, in the elementary schools, they use a book called *The Story of American Freedom* by Edna McGuire and Catherine M. Broderick:

The struggle between communism and freedom is the principal problem in the world today. It affects the relations of nations.

The Communists, led by the Soviet Union, create one difficult situation after another for the United States and its friends. They stir up trouble which they hope will divide the free world . . .

They fall back on "balanced" discussions, avoid undue stress on the UN, and take their time about coming to anything that might cause another furor. Policy in the elementary schools prohibits UNICEF campaigns, and the high schools excuse the handful of students whose parents object to the sex education unit, and they discourage political editorials in the school newspapers.

But the blandness and chauvinism of certain books, the caution of some teachers, and the precautions of the schools are only part of the story of education in Orange County. Fullerton fought battles about issues that many schools have simply buried or ignored—the United Nations, evolution, new courses, new taxes—*fought* while others capitulated. Even those most worried about attacks from the right now add that Fullerton is a community where parents value education—value it more than people did in Indiana or Michigan or wherever it was the speaker came from—and that Fullerton's troubles, now hopefully past, came from a minority who took temporary advantage of a divided opposition. In becoming slightly more conservative, the Fullerton schools have also become more cohesive; those who were there in 1960 and 1961 feel that the attackers produced a unity within the teaching force that had not existed before. The battles they generated are part of Fullerton's experience—a bench mark of its growth—but they have not eliminated the system's willingness to try courses and programs that many others do not—sex education is an example—and to tolerate, and even encourage, departures that would be exciting for any group of students anywhere.

Don Oseid and Jim Hines each conduct two sections of Tower English—small informal classes of advanced students who meet daily in the tower of the Fullerton High School, one of the most architecturally delightful buildings in Orange County. The school, originally erected in 1912 in the style of the Spanish missions of California, was rebuilt after a devastating earthquake in 1933, and it now educates 2100 students; its 23,000 volume library, modeled after the celebrated library at Salamanca, is among the most pleasant academic chambers to be found anywhere. Representative of what there is of old Fullerton, the school tends to be conservative and more reluctant to innovate than the newer schools with the younger staffs (and being old, it also has a serious parking problem). It has about it a well-heeled mustiness that the newer institutions lack. Unlike most schools of its own vintage, it resembles neither a factory nor a prison, and it may be the only American high school of its time which looks like an academic structure that belongs where it is. When Donald Cruickshank, the principal, says that "this school is a bit more conservative than the others," you are somehow glad it is. As he speaks he makes it clear that in his school there is no frenetic hurry to remake the world: it was among the last in the district to work with audio-lingual methods of teaching language, and to try the new math, and even now that it has started on them it does not seem especially excited about them. It enjoys a good reputation in college placement: about eighty per cent of its graduates attend some collegiate institution, many of them directly across the street at the Junior College (sometimes unjustly called a high school with ash trays) but some also at Yale and Wellesley and Pembroke and MIT—not to mention Berkeley, Stanford, Pomona and USC. And because there are many Mormons in Southern California several graduates from the Fullerton District attend Brigham Young. Some of the school's engineer parents insist that regardless of ability, their children be enrolled in the school's math-science track which places a heavy emphasis on those fields but, for the most part, they are willing to take the advice of the counseling staff. The pressure that exists is subtle. "College is the thing to do," said a guidance counselor in Fullerton. "From the time they're quite young, the kids are told 'when you get in college. . . .' After they leave here they almost have to attend college, because they're not prepared for anything else. We've done pretty well with the mentally retarded but the slow learners are simply getting watered-down versions of the regular program. We tried work experience programs but they suffered from low status. We offer industrial arts, but not vocational education."

Despite its relative conservatism Fullerton High has adopted the physics course of the Physical Science Study Committee, Chem Study (which a faculty member at nearby Harvey Mudd College helped draw up), the new math of the Illinois Mathematics Program and the School Mathematics Study Group, and other new courses. It is, like the other schools in the district, a beneficiary of Fullerton's national recruiting program and its high salaries, beginning at $6230 for a high school teacher with a master's degree, and exceeding $10,000 after 14 years.

But its most distinctive characteristic is the informal teaching of people like Don Oseid and Jim Hines, free-wheelers who thrive on California's informality.

The room where Oseid and Hines meet their advanced English classes is about halfway up the bell tower. No more than fifteen feet square, and isolated from most of the school's traffic, the room might be monkish if it weren't for the irreverence of the students and the two young teachers who encourage them. Don Oseid's two groups of seniors—about twelve in each—have hung Van Gogh and Degas reproductions on one wall; on the opposite wall Hines' competitive juniors have placed a large, elaborately lettered sign that says DOWN WITH GOOD TASTE, and next to it a poster: "Coolidge for President."

Tower English is a creature of the students themselves: two years before, they had come to Oseid and Hines and asked them to provide on opportunity to "talk about life and stuff," a request that ultimately coincided with a state program to encourage schools to institute special courses for advanced students. The state provides forty dollars per pupil in such programs: Hines and Oseid use the money to take their classes to concerts, the opera, the ballet and to other cultural activities in the Los Angeles area.

The twelve seniors in Oseid's class are reading Plato's *Republic*; before the year is out they will also read other dialogues, Thucydides' *History of the Peloponnesian War*, *Oedipus Rex*, the *Divine Comedy* and at least a portion of *Faust*. Like most kids in southern California, they seem bigger, blonder, and healthier than kids of the same age elsewhere; as they come to class they move haphazardly into the chairs that are scattered around the small room. Two or three sit on the flight of steps that leads from the room farther up into the tower. Oseid, already there, sits at one end of the circle that begins to form. He wears a sport shirt, but one sleeve is empty: a former Fulbright Fellow to Greece, and a graduate of the University of Michigan, Oseid lost the arm bailing out of a plane when he was a Marine fighter pilot. There is talk about Johnson and Goldwater, and about Proposition 14, which would—and did—make California's law against discrimination in housing unconstitutional, and about the visitor, who soon abandons his effort to make himself inconspicuous. Everything that walks into the room is a resource.

"Sure there's a form of class breeding in this country," says a boy as the conversation begins to shift from Lyndon Johnson to Plato. "Obviously there's a difference between a Mexican-American and a Newport debutante."

"But Plato talks about depriving inferior children so that superior children can grow up to be the guardians" says another. "That's not the same thing. . . ."

"Does our society encourage the practice of locking people into classes?" Oseid asks. The talk shifts temporarily to the feudal class structure of Japan, then drifts back to America.

"Has anyone heard of the Establishment?" Oseid asks.

"Goldwater speaks of the hated eastern establishment," a boy says. "I suppose he means people like Lodge."

"What is the Establishment?" asks Oseid.

"I suppose its people like the big bankers," a girl replies.

"They talk about control of the Republican Party shifting to the west."

"Do you get born into the Establishment, are you elected to it . . . how do you get into it?" The visitor has been identified as an Easterner, and Oseid, in asking his question, shifts his glance from the students to him. The visitor cites Richard Rovere's article called "The Establishment" which defines this institution —partly tongue in cheek—as an entity with no formal standards of admission but with particular characteristics. The Ivy League, *The New York Times,* the Ford Foundation, the Foreign Policy Association are all part of it, and John J. McCloy, chairman of the Board of the Ford Foundation, an officer of the Foreign Policy Association, former United States High Commissioner to Germany, and former chairman of the board of the Chase Manhattan Bank, is its most characteristic figure.

"Then," a boy says, "the Establishment is pretty much everything that the Birchers don't like."

"Are we becoming like Plato's *Republic* in being conscious of class?" Oseid asks.

"More so in the East," a girl says. "I think the East is much more formal. They're more conscious of it there. Take Fitzgerald —Gatsby was conscious of class . . . I don't think it's so true around here. . . ."

Fifteen minutes later Jim Hines' juniors come into the same room. More irreverent than Oseid, Hines begins talking to a couple of students about intelligence tests; the rest are still drifting in. "Can you increase intelligence?" Hines asks, looking at an article that someone brought him.

"Dr. Crane [a syndicated columnist in the local paper] thinks you're born with a fixed intelligence and that the stupid people are taking over America," says a boy with a grin.

"Now here's Dr. Upton," says Hines, looking at the article, "talking about how 'we literally lifted ourselves by our own bootstraps' into space. That's an interesting phrase. It shows you how we use metaphors."

The topic shifts to the term papers that the students will write for English and history—it is supposed to be one paper for both courses—but Hines has been conducting a sardonic attack on the topics suggested by the history teacher. "The first thing you discover about historians," he says, "is that they're all simplifiers. . . . I think the History Department wants something like 'The Civil War: Democracy vs. Totalitarianism.' I've made up my own suggestions." He passes the list around:

Your topic can be developed in many ways, of course.
Here are three possible approaches:

1. Checking up on your history book—Was the camel experiment really "Unsuccessful"?
2. Conjecturing the motives behind a given action—Was the "Ostend Manifesto" a gimmick to grab Cuba?
3. Contriving a relationship between apparently remote events —Did Cromwell cause the [U.S.] Civil War?

With these approaches in mind, consider the following topics—
as directions only, not as boundaries.

Was Sherman really the biggest booster Atlanta ever had?

Was John Brown a martyr or an irresponsible lunatic?

How did Cupid keep Rezanou from turning California into a
Russian Colony?

In what way did *Uncle Tom's Cabin* appeal chiefly to illit-
erates?

Why did the Westerners, rather than New Englanders, demand
a war to defend our rights at sea [1812]?

What should be the official name of the Civil War?
War to Repel Yankee Aggression? . . .

It should be noted that these are hints only—items of interest to
the compiler of this list. Your personal curiosity should guide
you to many other topics in the course of perusing your text.
Any event or conclusion or reason or relationship which makes
you wonder—that is the source of your topic.

"There are lots of others, of course," Hines says. "It's up to
you. 'How the UN is detrimental to world peace' or 'How Goldwater helped integration' are possibilities. . . . Now where are we?
Scene I in *Caesar*. Look at the depth to which Shakespeare char-
acterizes a person with a line or two—you can recognize the person the next time he speaks. Flavius and the Cobbler. What was
his attitude toward the mob?"

"They're fickle," a student says.

"Maybe the crowd wasn't as fickle as it seems, but he thinks
they're fickle." Hines reads:

> See whe're their basest metal be not mov'd.
> They vanish tongue-tied in their guiltiness.

"Is that a pun?" a student suggests.

" 'They vanish tongue-tied in their guiltiness. . . .' Why the
emphasis on guilt?" Hines says.

"That's part of the pun," the student says. "Gold, guild,
guilt . . ."

"But how do we know that it was intended that way," another student asks, interrupting. Hines responds by quoting Lady Macbeth:

> I'll gild the faces of the grooms . . .
> For it must seem their guilt.

Hines does not press the point; roaming through words and phrases, he lets the students suggest, never anxious about touching bases: mettle, metal, base metal, basest metal be not mov'd (alchemy?), gold, guild, guilt. Out of it comes a metaphor of conversion, and thereafter of fickleness. Later in the play the metaphor recurs; but Hines does not press it now, he does not club anyone with the importance of Great Literature, or with any version of How Books Are Our Friends, but neither is he trying to be One of the Boys. He says *look,* letting Shakespeare, and Hines as a reader of Shakespeare, stand as separate exhibits, the one of poetry and language, the other of the intelligent reader, saying the metaphor is a way of making order, and suggesting, as Robert Frost said, that poetry is a momentary stay against confusion.

Despite freewheelers like Oseid and Hines, and despite the relative conservatism of the Fullerton High School, the schools of the Fullerton District share a common mood and a common function: the mood of the Good Life; the function of preparing for its ultimate achievement. Almost every teacher and administrator in Fullerton eventually comes around to the statement that people in California, and especially in southern California, demand more of their schools than people in other parts of the country, meaning not that they expect them to be the Institute of Advanced Study, scholarly academies dedicated to perennial cerebration, but that they want the schools to be launching places for the rich and varied existence that California has promised, and to deal with the anxieties which it has often imposed. "College administrators and college professors," Lake wrote in 1962, two years after becoming superintendent, "are welcoming the opportunity to revive the stiff subject requirements of our prewar days, *the same standards that for so many years kept our high schools from being truly comprehensive institutions.*" (Italics his.) This kind of comprehensiveness includes the functions of social hall, art center, and country club, for the strands of status are woven into the theme of the Good Life. "The schools," said an elementary school principal, "are supposed to pick up all the loose ends of the community. They come to the high school dances in tuxedos and Cadillacs; there's even pressure on us to have dances in the elementary schools . . . From whom? From the parents. The kids are status symbols and their lives are supervised to death."

Given such considerations, the concept of the comprehensive high school begins to take on a special meaning. The school must serve not only a set of academic and vocational requirements, but it must train students in all the skills which a prosperous community most values; it must deal with the newer forms of technology and with the scientific background that the technology demands; it must take into account the society's expanding opportunities for leisure and recreation, and it must cope with the loneliness and the insecurity it often creates. In this kind of comprehensiveness the football band, the class in painting, the girls playing tennis at eight in the morning, Tower English, and the Birch attack are all logical elements. "We consider the school a preparation for life, rather than for a prestige university or a vocation," said Donald Cruickshank, the principal at Fullerton High School. And, given the conditions of southern California, that is what it is.

At Lowell High School, a few miles northwest of Fullerton, Donald Kennedy, the young principal, is trying to help fifteen hundred students develop a sense of identity in an area where few other institutions exist to help him. Lowell, erected in 1961, and actually located in Los Angeles County—California's jumbled school district lines honor no man-made geographical boundaries—faces outdoors and, in great measure, lives outdoors. The students are well dressed, the boys in fashion-ad sport shirts, the girls in dresses or blouses and jumpers. A few have already started bleaching their hair platinum or white; high heels are not unusual, but shorts or slacks are against the rules. Every now and then, Kennedy reports, students coming from other parts of California have to be retrained. Some, apparently, are used to even more informality than Lowell will tolerate. "We had one senior from a nearby district," he said, "who thought it unusual to take his books to class."

But Kennedy's major concern is "to try to be sensitive to the relationships in each class. We're dealing with fifteen hundred separate universes. These kids are craving personal identification. That's one of the advantages of the athletic program; in football or the drill team the kids have something to identify with. They don't want to be just a pack." Ideally, Kennedy feels, the sense of identity should also develop in the classroom, but frequently it does not. He speaks about students who "suddenly caught fire" in a Great Books class but frequently, he adds, teachers talk too much without being aware of student differences and interests. "The average age of the houses around here is less than ten years, and there are conflicts and frustrations everywhere. Our public is different from other parts of the country; they're more demanding of the schools in southern California than elsewhere. At the same time there's a greater informality in the teacher-pupil interaction. In the northeast the teacher was the law. That's not the case here. You have to be concerned about what happens when a kid asks a question."

Kennedy and his staff have instituted some para-academic enterprises to overcome the students' rootlessness and anonymity, and to generate excitement about the bigger world, a world sometimes hard to reach and perceive in the confusion of southern California. In addition to Great Books there is a venture called Seminar in which the monthly discussion sessions are supplemented by monthly trips to cultural events in Los Angeles, including, even in this land of Birchers, a rehearsal of the Leningrad Ballet. Dramatic groups perform regularly at Lowell, and every spring the school runs an ambitious festival of fine arts which includes dance, drama, music and art. But the shaping motif of these activities is not so much the development of rigorous discipline in the arts and literature as it is exposure to the Good Life, like instruction in swimming or tennis. There is a sense that the workdays are going to be short and the weekends long, and an implicit recognition that the problem isn't to make a living but to occupy a lifetime. "We work the hell out of them during the week," said a Lowell administrator, referring both to the staff and the students, "but we like to get them out on weekends to professional football or professional theater or other events." As a consequence the intellectual life at Lowell and at the other schools tends to be relaxed rather than passionate; at its best—as in Oseid and Hines' classes—it is highly stimulating; at other times it tends to be random and haphazard. In an American history class:

Q.   The colonists then turned to political theory. Who did they turn to?

A.   Writers.

Q.   Who?

A.   John . . . John . . .

A.   John Locke.

Q.   Who was Locke in opposition to?

A.   Hobbes.

Q.   Hobbes was the man whom all rulers of that time looked to. Hobbes did not speak of natural rights. . . . But Hobbes and Locke started out in the same place. Where would you start in drawing a system for governing man?

A.   Don't you have to understand people?

Q.   You start with man in nature, by saying that man is naturally a nice guy or a bad guy. [He starts to explain Hobbes' idea of the social contract, drawing a circle with ten figures on the blackboard.] Say there're only ten people in the world. There's chaos and confusion. Now Zeke over here is tough and smart, so you get together. . . .

Some of the students are sharp and quick, and Lowell's informality can't dampen their curiosity; they ask fresh questions, and often they challenge the teacher's wisdom. ("Christianity as set down in the beginning with Christ and all that jazz was all right," says a blonde in a world history class. "But the Church messed it all up.") Yet it is just as tempting for some to be academic spectators, to enjoy the classroom buddyship, looking healthy and alert, saying little, and escaping unscathed from the scenes of their intellectual crimes. They are expected to write research papers and to read supplementary books, but tolerance sometimes takes advantage of standards, and informality undermines structure. "We try not to discriminate against kids who can't express themselves," said a Lowell teacher. "Society is geared to the high school diploma, and so we judge kids on effort and give them assignments they can handle."

The Fullerton elementary schools—and this is true of elementary schools almost everywhere—are exempt from many of the special demands that the community makes of the high school district. They are, in a sense, more conservative in that they stick more closely to instruction in academic skills. Most of them are new, bright and innovative, but since they are relatively free of special burdens, one could pick them up, exchange them with the better elementary schools of Macon, Georgia, or Newton or Rochester, New York, and hardly know the difference.

At Ladera Vista Junior High School, Mrs. Virginia Domsic, who once taught in a one-room school in Idaho, is asking her seventh grade social studies class about the civilization of ancient Egypt. The kids, among the most physically attractive youngsters anywhere, look like an animated school equipment advertisement out of *School Management* or *The Nation's Schools*.

"Did everyone get a nice tomb?" she asks

"A lot of people weren't as rich as the pharaohs," a boy answers.

"After death they thought the pharaohs would still be pharaohs, and the little people would still be little people," someone else adds.

"The Christian and Egyptian religions were alike," the first boy resumes without prompting. "They both believe people go to heaven after death and find God. . . ."

A few steps across the campus, Adella Hase, a mathematics teacher, has written some symbols on the chalkboard:

$$A = \{0, 1, 2, 3, 4, 5, 6\}$$
$$B = \{4, 5, 6, 7, 8, 9\}$$

She calls on one of the eighth graders to write down the intersection of the two sets. Many hands are up. One student comes to the board and writes:

$$A \cap B$$
$$\{4, 5, 6\}$$

Then she asks for the union of the sets and someone else writes:

$$A \cup B$$
$$\{0, 1, 2, 3, 4, 5, 6, 7, 8, 9\}$$

Then she writes:

A = {all blonde girls in Room 12}

B = {all blue-eyed people,} saying to the class, "all those who are in the intersection of the two sets stand up." All the blue-eyed blonde girls stand. "All those in the union of the two sets stand up." All the blonde girls, and all the blue-eyed kids stand.

At Acacia Elementary School, which feeds Ladera Vista Junior High, and where the fifth graders are learning Spanish via television and tapes (next year, by California statute, every child will have to be taught a foreign language beginning in the sixth grade) teachers are experimenting with book length novels and nonfiction, beginning in the primary grades: *The Red Balloon* and *Rumpelstilskin* in the second grade, *Robinson Crusoe* in the third, *Kon Tiki* and *Robin Hood* in the sixth—getting away from Dick and Jane, and trying to find what the professionals call "high interest, low vocabulary" materials.

At the Maple School, which has the only concentration of nonwhite children in the Fullerton District (it is 83 per cent Mexican-American and 13 per cent Negro), the principal, George Lesikar, has set up programs to build verbal skills for kids who, for one reason or another, have difficulty expressing themselves and are not yet ready to read. In what the school calls a junior first grade (to eliminate the humiliation children feel if they are held back after kindergarten, or not entered in first grade with their peers) Jane Kleinheksel tries to stretch the vocabularies of twenty-one kids of whom at least one has never said anything at all:

Q.   We have some more butterflies in our cage this morning. Where did we get our butterflies?

A.   From caterpillars.

Q.   *Where* did we get them? . . .

A.   They climbed up the side.

Q.   This is what?

A.   A pan.

Q.   When we put it on top, what do we call it?
A.   A cover?

The kids who do well in Miss Kleinheksel's class are eventually transferred into a regular first grade, or promoted into the second grade at the end of the year. Those who continue to have difficulties will begin their second year in a regular first grade class.

The elementary schools all have television sets, and they use them regularly to receive educational programs in mathematics, science and language, they are teaching the new mathematics, and trying out other curricular innovations (Russell Parks, the superintendent, is a member of the State Curriculum Commission) and they attract competent and often outstanding teachers. But their prime asset, aside from the community's wealth and education, are principals like George Lesikar at Maple, Herman Anderson at Ladera Vista, and Alan Elliott (who used to be Anderson's assistant principal) at Acacia. It is impossible to estimate the difference they make in their schools and the neighborhoods they serve, yet it is clear that each has a vivid understanding of the relation of his school to the community *and* to the larger world that surrounds them. They are aware of the demands the community makes, but they have retained their perspective about those demands, knowing that the school must not only make connections *within* the community, but also must reach a larger universe which transcends local understanding. Lesikar, a Texan, is perhaps the most imperious of the three; since he deals with minorities, he is almost immune to parental pressure. "We can run the school," he says, "without having parents telling us what to teach. They generally recognize us as professionals." Lesikar is concerned about ways to introduce his kids to the dominant social order, impatient with some of the conventional materials—like Dick and Jane readers—and therefore eager to bring his kids all the cultural enrichment he can. (It is an odd commentary on the local culture that teachers of advanced high school students from affluent families feel a need to take their classes to the same kinds of events that Lesikar takes his. Where there is no genuine community everyone is, in some measure, underprivileged.)

Herman Anderson and his friend Alan Elliott are, by con-

trast, charged with schools that serve mostly affluent kids. Both
are young Californians; and as they sit in Elliott's office watching
the kids go home, neither can speak without an occasional reference to Fullerton's difficulties with the Birchers—almost no
teacher can—and to the occasional attacks from maverick parents. "We spend a lot of time explaining," Anderson says. "Some
think the work is too easy, and some think it's too hard, but once
we explain it they usually go along. We had our biggest problem
three years ago [1961] when a group of parents really started
book hunting—going after the same old books in social studies—
and after personality tests. The schools have more status now;
despite the extremists, most parents are happy with the results."
"For a long time the principal's function has been to placate
the patrons," Elliott adds. "There are times when we should tell
some people to jump in the lake. . . . Yes, the public should control the schools but there are real frustrations associated with
this." Elliott speaks of the things being tried out in the elementary schools—experiments with programmed materials, new
mathematics—and of the six-weeks long summer school for elementary school kids, but one of his greatest concerns has to do
with the impact that the area's status-seeking makes even on
elementary school children. He speaks of the structured lives of
children—of their riding and swimming and dancing lessons, of
the fact that girls begin to wear silk stockings in junior high
school, and of the subtle parental pressures that tend to turn
children into trainees. There appears to be no escape from these
pressures; they are not unique to southern California, but since
the schools are newer, and the communities less settled, tension
is more apparent.

Fullerton and the surrounding communities are, most of
them, affluent elements of the new society that southern California has started to produce and which some people predict is
the prototype of American culture in the year 2000. In the last
few years they have experienced all the conflicts and frustrations
that could be expected of new communities. But the thing that
will linger after the Birchers have been routed and the political
issues settled is the tension between ambition and the casual life,
between the dream as reality and the dream as promise. This
tension is, perhaps, the central element of the social psychology

of Orange County—and, increasingly, of many other places. In some ways it is old and familiar; even Faust discovered that he had made a bad bargain. But historically frustration and disillusionment were personal rather than social problems. In Orange County, the land of perpetual fun and happiness, the tension is collective: this, after all, is the promised land, and there is no place left to go. (And have we not always associated social and economic mobility with geographic mobility, with the place, farther west, where things are better?) The society *is* affluent; everyone *does* have a car; the mortgage payments *are* (usually) met on time, and even if it were possible to make more money, it sometimes doesn't seem altogether worthwhile. The weekends get longer, there is more time to fill, and, perhaps, a little guilt that one is not improving himself and his station. Leisure itself has become a career, and the schools must become training grounds for success in it. The accomplished man of the future will be the one who knows how to fill his lonely moments.

III

"Why should I travel," the Boston lady is supposed to have said, "when I'm already here?" but she could have been a San Francisco lady just as well.

San Francisco: its travels are modest and cautious, knowing it has arrived, and only dimly aware that the problems that plague other American cities affect it also. San Francisco is probably the most selfstanding of American cities—Kenneth Rexroth, the San Francisco poet and writer has compared it to a Renaissance city–state—and its reputation remains unmatched by any other American metropolis. It is the place where everyone wants to go, where European visitors are said to feel at home, where the price of cosmopolitanism is not exorbitant, where distances are short, the hills beautiful and the population urbane. Because San Francisco faces west—faces the Pacific and the Orient—its internationalism is less self-conscious than that of the eastern cities. New York's contacts are with a world from which Americans escaped, on which, in some sense, they turned their backs; San Francisco *faces* another world, and it is not the one which Americans have always associated with the things they wanted to leave and reject. The city has sometimes treated its 60,000 Ori-

entals (no one is sure exactly how many there are) in rather sha
by fashion, but it is now taking pride in its tolerance of Chine
and Japanese, and of an increasing influx of Latin America
It is likewise proud of its culture—of the opera and the sy
phony, of cabaret establishments like the Committee, of sm
theaters, art galleries and chamber music societies, of the jazz
North Beach, where Italians and Orientals live side by side,
the distinctive neighborhoods, of the Edwardian cablecars an
most of all, of the city's architectural and topographical beau
The surrounding water, the bridges, the magnificent hills, t
view from the Coit Tower on Telegraph Hill, the civil and (;
cording to general belief) the ever-responsible, ever-middle-cl;
decorum of the Chinese, the absence, until recently, of ci
rights agitation—all these things contribute to San Francisc
sense that the city was and ever will be thus, a feeling that thin
couldn't be much better, and, consequently, to a reluctance
change. Although almost 100,000 Negroes have moved in sin
World War II, and though most of them live in the ghettos
the Fillmore and Mission districts and Hunter's Point, San Fra
cisco still sees its problems in the soft light of the early morni
fog: they are becoming plainer, but are not yet overwhelmir
Mention Negro housing segregation to one of the boosters, a
he will tell you how happy the Chinese are; he will also say th
San Francisco still has genuine neighborhoods with their ov
little groceries and restaurants, each with a sense of communi
and its own pride in being San Franciscan; and he will expre
his concern that new high-rise buildings are marring the sl
line, that architectural changes will ruin the parks and that fre
ways will, and already have, done a little of both.

This kind of conservatism affects most of the city's insti
tions, the schools, perhaps, most of all. "The schools," said a S
Francisco newspaper reporter, "are in a sort of doldrum sta
Harold Spears, the superintendent, is a nice man, an honest ma
and he knows he's a capable superintendent. But the basic cc
cern here is not to push things too fast, not to raise the tax r;
too much. The school administration, in my opinion, is mc
conservative than the community." Unlike many California co
munities, San Francisco has a unified school district serving t
entire city (the population, despite California's general growt

has remained at 750,000 since World War II, although the ethnic composition has changed). The mayor-appointed school board is thus responsible for its junior college, ten high schools, fifteen junior high schools, and approximately one hundred elementary schools, educating a total of about 100,000 students. It discharges that responsibility by moving conservatively, allowing Spears and the administration to run the system. San Francisco does not go out to recruit teachers—indeed its salary structure tends to penalize experienced teachers who come into the system—and it rarely goes to the city's universities for academic advice. Berkeley, a thirty-minute ride across the Bay Bridge, might be on the east coast judging by its influence on the schools—and it draws its administrative staff almost entirely from the ranks. "The idea people are leaving," said the reporter quoted above. "There are still some good teachers, but many of the reformers are gone. If someone takes an idea to the administrators . . . why it's like murderers' row."

Despite this conservatism—"of course, we're a little smug," said a member of the school board—the schools have started to feel tremors from the teacher's union, from the community and from the outside world. The area Parent-Teachers' Association, the Downtown Association, and other groups have campaigned hard to support recent bond issues and have supported the schools on other matters. At the same time the racial problem has moved into the city with the Negroes; there is a growing consciousness of the problems of cultural deprivation (in San Francisco cultural deprivation comes in three colors of skin), and there is a new concern with quality education, generated in part by the pressure from the teachers who, in 1958, began to rebel at classroom interruptions and interference caused by school rallies and athletic contests, and in part by a reaction to the administration's attempt to convert Lowell High School, the city's only selective academic high school, into a neighborhood institution. Lowell, which has traditionally been *the* San Francisco High School—it traces its history back to 1856 and is said to be the oldest high school west of the Mississippi—is sometimes considered a secondary school equivalent of Stanford University: the school colors and some of the songs are the same, and when alumni—among them are Pierre Salinger and Pat Brown—get together for reunions they are as likely to do it at the Palace Hotel as in the school gymnasium. When a new plant was built in 1961 and the administration let it be known that Lowell would become another neighborhood school, a group of parents began to organize in protest and in defense of high academic standards; out of that protest came an organization now called SCOPE (Service Committee on Public Education) and a slowly mounting interest in raising the quality of *all* the city's public schools. At the same time the administration, partly in response to Negro protests, partly on its own initiative, has begun to develop programs for the culturally deprived; it has appointed a human relations director; it has shown an increasing concern about the problems of de facto segregation and it has started to re-examine its academic and vocational courses in a number of areas. Spears and the board have supported and enlarged the city's programs in compensatory education (many of them launched under the Ford Foundation Great Cities Program) and they are encouraging the development of new social studies materials under the direction of Earl Minowitz, a Washington High School teacher who was given a year's leave to start the work. The schools have also begun to develop and publish urban-oriented pre-primers, illustrated with pictures of Negro and Chinese and white kids playing in the city going through a supermarket, and so on; they are conducting an exciting and broad-scale art program; and they are expanding their classes for gifted elementary school children. But the inertia of the administrative staff and of many school principals and the city's conservative tradition dampen efforts to make substantial changes. Local initiative by teachers is usually tolerated and sometimes encouraged, but no one has yet shaken the system from a kind of competent lethargy. Its critics have charged that it sometimes graduates students who can neither write nor read, that the junior high schools are overcrowded, that the new curricula in science, mathematics and other fields are not being introduced fast enough, or not at all, that the school board is complacent about segregation, that school libraries are inadequate, especially in those areas where there are no ambitious middle-class parents to take an interest, and that the system as a whole is not interested in bringing in new people and new ideas. Many of the city's four thousand teachers are comptent, and a few are outstanding, but there are also many others who teach routine classes with routine materials and routine attitudes. Equally important, the city has made only marginal use of its ethnic diversity and of its rich resources; trips to cultural centers and other places of interest are becoming more common for children in the compensatory program, but most classes function strictly by the textbook. They could as easily be in Omaha or Wichita where there are no Japanese, no Chinatown, no docks, no ships, and no sense that one is in a great city. "There's no real dynamism," said a high school teacher, "no direction, no leadership. The schools just aren't as good as this community could support." "The administration," said another teacher, "doesn't know how to exploit the opportunities around here. They don't know how to use the diversity; there are a few cultural programs—assemblies, pageants and so on, but no real effort to take advantage of this city and its resources." Many of the members of scope tend to agree with these assessments: there is a general feeling that the schools are good, but that they could be better. "This could be one of the great school systems in the world," said one parent. "Now it's just all right."

And yet San Francisco tolerates and sometimes fosters outstanding individual efforts in the classroom. At Lowell and George Washington high schools, at O'Connell Vocational High School, at Spring Valley and McCoppin and other elementary schools, individual teachers and administrators have been given the freedom to develop exciting programs and courses, functioning almost like independent agents who are not part of any system:

Maurice Englander, chairman of the English Department at Lowell, and former president of the State Federation of Teachers, directs courses with ordinary labels: Advanced Composition, Literature, or just plain English 6. But the questions he asks and the intellectual substance of his approach make each a kind of special exhibit. Englander's technique tends to be structured rather than freewheeling, and he is anything but flamboyant. In class he is simply a civilized man with a civilized and thorough understanding of literature and good writing.

In a junior English course:

Assignment: Henry IV, Part 1

One of Shakespeare's most celebrated virtues as a dramatist is his skill at depicting the range of Elizabethan society, from highest to lowest: Henry IV includes such a range. But it also includes Falstaff, an individual who slips outside the confines of history because, in a most important sense, Falstaff is an a-historical man.

Thesis: If Falstaff is right, then Elizabethan England was wrong; if Falstaff is wrong, then humanity is dead.

Part 1—How might it be said that Falstaff fulfills the classic role of heretic? What is his heresy, and what would be the consequences of such a heresy as his for the Hotspurs, the Prince Hals, and the Henry IV's of this earth?

Part 2—As great as the range of character in the play is the range of language. Comment upon Shakespeare's discriminating use of prose and poetry in the play. What do you think the shifts from prose to poetry and from poetry to prose signify? Why?

Part 3—Hotspur consistently states views which give support and credence to his character and activities. Quote from the play those lines which, in your opinion, set forth Hotspur's views of life and death so clearly that, while we might question the essential rightness of his views, we recognize them to be essential to the kind of man that Percy is, so that he exists as a "real" and not a cardboard construction to fit the uses of the playwright.

In another assignment:

No one in *Pride and Prejudice* commits a crime for which he pays a legal penalty; yet not all the persons in the novel are virtuous. In the world of this novel, what merits Jane Austen's disapproval? i.e., what kind of action in this genteel world does Jane Austen consider "wrong"? Justify your answer with reference to specific situations in the novel.

The first sentence in the novel is, "It is a truth universally acknowledged, that a single man in possession of a good fortune must be in want of a wife."

A. How might it be considered a key passage in the novel?

B. Why does Jane Austen use the word "must," instead of "is," in the appositive clause? (Re-read the sentence substituting "is" for "must" to see the difference in meaning.)

C. Whose point of view does Jane Austen assume in the writing of the sentence?

D. Are there persons in the novel who might take exception to the statement, for any reason? If so, who? Why?

Although the title of Jane Austen's novel is *Pride and Prejudice,* could it be called, with any justification, *Appearance and Reality?* (Consider the following pairs of opposites in your answer):

1. Good and Evil
2. Truth and Falsity
3. Beauty and Ugliness
4. Love and Hate
5. Life and Death

Which, do you think, is most important in the novel?

Justify your answer with reference to the development of incident and character in the novel.

"To write," Englander says about the composition course, "you have to have some controling ideas. I got them to write a series of four papers on San Francisco—and to avoid the magazine and tourist clichés. Their tendency is to run off in wild generalization; I've been talking to them about what is observable, to teach them that composition really means arrangement and that by arranging materials a writer can come close to the essence of an experience. In writing you can't do what they do in physical education, throw the kids a ball and say 'go play.' " The students, he explains, write once a week; between compositions they read Shakespeare, Dickens, Fielding, Jane Austen. "I have them write about their own reading," he says. "Then I give them commentaries about the literature afterward."

In a small room of the second floor of the George Washington High School, Elgin Heinz, a man in his forties with red hair and a passionate interest in the Far East, teaches a course called Advanced World History. The walls of the room are plastered with pictures of China, Japan and India, but the dominant motif is represented by a sign across the front wall:

THINK—IT MAY BE A NEW EXPERIENCE

There is no text for the course; everything comes in paperbacks and journals, and it comes fast: Herbert Muller, *The Uses of the Past*; Robert Downs, *Books That Changed the World*; Crane Brinton, *The Shaping of the Modern Mind*; Eric Hoffer, *The True Believer*; Machiavelli, *The Prince*; Houston Smith, *The Religions of Man*; Herlee Creel, *Chinese Thought from Confucius to Mao*; E. H. Carr, *What Is History?*; V. Gordon Childe, *What Happened In History*; Edward T. Hall, *The Silent Language*. The object of the course is to discuss three questions: What is man? What is history? and How can men live with one another? It centers on three papers the students are asked to write:

1. Views of Man: Ancient Mediterranean, ancient Asian, Judeo-Christian, and modern.
2. Views of history: cycle or progress, the myths of history, objective or subjective, uses of the past.
3. Civic Man: Locke and Rousseau, Mill and Machiavelli, Thoreau and Hitler, Confucius and the Legalists.

The title "Advanced World History" is, obviously, a kind of dodge to accommodate the bureaucrats who oversee curricular requirements; if it were called "philosophy of history" or "history of ideas" there'd be no place for it.

"All human notions of God are projections," Heinz says to the class, discussing the article they have just read. "All scientific theories are projections. Man projects meaning and a pattern on a life of which he is basically ignorant. . . Given a list of facts, what do we try to do?"

"Draw the facts together," a student says.

"Forming a category," another interrupts.

"The scientist doesn't discard his preconceptions as new data comes along," Heinz says. "He salvages what he can. If we debate between gravity and God as an explanation for falling bodies we're debating about the form of projection we're going to use. (There are many paths up the mountain, the Hindu philosopher said, but there is only one summit.) Each civilization has had to make new projections."

"If everything is a projection," a student asks, "then nothing is real?" Discussion ensues, and someone concludes that "there's reality behind the projections."

"Then you share nothing with anybody," the same student says.

"You agree on a projection," says Heinz.

"But how do you know the difference between projection and illusion?" the student asks. The bell has already rung, but the students cluster around him as he packs away his papers. Walking to the door he is saying "the point of the article . . . is that we all accept the projections of our culture."

In a room on the west side of the same building Mrs. Richard Meister is teaching another small group, but one that is several worlds away from the group that Heinz has just left. More than half of them are Negroes, and though they are of high school age, and sometimes a year or two beyond, their reading level begins at the fifth grade and goes *down*. This is called Remedial Civics I and the current "text" is California's official publication listing the pros and cons of the seventeen propositions on the 1964 ballot.

Q. Proposition 15: what is it usually referred to? [Mrs. Meister asks].

A. Keep TV free.

Q. The people who say that, are they in favor or against the proposition? Who says "keep TV free?" How did it get on the ballot? What's the word?

A. Initiative.

Q. How does initiative work?

A. Pass a petition.

Q. José, what goes with it?

A. Referendum and recall. [He reads a summary of the proposition in a Spanish accent.]

Q. Herman, if you vote yes on this you're saying what?

A. No.

Q. If you vote no?

A. It stays the way it is now.

Q. Let's go back; what is Pay TV? [There is uncertainty in the class, and she helps explain the system. The kids groan when she explains that pay television programs sometimes include first-run theatrical and operatic productions. Opera is not their dish.] How do you suppose the theater owners feel about this?

A.   They don't like it.

Q.   Remember the argument is not on quality; it's whether there should be a law to prevent pay TV from operating.

[She goes on to discuss Proposition 16, which would establish a privately operated state lottery ("Don't they have those things fixed?" a student asks) and, on the next day, proceeds to discuss the state's most controversial issue, Proposition 14.]

Q.   What does Proposition 14 actually do?

A.   Gets rid of the Rumford Act.

Q.   What else?

A.   It says a person can rent or sell to whoever you want.

Q.   What does the law do now?

A.   You can't discriminate.

Q.   If Proposition 14 passes, you can sell to whoever you want? [The students all say yes.] Yes on 14 means you have the right to discriminate. Who's in favor of it?

A.   There's a club—wealthy businessmen.

Q.   Yes, it's a club and it starts with a C [no takers from the class] . . . The Commonwealth Club. You might tell your parents about Proposition 14—I don't want you to get it mixed up in your minds. . . [As she finishes there is something of a plea—not a pitch to vote—but rather a tone that seems to say that these kids will never get such help again, and that suggests the self-defeat of people who are already overwhelmed by the surrounding world.] Don't get it mixed up in your minds. It's worded so that you might vote opposite from the way you want to.

Within the shadow of the lights at Candlestick Park, where the San Francisco Giants play baseball, and where the wind blows off the bay, Julita T. McLeod has just told a Negro boy that if "you say 'hisself' again, out you go." Mrs. McLeod, a Filipino married to a Scotsman, teaches the compensatory class at the Bret Harte School, composed almost entirely of Negro children from the surrounding housing projects. The room is cluttered with displays, charts, photographs; twelve kids—nine Negroes, two whites, and an Oriental—and Mrs. McLeod, who is a combination of Carmen Miranda, Carrie Nation and Eleanor Roosevelt. "Sure I get mad," she says to the visitor, "if those parents don't help their kids with their work or if they don't let them work. I have kids of my own. I help them with their spelling at home while I'm chopping onions."

Every day she teaches five groups of twelve, all of them children who are well below grade in reading, and who, because they are supposed to have IQ scores above 85, are considered underachievers. The class is one of about 500 now being conducted by 100 teachers in various schools throughout the city—Isadore Pivnick, who administers the program, is constantly trying to establish more—but those led by Julita McLeod are generally regarded as the most successful, a distinction which earns her a parade of visitors as well as the envy of some other teachers. When kids come into her class—each spends an hour a day with her, the rest of the time in a regular classroom—she sends home a letter of instructions and a form to be returned by the parents. In the form, the parents must set down the time when they will meet with the teacher so she can impress them with the importance of supporting the work of the class. If they don't return the form Julita McLeod goes after them: she phones, and writes until, at last, most of them agree to cooperate.

The class itself is played staccato, reflecting the personality of the woman who directs it; but all of it is keyed to give kids enough command of the language, and enough confidence so that they can function in a normal classroom (since they are no longer ignored, or treated like the class dunces, the compensatory children consider this class a kind of status program).

The word *rare* is on the board, and the children are trying to understand its various meanings:

"Mother has a beautiful ring that has a rare stone in it," she says. "What kind of a stone is rare?" Words tumble from the kids: ruby, emerald, diamond, and somewhere on the board she finds room to write them out.

"On rare occasions, the elephant is given alfalfa at the zoo. . . . Ignacio, what does rare mean? Now please *don't* help." Ignacio, a Latin American immigrant, is obviously shy. "Come on Ignacio. . . ." There is some silence. At last Ignacio says, "sometimes."

Since the class has recently taken a trip to the zoo—field trips are a staple of all compensatory classes—there is a lot of talk about animals, and long lists of words and phrases taken from the zoo director's talk to the class, and photos, taken by Julita McLeod, of animals and cages. "Tell us the story of the brown bear ... say it in a sentence ... what does carnivorous mean? ... how do you pronounce it? ... what did we say an antonym was, Darryl? ... what does he eat? ... where did you learn *that*? ... I'm going to give you a book that will change your mind." The kids take notes on their trips, and copy signs, and when they return to class they make up collaborative stories that Mrs. McLeod sets down, always with the intention of making them talk, and talk correctly:

As we walked in the zoo, we saw a building with the following inscription. It said:

DEDICATED TO THE
MEMORY OF DELIA FLEISHHACKER
BY HER SONS

Mrs. McLeod said, "Let us read the words on the building." She passed the pencils and we copied the inscription.

Then we walked on and we passed by Storyland. There were slides, seesaws, a merry-go-round, and a toy train.

Mr. Baldwin, Director of the San Francisco Zoo, asked Mr. Mason to be our guide. Mr. Mason took us inside Monkey Island. He showed us where the zoo keeper feeds the monkeys and the place where the monkeys sleep.

Monkey Island is a man-made mountain. Monkey Island was built to make the monkeys feel at home in the zoo. The waterfall flows down into a lake where the monkeys drink and where they wash their hands.

Spider monkeys have very long tails. They use their tails for holding on to a branch or for grasping. These are called prehensile tails.

We read and copied the name plaques. Sometimes there was a little map on the plaques to show where the animals came from,

Mrs. McLeod gave us two keys for the talking boxes. We took turns listening to the talking story books.

We had lunch on the picnic tables. Some of us bought popcorn, sugar candy, milk, and hot cocoa. After lunch we went to see the other animals at the zoo.

The Andean Condor is a big bird that comes from the Andes Mountains. The blue and yellow macaw and the toucan barbet are beautiful birds that come from Tropical America.

The white-breasted sea eagle is a big eagle that comes from South East Asia, the Philippines, and the West Pacific.

Gibbons travel in groups of thirty to one hundred. They have family groups and tribes. They are active at night. Like the spider monkeys, gibbons eat insects, fruits, and seeds.

The rhesus monkeys come from India. Like the guinea pigs, the rhesus monkeys are used for medical research and experiments.

It was a rhesus monkey that rode the nose cone of a United States rocket that was shot into space. The monkey returned to earth alive.

After each trip or visit by an outside speaker the kids spend weeks exploring the language of their new experience; after a visit from a NASA astronaut the class wrote and performed a dramatization of its idea of a trip to the moon, a production that, to a visitor reared on the serials of another time, seemed aesthetically at least even with Captain Midnight, Jack Armstrong and the other adventures that used to come from the gothic box: "We sure left the earth at terrific speed . . . twenty-four thousand miles an hour . . . the first stage rocket just dropped off . . . our radar is picking up something . . . how about garbage? . . . don't worry, we won't have much because all we eat is capsules . . ."

"Each time the boat whistle blew," said a San Francisco school official recalling the days of unlimited immigration, "the principal would say, 'I need a new teacher.'" For him, as for so many others, the Americanization of immigrant children and, through them, their parents, was one of the great achievements of the public schools. Although that function, like large-scale immigration itself, is now officially over, it continues in the larger cities, and in some of the smaller ones as well. This is what Julita McLeod is trying to do at Bret Harte, and what some of the teachers are doing at the Frank McCoppin School, not far from George Washington High School, and at the Spring Valley School, located in the cleavage between Nob Hill and Russian Hill. McCoppin's six hundred children represent almost every nationality on earth; Spring Valley is predominantly Chinese, some of them recent immigrants, some offspring of third-genera-

tion parents. At McCoppin, Marjorie McLeod, the assistant principal (no relation to Julita), teaches a class called English for
Non-English Speaking—among the pupils are a Russian, a Pole,
a Czech, an Argentinian and an East Indian—working with
words like *comb* and *brush, chalk* and *eraser, blackboard* and
paper . . . asking, "What day is it? . . ." "What *kind* of day is
it? . . ." At Spring Valley Cecilia Fung teaches a compensatory
group which, unlike most, is not composed of American Negroes
or Puerto Ricans, but of Chinese immigrants from Hong Kong,
children of families who have come to this country in the past
decade, and who speak no English. Like Julita McLeod, Mrs.
Fung takes her class on trips, and encourages them to compose
their own literature, always with the intention of teaching them
the language, and giving them the experiences on which the
language depends:

> This is a story about Steven Orange. When I was a large
> Orange some people picked me down from the trees and the
> people put me in the box and took me to the store for sale. One
> day a woman came in with three children. When they saw me
> they all liked me because I am very big and red in color. So they
> bought me. Since all three wanted to eat me the mother cut me
> in three parts and so all three of them got their share happily.

"What's going to happen to these other oranges?" she asks
the kids sitting in the circle before her. There has been some
dissatisfaction about the prospect that Steven will get eaten.

"The oranges jump out of the boy's pocket," says one.

"They go back on tree?" a girl asks.

"They going to step on it," says another child.

"Do we want Steven and Tony to get stepped on?" Cecilia
Fung asks. They all say no.

"They under the chair," someone suggests. "They go to
school."

Both McCoppin and Spring Valley have their quotas of ex-
ceptionally bright kids, and both offer their special clienteles enrichment programs. At McCoppin small groups composed of pupils of every ethnic description meet daily in accelerated reading
classes, examining, for example, the discovery of a Japanese boy
that a story they are reading in the Arabian Nights is similar to

one of Aesop's fables, or the similarity of Johnny-a-Cake to the tale of the Gingerbread Boy, learning that common themes run through the folk literature and mythology of every country on earth. At Spring Valley, which has a special literature program conducted by the assistant principal, John B. Dougherty, fifth graders—most of them Chinese—read or listen to selections from *The Prince and the Pauper* ("Do you believe that Tom would have accepted the Crown of England if the real king had not appeared when he did?"), *Two Years Before the Mast* ("Do you think the Captain was right in ordering the flogging—or do you think he should have ordered some milder form of punishment?"), *Aïda, Amahl and the Night Visitors, The Wizard of Oz,* and other works, operatic and literary. Both schools encourage the use of new mathematics techniques, and debating and other programs tailored for special interests.

Although the Hong Kong children at Spring Valley are a small minority, and although their numbers are declining as the Hong Kong migration—resulting from a special quota dispensation granted by the government—comes to an end, Spring Valley will remain indefinitely Chinese. Thus it will always include, as it does now, some of the most highly motivated and intelligent kids in the system—and some of the most enigmatic. In the office of the new principal, Elizabeth Hall, who is Chinese herself, you meet an eleven-year-old named Kenneth who is president of the student body, an outstanding student who spends one afternoon of the week attending advanced science classes at a public high school, and the other four going to Chinese school so that he can learn something of the language and traditions of his people. Although Kenneth, who hopes to be a doctor, is unusually bright, he is just one of perhaps 10,000 or 12,000 Oriental children in the city schools, children who are regarded among the most respectful, ambitious and able students in the system. Until they are in the third or fourth grade their test scores are generally below average; then they begin to catch up, as the language limitations of the home—where even second- or third-generation parents still try to conduct affairs in Cantonese—begin to break down, and as high motivation begins to assert itself. "The Chinese people have always had a great deal of respect for education," Miss Hall says, explaining that children beginning first

grade are sometimes disappointed if they don't get a book to
read the moment they come to class; in Chinese, she says, school
means "to read a book." (The old Commodore Stockton School,
which serves the heart of Chinatown, is one of the most respected
buildings in the community, and when it celebrated its fiftieth
anniversary a few years ago it attracted scores of old students who
had become successful San Francisco citizens, some of whom still
knew it as the King's School or the Emperor's School, the name
that emigrants from the Manchu period gave it half a century
ago.)

The descriptions of contemporary Chinese kids vary—and
sometimes they are as contradictory as southern descriptions of
the Negro—but they often bear a strong resemblance to descriptions of Jewish life in eastern suburbs. In Newton, someone said,
extracurricular involvement consists of Hebrew school and trips
to the orthodontist; at Spring Valley it is Chinese school and trips
to the orthodontist. There is uncertainty whether the old family
traditions and ties are being maintained as young couples move
out of the Chinese community and into mixed neighborhoods—
which are slowly opening up—but the image of the Chinese as
hardworking, pleasant and well-disciplined citizens remains, and
it is often used, at least implicitly, as a reproach to the militant
Negro activists who are impatient with de facto segregation and
life in the ghetto. (A desire for straight teeth is at least one indication that Chinese parents, like most others, are interested in
prying open the gates to a thoroughly middle-class life for their
children.) The Chinese, however, have never been politically
militant, chosing, rather, to establish themselves through economic power and block voting: the tight Chinese family associations of San Francisco known as the six companies have maintained order and welfare services in the community, and there is
little juvenile delinquency. "If a Chinese adult sees a kid misbe-
having on the street," someone said, "he'll speak to the kid
about it, whether he knows him or not."

It is all quaint and wonderful, and San Franciscans are delighted. But in recent years attitudes emerging from the civil
rights struggle have started to put Chinese docility in a new light.
"I'd like to blast those myths," said Reginald Major, who was a
leader in the city's NAACP before he resigned his office in a fac-

tional split. "The failures in Chinatown are better hidden than the failures in the Negro community, but they're there. The white power structure has been playing off one minority against another. They say the Chinese have pulled themselves up by their bootstraps but the fact is that most of them are small marginal merchants who are working their tails off. The Chinese have developed a small middle class which serves as a buffer between the whites and the rest of Chinatown—there's a bunch of guys who control Grant Avenue—but they couldn't function if it weren't for Chinatown, and Chinatown, however you call it, is a slum." Major describes a city which is being caught from behind by its problems. "This place is manipulative without any real basis in work," he said. "It's boomed on trade, there's always been a labor shortage, and never any real labor trouble. There's a pleasantness about the architecture—you sort of get bemused by it—and because the weather's mild the streets never go to pot like they do in other cities. It's all sort of Mediterranean—slow development, no real industrial competition, and never a lot of people to care for."

This kind of slowness, the critics feel, has allowed problems —which have never been insurmountable in San Francisco—to accumulate. According to NAACP figures, half the city's schools were built between 1895 and 1925, 23 of them in 1911 and 1912 (all of them are still being used); there is a high rate of teacher turnover, especially in the Negro schools, and there were, until recently, major inequities between schools erected in white neighborhoods and those in Negro areas like Hunter's Point. Characteristically, white middle-class parents in Twin Peaks work hard to assemble good school libraries, but little has been done in Negro schools. Despite teachers like Julita McLeod and despite the compensatory program, a school like Bret Harte has more in common with similar institutions in Chicago or Harlem or Roxbury than it does with Spring Valley or McCoppin, let alone the schools of Twin Peaks. Upstairs, Flip is saying bow-wow in the first grade reader, while the teacher is saying, with some exasperation, "Did you hear me, David?" Every year the neighborhood vandals take a large toll in school windows (the building, erected a few years ago, is bright inside, but auto-assembly-plant-modern on the outside); teachers, many of them highly competent, complain that lack of adequate staffing leaves them overworked, usually with at least one or two pupils with an IQ below 70 who should be in special classes; and there is no full-time social worker, although many of the school's 680 pupils—another 240 are being bussed to other schools to relieve crowding—bring to class all the problems of the surrounding housing developments. Some of the teachers are not sure they will stay, although they all say they would like to if they had more help. One, who has been there a number of years, is only hanging on until an administrative position opens up.

Like all major cities, San Francisco faces problems of cultural deprivation (among Latin Americans as well as Negroes); it has not yet found a working solution for kids caught between the inadequacy of the old vocational-shop training and the irrelevance of college-prep academic courses, and it has not yet eliminated the coincidence of Negro teachers, Negro classes and Negro schools. With the increasing Negro population, the problems of de facto segregation have increased, and pressure to alleviate them is mounting. In 1964 Negroes threatened a school boycott which was prevented only through a last-minute compromise, but the possibility of a real boycott remains. Since San Francisco is highly sensitive to such blots on its reputation, even a threatened boycott is something of a disaster.

> During the past two decades [wrote Wilson Record in a study published by the University of California], the Bay Area, as perhaps could have been expected, has lost much of its uniqueness. Its physical appearance has become less distinctive; its new buildings are in the concrete and glass packing box style; its freeways are as crowded and ugly as any to be found in eastern cities. Its culture has tended toward standardization. Deviant movements which seem new and creative all too frequently turn out to be fads whose chief support eventually rests on those who see an opportunity for commercial exploitation. Finally, its social forms reflect little of an unusual history or of a distinctive way of absorbing new peoples and relating them to those already there.

> There is no better evidence of the Bay Area's having joined the national society and having been caught up in the metropolitan main drift than the local emergence of national patterns of

racial discrimination. In that respect, too, the Bay Area has arrived. Citizens of Oakland and San Leandro, San Francisco and San Rafael, Richmond and North Richmond, need no longer feel that they are being outdone by New York, Cleveland, Detroit or Chicago. In the circumstances it should come as no surprise that the pattern of Negro response in the Bay Area is not significantly different from Negro response in other metropolitan communities.

Whether or not Record's assessment is correct (and he credits Bay Area school systems with an increasing awareness of the problems of minority group education), most San Franciscans—critics and defenders of schools—feel that the city's problems are, and will continue to remain, less acute than those of other cities, and that they will be solved more easily. "What developed here developed out of apathy," said William L. Cobb, whose job as assistant superintendent for human relations was a byproduct of civil rights agitation. (Like most school human relations directors, Cobb is a Negro.) "Maybe we just didn't sense the problem." Cobb feels that San Francisco does not have hard-core resistance to integration "and so it's unlikely that we'll ever have a situation like New York or Chicago." Many others agree: James Benet, the education writer of the *Chronicle*, said the city's problems are rooted in inertia rather than active resistance, and he believes that San Francisco could be a model city because the Negro population is sufficiently small to make genuine school integration acceptable to almost everyone.

Other than Cobb, the person most responsible for providing equal educational opportunities to underprivileged children is an imaginative former teacher and school principal named Isadore Pivnick, who supervises the entire compensatory program and is one of the fastest-moving individuals ever to set foot in a schoolhouse. "I read one night that I had become principal of a slum school," he said, recalling his initiation to the compensatory business. "Many of us weren't attuned to the fact that a problem even existed; people just grow up with it and never recognize it. But things have changed. We take many things for granted now that we had to break our necks for a few years ago." As people become more aware of the effects of cultural deprivation, he says, "we have to be careful not to become too mechanical. The

Hong Kong refugees—many of them peasants—have different standards from the middle-class Orientals, and they're different from the Spanish community, and so on." The compensatory program now involves some 6000-7000 kids in the elementary and junior high schools, the cooperation of a variety of welfare agencies, child-care centers, and community-based study centers, the Junior League, almost one hundred teacher aides and a host of other resources. The program operates according to no formula, although its major ingredients are cultural enrichment, small classes and a great deal of social work. Pivnick has used all sorts of techniques to build the program; he calls in consultants like Martin Deutsch and John Hope Franklin, he runs from school to school and group to group making speeches, meeting with teachers, and occasionally saying to someone "what if those children move to *your* neighborhood?" New pre-primers and readers with an urban, ethnically diverse setting, are being written, classes go on trips around the city, there is a special drama project (which allows kids to act out some of the feelings they have trouble expressing otherwise—a technique similar to psychodrama, and now being used in a number of places), and a special psychiatric clinic to help disturbed youngsters. Pivnick hopes to expand his program—many children who need it are not yet being touched—but he has made an impressive start. "You bootleg a lot of stuff until you get your foot in the door," he said. "Then you move."

A growing minority of San Franciscans would like to see more motion. Controversy over segregation, admission policies at Lowell, and school standards generally have produced a new concern with the system's problems. While other California communities have flirted with the "fundamentals" of Raffertyism— grabbing formulas and solutions—San Francisco is asking questions. The response of organizations like SCOPE is not to rabble-rouse, but to study, not to demand, but to suggest. Nevertheless, they are letting the administration know that they are not happy. "We have asked Superintendent Spears," said a member of SCOPE, "why he always has to follow; why can't he lead?" expressing concern not only with cultural deprivation and segregation, but with inadequate school libraries, with the tendency to choose physical education teachers for administrative positions and principalships, with what the organization considers inequities among different schools, with inadequacies in education for gifted children, and with what one of its leaders called "unimaginative, plodding leadership." Although SCOPE is still in its infancy —it now has study committees working on various school matters —and although it has tried hard not to become the voice of any segment of the community, its membership includes a high proportion of professional people, housewives—and Jews. Its leaders, people like Mrs. Morris Kadish, the wife of a paint contractor, and Warren Saltzman, a young attorney, are sympathetic to the problems of the administration, and they hope to make positive contributions rather than functioning as negative critics. They are critical of the school board's dependence on the administration for information and on the general inbreeding of the system, and they have started to look with some interest— and envy—at the Berkeley System where Neil Sullivan, who directed the reopened Negro schools in Prince Edward County in 1963–64, is presiding over a system with a reputation for imaginative and exciting instruction.

Although SCOPE is just one of several groups with an interest in the city's schools (the chamber of commerce has a committee on education headed by a realtor named John Levinson who is more interested in good schools than in promoting business-education day; the San Francisco Federation of Teachers has demanded better instructional standards, as well as better pay; and the NAACP remains active) and although their impact is still marginal, there is every indication that their effectiveness will increase. Most of their leaders agree that Spears (who will retire in the next year or two) has been an efficient administrator, but that San Francisco, which has always had an adequate system, is being overtaken, that its good salary standards are not as good, comparatively speaking, as they were a decade ago and that, as an officer of the teachers union said, the city has become a training ground for other systems. "Ten years ago," said Dan Jackson, president of the union, "people would forgo some other advantages to come into the system; we were in a good competitive position. But it's not true now. The state retirement system is as good as the city's, while the teaching situation here has declined."

The critics also charge that the administration lacks pride in scholarship, and that it refuses to encourage academic improvements. ("They'll bring in experts on salaries," a teacher said, "but they won't give a guy a quarter to ride across the bridge to Berkeley to talk about the English curriculum.") But what they most dislike is simply the system's inertia and, as they see it, the board's refusal to do anything about it. "I know the system tends to be ingrown," said one board member. "It's probably good for morale, though it's not good for new ideas, but you can't turn the relation of the board and the superintendent into a contest." The board—chosen to reflect the city's identifiable interest groups, Catholics, Negroes, Jews, labor, business—has always defended the academic freedom of San Francisco's teachers. In 1959 when the names of a few city teachers appeared on one of the blacklists of the House Un-American Activities Committee, which, in other California communities was ample cause for suspension, the board defended them; there has never been any bookburning in San Francisco, no signs of Birchism around the schools, and no intimidation of teachers on political grounds. But the board has never yielded to other pressures either. As in other communities where school boards are relatively inaccessible and conservative, the San Francisco establishment has protected the schools against outside influence of every kind.

And yet there is a kind of sanity about it all. Neither Max Rafferty nor Sputnik has made much of an impact. There is no consuming passion to use the schools to fight the cold war, prevent brainwashing or close the missile gap, and no overwhelming sense that the schools are the only instrument for saving the city. Harold Spears' reluctance to innovate is based at least in part on his feeling that no school system can be a patchwork of special programs, and that no genuine reform will be dictated from downtown. As a result the system has relaxed into a somewhat decentralized organization which depends on individual teachers and principals for success. If this sometimes leads to mediocrity, to a preference for safety over innovation, it also tends to eliminate the tensions to which other systems often commit themselves. San Francisco shares with southern California a passion for the Good Life and a reluctance to make the public schools exclusively academic institutions, but it is free from the insecurity that dominates the palmy southern suburbs. What the city now has to do is reconcile education for the Good Life with education for the realities of urban life, to fit the California style to industrial and technological necessities. The real virtue of that style lies in its comprehensiveness and tolerance, in the willingness of schools and colleges to offer education for any person at any level in almost any subject. But this style is only an alibi for low standards and well-rationalized academic games if it cannot be adapted to the underprivileged, to Negroes and Mexicans and Orientals. Comprehensiveness and tolerance are worth nothing at all unless they can comprehend genuine diversity, tolerate real differences, and offer relevant education to every child.

7

The New Quest in Jeffco

"JEFFCO isn't going to build just an experimental school. We want to build an experimental school system. Most schools don't like to go all the way. They want to leave things as they are, and then add special programs for the gifted or the disadvantaged. Whatever we try out we expect to use for every student. We're going to get a different kind of kid with a different kind of attitude. None of us fully understand it, but that's what's going to happen."

The speaker is Lawrence M. Watts, the assistant superintendent of schools in Jefferson County, Colorado, and what he describes may well be the most exciting public school system in the United States.

On the map Jefferson County looks like a wedge between Denver and the highest peaks of the Colorado Rockies. It encompasses an area two thirds as large as the State of Rhode Island, a landscape that rises from ticky-tacky suburban to evergreen forest, and an exploding population that speaks in the accents of every region of the United States. In pioneer days this was a campground for the Indians and, according to a well-nurtured local legend, a one-time hideout for Jesse James. The miners still bring gold and lead out of the mountains and the ranchers still raise cattle, but the local economy is now far more dependent on the Martin Company and the missile market, a huge Federal Center with six thousand government employees, the Coors brewery and porcelain plant, and downtown Denver. With a population approaching 200,000—it *quadrupled* in the last ten years—Jefferson County, usually called Jeffco, now has more kids than coyotes, and more ranch houses than ranches. Wheat fields have become housing developments, and country lanes are now arterial roads.

In its eastern half, which abuts Denver, Jeffco is flat and residential; but in the west it rises through the sparsely settled forests of the Front Range to an altitude of 10,000 feet, its roads marked by places named Pine, Bear Creek, Conifer, Evergreen, Coal Creek and Red Rocks, approaching some of the most spectacular scenery in the United States. On a clear day one can see Pike's Peak to the south and the slopes of the Continental Divide against the sunset, perennial reminders of place, of the country's history, and of its promise. "Welcome to Golden," says the pennant the boosters have hung over the main street of the county seat, "where the West remains."

And it does, though not the way they mean it in Golden. The pioneer has come and passed on, and the frontier is closed. The homestead has become a corporate farm, the mine a highly mechanized, scientific enterprise, and the village a city where depersonalized professional services have replaced the volunteer. The self-made man, we have been told, was usually a Horatio Alger fabrication who got lucky at the right moment, or a public relations gimmick for a gang of industrial buccaneers who plundered natural resources and cheated the public. But out of it all, part romance, part wishful thinking, came an optimism, a confidence in possibilities, an excitement about the new things. "American democracy," said the historian Frederick Jackson Turner, "is fundamentally the outcome of the experiences of the American people in dealing with the West." The frontier, he believed, was the single most important element in shaping American institutions and character, producing a society "of which the most distinctive fact was the freedom of the individual to rise under conditions of social mobility, and whose ambition was the liberty and well being of the masses." Turner's thesis about the importance of the frontier has been attacked, modified, revised, and then attacked again; attempts have been made to verify it through sociological studies of the behavior of tenants in new housing projects, and to discredit it with descriptions of the vicious anti-social behavior of those who were closest to the forest.

The rural slums are as much a product of the frontier as the industrial entrepreneur, and the one-room school as much its legacy as the University of California. But in each instance one is left with a vague feeling that Turner was right, that, in speaking of "that coarseness and strength combined with acuteness and inquisitiveness . . . that buoyancy and exuberance which comes from freedom," he was indeed a romantic, but that, at his best, the American himself was always a romantic, a man who, like Melville's Captain Ahab, would strike the sun if it suited his purpose. "In spite of custom," Turner wrote in 1893, "each frontier did indeed furnish a new field of opportunity, a gate of escape from the bondage of the past; and freshness and confidence, and scorn of older society, [and] impatience of its restraints. . . ."

Something of that remains in parts of the American West, and especially in its schools. In some places it has soured into frustration and dogged political fundamentalism, producing Birchers and superpatriots, Christian Crusaders and social paranoids, and elsewhere it has been replaced by urbane cynicism, turning to the kind of moral muckraking that is itself as repressive as the moralism it attacks. And yet, one is often impressed by manifestations of what Turner called the striking characteristics of the American intellect: by the confidence in human potential, by the often ingenuous trust and the unbashed innovations, and by the places where people behave as if the world had not yet been finished, all the lessons learned, or all the mysteries solved.

In Jefferson County, the schools function as if they were still on such a frontier. Operated by a single district which was created in 1951 through the merger of thirty-nine separate systems, they serve an area of 791 square miles and educate 50,000 students—there were 13,000 ten years ago—in 105 schools, a planetarium, and a 550-acre mountain ranch, the "Outdoor Education Laboratory School," which every sixth grade pupil attends for a week. The phenomenal growth of the district—in other communities often a source of paralyzing controversy—has been accompanied by equally rapid academic innovation, all of it carried out to fulfill a promise made at the time the merger took place: that educational opportunities in every part of the county would be equalized, and that no child, whether in the mountains west of Evergreen or in the flat suburbs of Wheat Ridge or Applewood, would be deprived of new material or improved teaching techniques. The implications of this promise and the problems that attended the creation of the district have produced innovations and attitudes that leave conventional school administrators in varying

states of apoplectic shock. According to all that's true and beautiful, it is impossible to run a school system in the way Jefferson
County is doing it. Its administrators are opportunists, prospec-
tors of curricula, and assayers of ideas, who have learned to ignore
the rules of orthodox school management. They enlist hundreds
of ordinary people—the self-proud "citizens and taxpayers"—in
the process of planning new schools or discussing new projects,
and they have the patience, and the democratic faith in popular
judgment to let them talk themselves out; they invite their most
vocal critics to serve on advisory committees, ask the economy-
minded chamber of commerce to review the budget, and to suggest cuts, and they are willing to listen to anyone's complaint or
suggestion. They have experimented with new designs in school
construction, instituted new courses, and applied new administrative and pedagogical techniques, not because they wanted to
keep up with their neighbors, or because college-ambitious parents pushed them, but simply because, being almost entirely
new themselves, and thus not burdened with academic tradition
or the heavy hand of "reputation," the schools were able to judge
every program and idea, new and old, as *if it were* new. They were
able to initiate a new physics course because it was to them just
one of several equal choices, not something that would replace
another course that had been conducted for generations; they
were able to build schools shaped like barbells for team teaching
because most of their plant is little older than the idea of team
teaching itself, and they were able to persuade themselves and the
community that a planetarium was an important teaching device
by studying others around the country and then inventing uses
for it that went well beyond just the teaching of astronomy. As a
result they have established not only new, or, perhaps, indeed,
very old, techniques of generating community support, sometimes in the face of serious difficulties, but they have also begun
to generate an entirely fresh kind of classroom attitude. Although
they have not yet started to produce the "different kind of kid,"
ready for shipment, each with a sharp, shiny inquisitive mind,
they have seen the possibilities, and the common intellectual
roots of the many new courses which have appeared in recent
years, and which have produced a riot of alphabet designations.
Most of these courses—though not all—have been drawn by na-

tional groups of university scholars and secondary school teachers: the Physical Science Study Committee (PSSC), whose course
is now used in all Jeffco high school physics classes; the Biological
Sciences Curriculum Study (BSCS); the "new math"; the Earth Science Curriculum Project (ESCP), which will probably be used in
all ninth grade classes beginning 1965; Educational Services, Inc.,
(ESI), which administers the physics course, and is now producing
social studies materials for elementary and junior high schools,
and a new eighth-grade physics course. Although prepared by different organizations, all of them rely heavily on Socratic questions, on Cartesian induction and, more immediately, on the
twentieth century writings of Alfred North Whitehead and the
Harvard psychologist Jerome S. Bruner.

> Intellectual activity anywhere [Bruner wrote in *The Process
> of Education*] is the same, whether at the frontier of knowledge
> or in a third grade classroom. What a scientist does at his desk
> or in his laboratory, what a literary critic does in writing a
> poem, are of the same order as what anybody else does when he
> is engaged in like activities—if he is to achieve understanding.
> The difference is in degree, not in kind. The schoolboy learning
> physics *is* a physicist, and it is easier for him to learn physics
> behaving like a physicist than doing something else. The "some-
> thing else" usually involves the task of mastering . . . a "middle
> language"—classroom discussions and textbooks that talk about
> the conclusions in a field of intellectual inquiry rather than
> centering upon the inquiry itself. Approached in that way, high
> school physics often looks very little like physics, social studies
> are removed from the issues of life and society as usually dis-
> cussed, and school mathematics too often has lost contact with
> what is at the heart of the subject, the idea of order. . . .
>
> . . . the curriculum of a subject should be determined by the
> most fundamental understanding that can be achieved of the
> underlying principles that give structure to that subject. Teach-
> ing specific topics or skills without making clear their context
> in the broader fundamental structure of a field of knowledge is
> uneconomical. . . . In the first place, such teaching makes it ex-
> ceedingly difficult for the student to generalize from what he has
> learned to what he will encounter later. In the second place,
> learning that has fallen short of a grasp of general principles
> has little reward in terms of intellectual excitement. The best

way to create interest in a subject is to render it worth knowing, which means to make the knowledge gained usable in one's thinking beyond the situation in which the learning has occurred. Third, knowledge one has acquired without sufficient structure to tie it together is knowledge that is likely to be forgotten.

All of these courses demand responses from students that go well beyond those asked in a conventional textbook course. They place students in the position of practitioners, giving them laboratory materials, source documents, and other data, and ask them to make their own statements, and to draw their own conclusions. Almost everyone of them will say, in one form or another: "the stress will be on inquiry by you, the student," and each will say, in its own way: How do you know what you know? What don't you know? What are the limits of your conclusions? They will ask: What is a model? What is a number?

> In an investigation [says the introduction to the ninth grade earth science course] we are striving to create a picture of the cause of a phenomenon we are observing. This picture is called a model. As we strive for more and more detail in the picture, we find more and more that some of the details are inconsistent with new observations.... We have to remember that a new observation may require modification of an answer we had regarded as the true one.

In the new biology course:

> The facts of biology will not be presented to you as a series of foregone conclusions. Nor will theories be presented as though they were facts. Instead, we have attempted to present biology as an adventure in ideas, in which the ideas refer to specific observations and experiments about living things.

In PSSC physics:

> The laboratory manual provides a general introduction to the problems at hand, gives you a few technical hints, but leaves the thinking to you. You will be on your own a great deal.

And in the new eighth grade physics course:

> ... Over two thousand years ago the Greek philosopher Democritus conceived of small units called atoms. But Democritus

did not really know there *were* atoms, or how many different kinds there were. His ideas must have been important, because we still use the word "atom"; but the word in itself does not really explain anything. It did not help people to predict any properties of matter or to understand what kind of changes could or could not take place. If someone tries to explain [the workings of a television set by talking about gremlins] would you be satisfied? Inventing the word gremlin does not help you understand how a television set works. Nor does the statement that matter is made of atoms help you much in understanding matter or atoms. Modern chemistry and physics can give you a much more meaningful account of the properties of matter. If this account is to have meaning to you, we shall have to start at the beginning. We cannot just throw new words at you. Each step must be fllled in with many experiments that you will perform so that all the words and ideas will correspond to something real for you, and so that you can reach conclusions on your own and form your own convictions.

And in a report on an experiment in elementary school social studies:

> . . . We found the children almost nonchalantly facile in their solutions. To explain this we must remember that one major change . . . had already been enacted—they are being rewarded for *their* rigor in recognizing the authority of the data. This differs markedly from the teacher imposing an external framework of authority in inquiry. . . . The children were with an almost sadistic kind of freedom romping through cognitive tasks that under traditional conditions would take weeks to build up to. They were using intellectual techniques of inquiry *in process* that by the standards of some of the observers were traditionally considered to be *ends*. . . .

The sciences have led the parade in curriculum revision, and the humanities are still the most reluctant to change or even to initiate experiments. "If it hadn't been for the new physics course," a Colorado school official said, "my eyes would be still closed." And in Jefferson County, with its concentration of geologists and engineers, one would expect changes to begin in those areas, even if they hadn't in other parts of the country. But the attitudes of inquiry, independent judgment and experimen-

tation, and the idea that understanding in any discipline is a human construct, the result of a creative act, and not some pre-exist-
ing "subject" to be derived passively from a textbook—these
things are applicable to any discipline, and Jefferson County is
trying to make them part of every course; they are the new frontier, and the central object of education. "I'm not supposed to
give the kids answers," said a junior high science teacher. "I'm
supposed to let them make mistakes, and they make mistakes.
Some kids rebelled. When they asked for the answer, I just beat
around the bush. . . . The hardest thing for a teacher to learn is
to let the kids work, and not to go in and lead them by the hand.
. . . I fought like mad to get into this, and I love it."

"Knowledge," Whitehead once said, "will not keep any better than fish."

II

It's all in a day's work. Building laboratory equipment in
your basement at night is part of the excitement of a new course,
compensation for not having to lecture every day to an assembly
of droopy minds who know that you know that they couldn't care
less. And so change has become conventional and heresy is normal. There are hundreds of other teachers taking in-service training so that they can teach the new math or pssc physics or French
by audio-lingual methods, knowing that whatever happens, the
place won't be the same next year as it is now..There will be new
kids, new schools, and probably new courses. Some teachers don't
like it, and they move on, usually to California where the pay is
better and the water warmer. But whatever you do, the place is
changing, and while you're there as a teacher, you will probably
change with it. By 1970, said Forbes Bottomly, the Superintendent of Schools, the entire system will be nongraded, and some students will spend only eleven, and perhaps ten, years in the public
schools. (Bottomly resigned in 1965 to become superintendent in
Seattle.) Grade designations have already been eliminated in foreign languages, in some primary classes in the elementary schools
and, at one high school, in English. When a student has mastered
the work he is doing he moves to another subject, or to a higher
level, either with the same teacher or with another. The English
classes at Arvada West High School have been organized in nine
week units (and this is now contemplated in social studies), each

concentrating in depth on some area or activity: Shakespeare I, Shakespeare II, American Drama, American Poetry, Mythology and Folklore, English Novel, Composition I, II and III and so on —and every student can choose his areas of concentration in the order he wants to study them. Team teaching is spreading and new schools are built to accommodate it in "quads" and "triads," rooms with movable partitions which can be combined for large lectures or films, or separated for small group discussions. Elementary school teachers are making tapes for language arts classes so that children can work independently while the teacher gives individual instruction to others; Cuisenaire rods are used in primary arithmetic lessons to teach first and second graders numerical relationships, and even the concept of fractions; and the entire junior high school program is being revised. But perhaps the greatest heresy of all is the idea that innovation is for everyone, not just special students; that you can teach any child the new math, that any physics student can carry out relevant laboratory experiments and find his own answers, and that only by tolerating confusion, and asking meaningful questions, can you teach anybody anything.

Chris Samples teaches a class of bright ten-year olds at the Wilmot School, a new glass and brick building in the mountains west of Evergreen, but she has a way of making them seem even brighter than they are. Chris and her husband Bob, who met as students at the University of Connecticut, came to Jeffco several years before; she now teaches the fifth grade, and he runs the planetarium. One of them is probably the best teacher in Jefferson County, but it is hard to say which.

The walls of Chris Samples' five-sided classroom are cluttered with photographs, maps and cutouts. On the floor stands a plaster and wood replica of an Iraqi village (the visitor might not know this, but the children tell him); the tables are covered with models of Iraqi huts which the children have made with clay, water and straw, and with materials for making more. Next to them is a cage containing a guinea pig. It is early afternoon: the subject is social studies, an experimental unit developed by Educational Services, Inc., which has assembled the photographs on the wall, the clay and straw, and the other material that the children use; all of it was shipped to Evergreen from Boston. Mrs. Samples has written three lists on the board; they are headed "land," "water" and "people." More than half the children have their hands up, and some of them are waving wildly.

Q. From the film and the pictures you've seen what would you say are the problems of the village?

A. Salt.

Q. Why salt?

A. The salt had encrusted on the soil and wouldn't let the crops come through.

A. There might be a lack of date palms.

Q. Why?

A. It could be a very dry year and they wouldn't grow.

A. Lack of rainfall.

Q. Is there another word you might use? What could you call this?

A. Drouth, dry season.

Q. Anything else?

A. Floods.

Q. What causes these floods? [As the kids answer she extends her lists on the board]: "floods" and "drouth" have been added under "water," "salt" under "land."

A. The rainy seasons; they get too much rain.

A. Lack of food.

Q. Why a lack of food?

A. Because there was a shortage of water, and crops wouldn't grow.

Q. Would there be any other time when there was a lack of food?

A. The cattle have to have something to eat. . . .

A. The wind might come along and cause a sandstorm. . . .

A. The floods sometimes wash out their crops. [The lists grow.]

Q. Anything else that might be a problem?

A. A lack of doctors and medical supplies.

Q. Is there a doctor in every village? Who takes care of these people?

A. There's one building in the village which is the school and also the post office and hospital. . . .

A. There might be tornadoes.

A. It's flat enough for it.

Q. We'll have to find out if they have tornadoes.

A. The buildings might fall down.

A. They don't have any stores; they can't go downtown to buy food.

A. The insects might eat their crops or something. . . .

A. If someone's sick and there's no doctor and they have to take them fast—there's no way to take them.

Q. Transportation—what kinds of transportation do they have?

A. Horses and donkeys. . . .

Q. Which of these problems would you try to solve first? [By now the lists have at least a half dozen items each.]

A. Probably the food problem.

Q. What other problems would you try to solve?

A. The smugglers; if you had food the smugglers might try to take it away.

A. The sandstorms.

Q. What could you do about the sandstorms?

A. Build walls to hold the sand back.

Q. Would this come before the food problem? How could you overcome drouth?

A. You could steal the water from another village.

A. You need water to keep alive, for everything, no matter what it is, animals or plants.

Q. Which is more important, water or food?

A. You could have a tank where the water flows in, then they could store it.

Q. Say you lived on Bear Creek and you had floods every spring from the melting snow. . . .

A. When it was dry you could dig and make the river deeper.

A. You could build a wall. [Now there is a question of whether the Iraqi bricks will resist water; several children want to take a brick home to bake it and see if it will survive, probably in Bear Creek.]

Q. Now remember, you can't leave the village to solve these problems. Think about them, and we'll come back to this tomorrow. [Several hands are still up, and a discussion continues

round Mrs. Samples.] "Why are all the huts in the village hud-
led together?" she asks. "For protection against smugglers," says
boy. "They've got to have irrigation ditches," says another.
They need most of their land for farming, they can't waste it...."

"I'm trying to get them to solve the problems of the village
without going to the city," Chris Samples says after class. "Later
we're going to study the early cities. By then I think the kids will
see how cities might have started, that they evolved not from an
equilibrium between land, water and people, but from a disequi-
librium. Even now their solutions often depend on the city." She
explains that the children made not only the huts, but that they
developed their own method of mixing the mortar for the bricks.
I just showed them the pictures, gave them the brick molds and
told them to go ahead. They've become so involved with the village that they've learned to sense the problems. I don't have to
tell them. Now they'll be able to go on to something very dead,
like the early cities, because they have an insight into people
other than those around them. The trouble with social studies
teaching is that it is so rarely about people."

Both Bob and Chris Samples have worked with ESI in developing materials, Bob in science, Chris in social studies. "The
scholars could have told us how to teach this," she said, "but they
didn't. Every teacher who is using it is following a different outline, and each of us is keeping a record of what we do, of what
works and what doesn't. This frightens some teachers; they're
afraid to break away from the straight and narrow, and the real
problem will probably be to train the teachers because many of
them want a script to follow. I like it this way because the children don't have to depend on my right answer." She explains that
she is not satisfied with all the materials, that the written descriptions of life in the Iraqi village are not adequate, and that she and
Bob have made their own overlays for the overhead projector
showing the topography and climatic zones of the Middle East.
"Tonight we're going out to the golf course in Evergreen," she
said. "They've had trouble with salt coming up through the soil.
We're going to get some soil in tanks and bring it over so the kids
can see how it takes place."

At the Creighton Junior High School, where visitors come to

see Cross Country, an interdisciplinary team teaching experiment (science, social science and history) Donald Osse's eighth grade science students are sitting at tables littered with simple wooden balances, beads, and metallic cubes.

> Try to decide [says the laboratory manual] by handling two cubes that look alike and have the same volume whether they have the same or different masses.

> Measure the masses of the cubes on your balance. Which has the greater density?

> Now, just by handling them, compare the mass of each of the cubes with a third object of different volume. Can you decide this way whether the third object is made of the same substance as one of the cubes, or of a different substance?

> Measure the dimensions of each of the three objects, calculate the volume of each, and then their densities.

At the Manning Junior High School, Albert McDowell's ninth-grade science class is working with two cylinders set at equal distances from a light bulb, acting as a source of heat. Each cylinder contains a thermometer. "When I turn the light off," says a student to the visitor, "that's sunset. The space is the atmosphere, and the cans are light and dark surfaces on the earth."

> Set up the black and white cans at equal distances from the lamp [says the lab manual]. Why?

> *You have to give each cylinder equal light [the student writes in his notebook]. Otherwise the experiment is off.*

> Be careful that you are not close to other sources of radiant energy, such as radiator or the sun. Why?

> *You have to measure the heat from your heat source only.*

> If the heat from the lamp represents solar heat and the black and white cans represent dark and light earth surfaces, what does the air inside the can represent? What is unrealistic about this representation of nature?

> *The light and dark areas are not round like the earth, and they don't receive the same amount of heat. They aren't equidistant from the sun or anything.*

"I know it's not like a natural model," the student says to the isitor, "but I don't think there's a better experiment for this. . . . t sure beats memorizing a lot of stuff." "What you know in this ourse," another student interrupted, "are why and how. *He* ever tells you anything."

At the planetarium, a $50,000 piece of equipment which the chool district bought for $6,000, two hundred seventh graders om all over the county are listening to Bob Samples. (Planetar-im classes are held every day; in the evenings there are public howings for the community; but this is not entertainment.)

"You'll have to use your imagination," says Samples. "We're oing to look at space as seen from some isolated place in the uni-erse, not from the earth, and we're going to see it not in terms f visible light; we'll pretend we can see infrared and ultraviolet ght. If we could see the infrared we could see the heat that's be-ng radiated; that way you wouldn't be able to recognize your est friend. . . . What you're seeing is not stars, but galaxies. . . . 'ou're looking at energy. . . . When men first saw this what would hey want to do? . . . That's right, they wanted to tell each other 'hat this was. They wanted to name the galaxies, to make a map, o put things in order. Let's pick one out and talk about it. . . . Now you can make some order out of this [one of the swirls pro-ected on the dome above is now enlarged many times]. How ould you describe this? That's right, a spiral. . . . How would ou describe this one? . . . Yes, a little bit like a spider. It has sev-ral arms. . . . Now astronomers called these spiral galaxies S gal-xies . . . and these elliptical ones E galaxies. . . ." He discusses the ubclassifications: E_0, E_1, E_2 by attaching the symbol to the visual epresentation of each, and then begins to describe the various heories of how stars are formed from energy and dust in space.

"Are those loose stars outside the galaxies," a student asks, nd his question is immediately followed by another: "What's eyond that?"

"What you're asking," Samples says, "is what's it like at the dge of the universe traveling at the speed of light. It takes cour-ge to ask that; I'm glad you did. . . . Now suppose that there are lot of kids in a playground, and they all begin to run in a radial attern, going in different directions. As you looked around you t would still seem as if you're at the center, and as if everything

is moving away from you gradually. That's the way the univer
looks. . . ."

The film is called *Fishing at the Stone Weir*. It is about tl
Netsilik Eskimos of northern Canada, and is still "experimental
the school district has just received it from ESI, which produced
for first-grade social studies lessons. (ESI photographers and a
thropologists spent months in the Arctic making movies of Esk
mos; sometimes, when the Eskimos had adopted more mode
techniques, the anthropologists made primitive tools and taugl
the Eskimos how to use them.) The film shows an older man,
younger man, a woman and a boy walking along in the tundr
All of them are covered with insects. They stop at a river, an
make camp. The two men begin to put stones across the rive
working a couple of days before the weir is completed. Fish begi
to collect behind the stones, and they spear them; soon they hav
dozens strung together and they give them to the woman wh
cleans them. As they fish, the boy wades into the water and im
tates their movements. The woman takes a piece of intestine fro
a fish, ties one end, and blows it up for the boy, like a balloo
Every part of the fish is used. The dog chews the heads; the woma
and child eat the insides, and the men cut large sections whic
they eat raw. The film has no narration, no verbal explanation o
any kind.

"Doesn't the boy go to school?" asked a first grader who sa
the film at a trial showing. "But he is going to school," anoth
replied. "He is learning to be like the men. . . ."

From the introduction to the BSCS Biology Course, now b
ing used in most Jeffco high school biology classes:

[The theory of evolution] is the most inclusive of the great un
fying principles of biology. It is so much a part of the found
tion of biology that the science can hardly be understood wit
out it.

The barometer dipped slightly during the night, the bo
says, and the wind is now about 10 mph out of the west, ov
there, where you can see the 14,000 foot peak of Mount Evan
The low early this morning was 29 degrees—Fahrenheit, that is–

ut now the thermometer stands at forty. He has recorded it all
n his notebook. He also says that they saw a herd of elk in the
valley the night before, and that he thinks he heard a coyote, but
he wasn't sure because someone in the bunkhouse was snoring.

Along with 120 other sixth-graders who are spending this
week at the Outdoor Education Laboratory School (once the C.
Phelps Dodge Ranch), the boy is keeping a record of what he sees
and hears, of the rock formations which the geologist described
on the forty-mile bus trip coming out, the mineral samples, the
trees, the animals, and the stars. He waits on tables in the cafeteria, hears talks on good timber practice—which trees to cut, and
which to leave standing—on map reading, safety in the woods,
astronomy and conservation. For this week his English classes will
be devoted to writing accounts of his observations, and his art
lessons will concentrate on representing what he has seen. At least
one evening he will study the sky with one of the school's three
telescopes (two six-inch reflectors and one eight-inch reflector),
but he has already been prepared for this at the planetarium. If
the sky is clear tonight, Bob Samples will come to the ranch to
conduct the astronomy class and set up the telescopes. The boy
and his classmates hike around the ranch; everywhere they can
see the magnificent mountain peaks in the west, many of them
covered with snow, and all week long someone is shouting "hey,
look at this" and "what's this?"

This particular morning he and the other kids will hear an
illustrated talk by Don Zielesch of the Fish and Wildlife Service
of the Department of the Interior. Zielesch has been coming to
the Outdoor School every week for several years.

"What is a predator?" Zielesch asks.

"It's an animal that eats another animal," a child says.

"There are four major predators in Colorado, the bobcat,
the coyote, and the bear. What's the worst predator?" Some guessing ensues among the kids. Finally one says "I'm not sure about
this, but could it be man?" Zielesch goes on to show slides, explaining that there are two reasons why predator control is necessary: damage to livestock, especially to sheep, and the danger of
disease. He discusses the behavior of rabid animals. "If the animal
just sits there and looks," he says, "don't try to pet him. If he's
healthy he won't just sit and look at you."

"How long will you live if you're bitten and you didn't have the shots," a child asks.

"Thirty to forty-five days. There was a girl who developed rabies in Tennessee. Her wound had been ignored and she died. But before she died she bit her own mother. You can't control yourself because the disease affects the nerves." Zielesch goes on to show slides and animal skins.

"What's this?" he asks.

"It's a bobcat."

"And this?"

"A badger."

"And this?"

"A timber wolf." The kids successfully identify the spotted skunk, red fox, silver fox, kit fox and prairie dog.

"What's this?" Zielesch asks.

"It's a buffalo."

"It's a bison."

"I don't think there's any difference," a boy says. "They're two names for the same animal."

Before the end of the school year three thousand five hundred kids will have had similar experiences; a new group of sixth graders and their teachers come each Monday morning and stay until Friday afternoon. (On weekends and in the summer the place is available to community organizations on a rental basis.) And each group that comes represents new converts to an idea that was questioned when the ranch was bought in 1963. The place, after all, was a frill, an interlude of fun and games, rather than serious study, and it is not even located in Jefferson County. But the ranch will pay for itself in a number of years, and Friday's tired kids with their crammed notebooks indicate it wasn't as much fun and games as everybody thought. Now no one questions the purchase any more. At the rate Jeffco goes, it is almost ancient history.

Everything moves in Jefferson County, and almost everything was created yesterday. Buildings move to keep pace with shifts in the population; teachers move to give specialized instruction in remote schools; equipment moves; children move; books move. A few years ago, when an old high school burned down in the mountains, the district assembled enough mobile units—frame buildings with fully appointed classrooms inside—to resume classes within two weeks. As people move within the county the mobiles follow them around. When a new residential development goes up, the district converts one of its houses into a "cottage" elementary school until it becomes economically and geographically necessary to erect a complete neighborhood school. Before the new consolidated high schools accommodated children from the mountains, teachers of Russian and other specialized subjects drove into the hills to conduct classes—all to fulfill the promise of equality. Children who cannot afford the fifteen dollar fee for the week at the Outdoor School attend for nothing. In two years Jeffco converted all its physics classes to the new PSSC, instituted a new elementary school science program, began the new math, and the modern biology program, operating one of the largest teacher in-service programs in the country. When the new math was adopted the district offered classes for parents, expecting perhaps twenty or thirty to appear. Instead six hundred enrolled, and every competent teacher and administrator was pressed into service to handle the load. Every year the district spends $20,000 on paperback books for its libraries—"sure they wear out," a librarian said, "but the kids are using them"; at Manning Junior High, where a student can read *U.S.S.R.* along with *Scientific American* and *Saturday Review*, one volume of Russian short stories was checked out twenty times in a year, and *Brothers Karamazov* was doing well. Two thirds of the junior high school program is being revised (next year there will be a full year of biology in the seventh grade, the new IPS science course in the eighth, and earth science in the ninth); high school social science and English courses are being reviewed—Jeffco is still looking for a really exciting English curriculum—and a new vocational program is under study. Each time a new national curriculum project is initiated someone from Jeffco investigates, offers assistance in trying out materials, and suggests that Colorado would be a good place to train teachers. Jefferson County has, or has had, teachers and staff members working with PSSC, ESI, the Illinois Mathematics Program, the Earth Science Curriculum Project, and other groups, and has been looking for an affiliation with new ventures in the humanities and the social

sciences, always on the assumption that an early start with a new
curriculum means that help from university scholars will be
available. Innovations are not made indiscriminately: ultimately
they must be more than experiments and must logically suit the
total program that the district is trying to develop, a program that
involves teachers as well as books and laboratory exercises, and
that requires a high degree of sophistication on the part of the
staff. At the same time there are advantages in getting there first.
"We've made an economically profitable venture out of innovation," Watts said. "It's like a hog market. If everybody got their
hogs to market you wouldn't gain anything. We try to get there
first. We got our data processing equipment free because the
company wanted to demonstrate how a school system could use
it. The same with the planetarium—the Japanese had just introduced this model into the American market; that's how we got
the big rake-off. Man, what a teaching tool! We knew we couldn't
use it like a college—as a scientific instrument, or like a museum
for oohs and ahs. But you can use it for all kinds of things. It can
recreate the past and project the future; what a stimulus to the
imagination. You can use it to take the kids back to Marco Polo's
time, or to show the connection between man's ability to navigate
and his political supremacy. . . When we started the new elementary science program we had six hundred teachers in evening
in-service courses. Teachers, supervisors, principals, everybody
showed up. We shipped guppies and chickens and balloons all
over the county. When they started the new ips eighth-grade science program we talked them into using Jefferson County as the
testing center for this part of the country, and told them we'd
help train teachers; and we're the only system outside the East
that's trying out the esi social studies. They wanted to keep it
close to home, but we got it. We tried to get them to develop
some stuff for the planetarium, but they said nobody had one but
us, and it wasn't worth it. So we'll try doing it ourselves. Curriculum development on the local level is inefficient, but we'll
give it a whirl. It's fun, isn't it? All this left handedness. But maybe there's a place for chaos."

But chaos extracts a price, and not every experiment is a
roaring success. A great deal of planning and study goes into the
various innovations—the trials and experiments aren't being

conducted for the purpose of titillation, an administrator said— and almost every one of them is accompanied by a major effort in teacher training and re-training. And yet, in trying to turn thirty- nine little systems into a space-age school district, Jeffco has some- times outrun its shoes, leaving parents frustrated and teachers breathless. Staff turnover is high—though Jeffco administrators point out that it is not as high as Denver's. In the elementary schools about one fourth of the teachers are new each year— partly as a consequence of growth, but partly also because many leave after three or four years, often for California, where the pay for experienced personnel is higher, the climate more attractive and the academic pace sometimes less frenetic. (Watts also points out that since the district seeks "adventurous" teachers it is likely to attract many who are reluctant to stay in one place all their lives.) The average teacher's salary in Jefferson County is $5870, somewhat above the Colorado average, but far below California ($7375); Jeffco pays a beginner with a master's degree $5150, but its top salary in that bracket (after twenty years) is only $8410. A Jefferson County administrator conceded that the district saves money on its teachers' salaries—very few are in the upper brackets—and that this is one way that the per-pupil budget is held down. (In 1962–3 it was $391, compared to $484 in Denver.)

In an effort to offset this loss, and to attract innovation- minded personnel, Jeffco recruits in thirty-six states, visiting universities and teachers' colleges, most of them in the Midwest and Far West (excluding California). "We make it into a chal- lenge for them," said Watts, who has done a good deal of recruit- ing himself. "We tell every person we consider for the sixth grade about the ranch. We don't make it a chore, but an opportunity. We tell them 'if you measure up, we'll take you.' " Despite this inducement there are teachers in Jefferson County who are not interested in innovation or change and who resent the demands that are implicitly or explicitly made of them ("Sometimes they cuss the hell out of us," an administrator reported with some de- light); others talk innovation but rarely practice it. Team teach- ing efforts in history, competently handled, are regarded as major departures for people who have become impatient with survey courses, but the questions they ask continue to focus on assimila- tion of data and on memorization of material—substituting rigid coverage of a unit "in depth" for coverage of all the names and dates from Columbus to Goldwater. Others merely replace the old math with the new math, and continue to present as the kids regurgitate, while still others try to force interdisciplinary connections where no such connections can be made. Even at the Outdoor School, with its almost unlimited opportunities for independent study, some teachers still walk their kids around in files—always fearful of the damage suit that might follow an accident, following a dutiful daily schedule, and behaving as if the Outdoor School (550 acres of timber, trails and opportunity located three miles from the nearest paved road) were no more than Miss Rigid's antediluvian classroom.

Within the community itself there is recurring concern that things have moved too fast, and this reflects a national reaction against the new courses. Some school systems have introduced new materials before teachers were properly trained to handle them; in the grade schools some of them were bombarded with three or four simultaneous innovations and, since they were too frightened to complain, they proceeded as best they could. Max Beberman, who directed the Illinois Mathematics Program, charged not long ago that faddist schoolmen were introducing his material before they had trained teachers to handle it, and that it was being improperly taught. Although Jefferson County, through its large in-service training program, is trying to avoid such problems some parents are still uneasy. "There was a feeling, and maybe there is still," said a PTA leader, "that we've had too much experimentation. They say this community likes experiments, but not too many at one time. A few years ago people felt that the system was trying to play on its national reputation and that new programs were started without adequate explanation to the parents. Some still wish they'd teach the kids plain old addition and multiplication rather than the new math. It was after some of those criticisms came up that the schools began the adult education in math. . . . This district began to grow during the days of the big academic push—Sputnik and all that—and I think we were doing it too fast for a while. We were among the first to start a Spanish program for all children K-12; when it was first introduced it threatened to become a colossal failure because the teachers just weren't prepared to handle it." "We've dug a lot of foundations," said a faculty member at the School of Mines in Golden. "Maybe we ought to build some roofs before we start any more holes." But this feeling is by no means universal. Most parents are delighted and, since they come from all parts of the country, they have ample basis for comparison. "The kids are learning," one of them said. "When they started the new math they suddenly got enthusiastic. I'm no mathematician, but the kids are sure excited."

In the rush to create an outstanding school system for an area that was, in many respects, born yesterday, and which is growing up with missiles, geologists and well-educated suburbanites, Jeffco placed virtually all its emphasis on developing its academic curriculum and almost none on vocational or technical training. The high schools offer industrial arts, a sort of overview of various trades, but no genuine vocational courses. Even though half of the county's high school graduates do not go on to college all students are being educated as if they were. The district is sufficiently sophisticated to understand that the old style of vocational training is likely to prepare people for jobs that no longer exist, and to teach skills that may imminently become obsolete, but no one is yet prepared to say just what should replace it. "The best vocational education," someone said, "is basic math and science. In some schools there's a tendency to give slow kids less lab work, but that's just the thing they need most." Nevertheless, there is mounting concern among the staff and in the community that a good vocational program is necessary. Many feel that although Jefferson County's dropout rate is somewhat lower than the national average for senior high schools, it is still too high, and that it can best be reduced by offering relevant training to students who are not academically inclined. "We're educating half our kids," said Mrs. Betty Miller, a former PTA officer who was elected to the Colorado legislature in 1964. "Those who don't go to college graduate with no real preparation of any kind." Although some Jeffco administrators feel that improved academic training will reduce the dropout rate, the district has begun to study the alternatives in vocational programs. A citizens committee was appointed in 1964 to consider the possibilities and, at least in part, to meet community criticisms (one of its first discoveries was that the district was already doing more than some members expected). Typically, the committee, composed of businessmen, professionals, housewives, also includes some of the district's most vocal critics. They received no instructions, no elaborate plans, but merely a promise that the staff would provide any information or administrative assistance the committee desired. At the end of its second weekly meeting the chairman, a Lakewood businessman named James R. Murray, asked one of the staff members: "What do you need our advice on? What are we supposed to be here for?"

"There are people in the county who feel that the vocational program needs to be beefed up. We're asking for your advice on how to do it."

"Well, we don't know what's going on," Murray replied.

"Maybe we'd better look at some of the schools," said someone else.

"I'd like to find out what's really going on in home economics," said a housewife committee member.

"We're ready to take you anywhere you'd like to go," an administrator said. "What days would be best for you?"

As the committee began its deliberations, the administration had already started trying out a new heresy. Instead of committing vast funds to furnish complete electronic and other shops in each high school (and once shop equipment is installed, it is almost never changed), why not put the equipment in trailers, leaving each trailer at a school for six weeks, and then moving it on to the next? The schools have been employing this technique with their driver education equipment and the Air Force uses it with its missile outfits, so why not use it also to supply a half dozen high schools with one set of equipment? In the winter of 1964–65 the first mobile shops were set up, and early indications were that the district may soon have a great part of its vocational plant on wheels. Jefferson County is far from solving all its problems, but it has thought of most of the questions.

III

When the Jefferson County School District R-1 was officially created in 1951, thanks in part to an act of the legislature that was later repealed (and then adopted again), it was saddled with a collection of problems that have all but destroyed effective education elsewhere: local jealousies, a huge geographical area, rapid growth, substandard buildings, no effective sense of community, inadequate state support, and a generally conservative political climate. Communities as far apart as Levittown, New York and Anaheim, California became examples of the paralyzing school controversies produced by rapid growth and inadequate community leadership and understanding. (A committee named by the National Education Association which investigated the Levittown controversy in 1961 called it a "community in confusion," and chronicled a history of rejected bond issues and budgets, low staff morale, political pressure on teachers, suspicion, and endless controversy.) Failure to provide adequate support for schools has impaired education in Oklahoma, Utah and Louisville, Kentucky, and in many growing areas where conservative groups have succeeded in resisting higher expenditures and academic improvements.

Jefferson County was ready-made for similar struggles, and it did not altogether escape them. Its rapidly rising tax rate and its penchant for experimentation, have produced attacks from right-wingers, from budget-minded tax groups, and from educational fundamentalists; its elimination of the inadequate schools of the mountains has affronted local community pride, and its chaos has sometimes bothered even the most sympathetic parents. Although the county gave fifty-six per cent of its 1964 presidential vote to Johnson and Humphrey it has its share of old conservatives and new-style right wingers. The Colorado School of Mines in Golden is among the more isolated and conservative educational institutions in the state—and one of two in which the students favored Goldwater—while much of Golden itself remains Goldwater country. Anti-communist "Freedom Schools" have been held in the Denver area and right-wing organizations like Colorado Patriots, Inc. and a "Committee Against Summit Entanglements" have been active, circulating the message of conservative extremism. In 1964 a group of Denver and Jeffco businessmen sent telegrams to fellow corporation executives in Colorado soliciting support for the Manion Forum (directed by Clarence Manion, a member of the John Birch Society), expressing concern about "atheistic alien philosophies" and asking for a return to "basic American concepts of personal rights, free enterprise and national morality."

But Jeffco never became Levittown or Anaheim, and it never will; although Colorado Patriots and other reactionaries opposed the most recent bond issue—which carried by a substantial margin—there have been no book burnings, no attacks on teachers and little ideological criticism of the new courses. When high school students arranged a debate between a member of the Fair Play for Cuba Committee (which is sympathetic to Castro) and a Castro critic, only three families complained, and the debate was held. The area's conservatism is milder than that of southern California; there are fewer utopians gone sour, fewer retired persons, and fewer people who have a stake to protect. But Jeffco has a high local tax rate, and a high bonded indebtedness and its success in averting damaging controversy must also be attributed in part to what, lacking a better phrase, one has to call the residue of the old frontier, in part to a hard-working and adventuresome school board, and in part to the influence of two unusual men, Robert T. Johnson and Forbes Bottomly. These two, along with Watts and other staff members, managed to convert controversy into productivity, chaos into purpose, and growth into progress. Johnson was the first superintendent of the unified district, succeeding a kind of interregnum which followed the merger. Bottomly succeeded him in 1962, and Watts, who is now assistant superintendent, served under both. Together they rewrote the maxims of proper school management, opened school decisions to community discussion, and invited anyone who was interested to serve on any committee that he had time for. "Every time they build a new school out there," said a flabbergasted educator who knows the district from several visits, "they set up a committee. First they invite all their critics to serve. Then they choose people more or less at random, sometimes by picking names from the phone book. They'll get the doctor and the town whore, and everybody in between. It's unbelievable." Architects are commissioned for new buildings with the understanding that they attend the citizens committee meetings, provide information when necessary, and that they have the patience to listen even to the most absurd suggestions. In each instance the committee is given cost estimates, alternative plans, and an idea of what each proposed economy will cost in educational opportunity and effectiveness. The architect feels that carpets throughout a new building, though expensive, might save money in the long run by eliminating the need for accoustical ceiling tile, and that they would generate an *esprit* not found in other schools. Most members of the committee are doubtful (for obviously carpets are frills—or are they?) and the debate goes on. . . . "Anybody can get on these committees," said Betty Miller. "But they'll have to work. I've seen them go for six solid months."

Following a pattern set by Johnson in the hectic days after consolidation, the dictrict misses no opportunity to involve the community in its affairs. (Creation of the district was first studied and recommended by a citizens committee.) School board meetings are jammed with spectators, PTA membership is high—sometimes reaching 400 members in schools with 500 children—and whenever a special problem arises a new citizens' group is created to study it. In the first four years after the district was formed Johnson attended hundreds of meetings, listened to complaints, and answered questions as honestly as he could, promising little but more problems as the region grew in population; and when Jeffco held its first major school bond elections in the mid-fifties, the entire school force was mobilized to support them. High school bands led torchlight parades through the streets of Golden and Lakewood and other towns, students produced singing radio commercials, and teachers and administrators spent evening after long evening at public gatherings, telling people why they thought art and music should be part of the school program, why new buildings were necessary and one-room schools inadequate. "When we had the little school at Bear Creek," said an old timer, "we felt the school was ours. It was part of the community. We had our parties and events there. The kids didn't play their instruments very well but *they* were playing and nobody minded their mistakes. Now they send that music teacher around and we have to hear him play. If he was any damn good he'd be playing in some orchestra and not teaching school." But Johnson, who was considered an autocrat by many teachers, succeeded in generating community interest and pride in the schools, and that pride justified itself. Bonds have been approved, the system has grown, and, although Jeffco's campaign techniques have become more sedate, community involvement has not diminished and the administration's attitude about the ultimate good sense of the people has not changed. "I've seen some angry protest meetings," an administrator said. "Usually we just let them keep talking. After a while someone will start taking your side, and often by the end of the evening they've talked themselves out of it."

The district's committee system has produced a certain amount of local cynicism; there are people who feel that because the administration encourages it, it must somehow be devious or dishonest, and that it serves the administration's purposes (which, of course, it does). "The committees," someone said, "get the school board off the hook." One committee took the schools to task because there had been a "widespread feeling that the administration had already made up its mind. . . . As a result the work of the committee was delayed while subcommittee members questioned the motives of the administration and debated their effect upon the purposes of the project. . . . This situation could have been made less difficult if the administration could have made it clear that it had no preconceived solutions of the problems involved. . . ." Despite such criticisms no one has seriously proposed doing away with the committees; moreover, Jeffco has been able to use them, rather than school board elections or budget controversies, as forums for criticism, and as a means of informing the public. When the *Canyon Courier*, weekly newspaper published in Evergreen, attacked the administration (charging excessive innovation), residents wrote letters defending the schools, and—when the paper did not print them—they bought a full-page advertisement answering the charges and telling the editor what they thought of him. "The many people involved on the citizens' committees," said the wife of a clergyman, "form a sizable and enthusiastic lobby. That's why we don't have more trouble."

The schools are Jeffco's only common enterprise. The county government, run by elected commissioners on the old rural pattern, provides no street lights or sidewalks and maintains only the most minimal services. Inadequate zoning laws are inadequately enforced, and some areas have become a stew of decaying houses, trailers and junk. There are no laws against keeping animals, even in the more settled areas, and whenever one is proposed most voters consider it an affront to their freedom and rural simplicity. Many suburban residents in areas like Apple-wood and Wheat Ridge—the prestige neighborhoods—keep horses. ("Status," someone said, "is determined by the pile of manure you have in your front yard. The bigger the pile, the more horses.") The schools have, therefore, become a surrogate for other forms of community activity and cohesion. In some measure this function is similar to that performed by schools in many other suburbs where they are the prime source of com-munity, but in Jeffco everybody can take part; the creative process is accessible to every resident, while academic snobbery and concern with admission to prestige colleges is a relatively small consideration. Almost all those who go to college attend a state institution and, as in California, there is little panic about getting into them. Where schools in eastern suburbs are stepping-stones to status (and admission to an Ivy League college is taken as a sign of parental affection and success) education in Jefferson County is a combination barn-raising, town meeting and initi-ation ceremony into the modern world. Virtually all high school football games are played at a central field (adjacent to the plan-etarium, the school of special education for retarded or otherwise handicapped children, and other schools) to eliminate the ex-pense of maintaining separate establishments and reduce pro-vincialism within the district. The schools provide the only com-munity-owned cultural resources, and they offer public services that the county is otherwise unwilling to provide. The only major library collections are those in the schools. The planetarium, used for classes all day, offers programs for adults three evenings a week. The Outdoor Education School is available for com-munity groups; school buildings are open for meetings, and almost every night citizens' committees assemble in some part of the county to discuss school building plans, more efficient use of staff, new materials, or a forthcoming bond issue. Even in the realm of transportation the schools are providing extra services; children who live only a few blocks from school ride the school bus because there are no sidewalks, and the roads are too danger-ous. "The schools are the only thing you can hang your hat on," said the president of a PTA unit. "They're it around here."

But the schools are not merely a means of keeping people

constructively busy and of supplying some cultural resources while retaining (in the county administration) the vestiges of rural purity—and thereby trying to have the best of both worlds —they are also the gate to the New World. The missile engineers concentrated at the Martin Company, the government geologists at the Federal Center, and the region's architectural and techno- logical modernity give these schools their natural proclivity to science and to innovation generally. Technology in Jefferson County is not a threat, a dehumanizing force, a source of alien- ation. It is rather the thing that brings water from the western slopes of the Continental Divide through a thirty mile mountain tunnel; and that provides rapid communication over 14,000 foot peaks and across a thousand miles of prairie. In other places it takes away jobs, but here it provides them; in other places it sepa- rates a man from his neighbor, but here it brings them together; in other places it has defaced the landscape, but here it has made it accessible. The sky is clear, and the mountains close, and man's art, rather than obscuring them, enlarges and heightens their impact. (Because real estate agents in Jefferson County have dis- couraged—and in some instances actively prevented—Negroes from moving in, it has no racial problems. Except for a few Spanish-speaking persons, there are no ethnic minorities, there is no industrial labor force of any size, and the poverty is reasonably well concealed: even the most knowledgeable residents have difficulty finding the slums, assuming they know about them at all.) This is not to say that Jefferson County has escaped the moral and cultural dilemmas that technology imposes on all of us. The tensions in the community, the chaos of neon from the motels and drive-ins on Colfax Avenue; the religious and political fundamentalism of the rightists, and the architectural barren- ness of the subdivisions make it perfectly clear that this is no utopian blend of nature and technology, of garden and machine. The county tax rate is high, and most of it already goes for schools: although chances were good that the legislature (where the Democrats won the lower house in 1964) would increase edu- cational appropriations in 1965, the state has traditionally furnished only a small percentage (twenty-one per cent in 1964) of the school budget, and every resident knows it. But the new- ness of the region, its freedom from sentimentality about a lost and lovely past, and from the social tensions of the urban present, and its proximity to the great western mountains, allow it to come to terms with technology and change (and even with rising taxes), to see possibilities in them rather than oppression, and, therefore, to side with the future instead of the past.

No one can be sure what the possibilities are, and perhaps it does not really matter. What is important is, rather, the *attitude* of possibility and of freedom, and the educational demands it makes. In a remarkable book called *Education and the New America*, Solon T. Kimball, an anthropologist, and James E. McClellan, a professor of education, explored the educational consequences of this attitude and the technology on which it now depends:

> Our nation, beyond any that has ever existed, offers freedom, order and opportunity. And beyond any other, our nation extracts a price for its goods. Our freedom from material want, from poverty, drudgery, disease, and ignorance will endure only so long as we pay the high price for these great goods, the price of submission to the discipline of a technological culture—not to technology *per se*—but to the forms of rational thought and action and to the ordered relations with others in the superstructures which channel and direct our energies. This discipline exhibits itself not only in the time clocks at the production end, but also in the need to surround oneself with innumerable physical objects, each of which demands care and attention.

If this is the condition of American society, they feel, then the individual has only two choices: "he can either be carried along as a passive passenger or he can be himself a moving force in determining his own destiny. The difference will be in the degree to which he *knows* what the system is." The only way the individual can be something more than "a mere slave in the society" he serves is through a lifetime of "productive learning" e.g. through continuous self-education, and this can only be brought about by reconstructing formal secondary and higher education in such a way that "productive learning is a usual and consciously prized result of study." They go on to propose four basic "disciplines": the formal disciplines of logic and mathematics; the discipline of experimentation; the discipline of

natural history (which includes social science); and the discipline of aesthetic form, all of which sound strangely like the old
school subjects tricked up with new names. What makes them
different is the concept itself: "These disciplines are not merely
(if indeed they are at all) academic studies. Rather they are the
primordial rules of thought that guide our most fundamental
interpretations of the world. They are substitutes in the contemporary world for the gossip and sorcery of primitive village
life; that is to say, these disciplines are for us legitimate modes of
social control." What Kimball and McClellan describe, finally,
is that "different kind of kid" with the different kind of attitude
that Larry Watts is talking about, the kid with the inquisitive
attitude, for whom no explanation is entirely satisfactory, the
kid who is forever on an intellectual quest and for whom *process*
is as important and meaningful as substance. Kimball and Mc-
Clellan reject the conventional symbols of public morality and
meaning. For example: "The symbols of Christianity and Juda-
ism make sense, give adequate expression to the demands for
interpersonal commitment within the family and local neighborhood. Within the larger structures of society and nature, no."
And again: "America is no longer the kind of place that easily
admits to the sort of personal identification we could call 'love
of country.'"

> Perhaps the final step in the democratic experiment is that
> the society no longer poses an ultimate meaning to life. Instead
> it builds within each individual such a complex sense of self
> that the person is forced to create meaning, order, and purpose
> for himself. . . .

> The culture has few or no compeling myths, superstitions or
> illusions to comfort [the individual]. But he may, on the other
> hand, find the *quest* for meaning, the freedom to *create* his
> own purposes the most rewarding life of all.

Jefferson County has made no official declaration of its intention to educate seekers rather than believers, and to teach
process as well as fact, and, indeed, it is still not doing it. But the
trend is in that direction, joining new educational techniques to
the conditions of social and technological change—things that

have long been part of the American intellectual landscape, but which have, heretofore, received only lipservice in the schools. A century ago American children learned the important things outside the schoolhouse, and everyone knew it; but that form of education is no longer available. Until recently, however, we behaved as if it were, and the schoolhouse continued to foster rigidity when everything outside demanded inventiveness, imagination and adaptability. Americans held the schoolmaster in amused contempt and gave him those tasks that were deemed educationally least important: the things that really mattered were handled at home, around the farm, in the craft shop, the church, and in the forest. As each of them declined in importance, it relinquished its educational function to the schools, which are now saddled with conflicting burdens they cannot possibly handle: moral instruction; vocational education; political brainwashing; fighting the Cold War. Each task was simply added on, to be taught in the same way as the three Rs, cleanliness and George Washington. Until recently it rarely occurred to anyone (except perhaps someone like John Dewey) that the decline of informal education demanded not merely quantum increases in the school curriculum (and this still goes on with anti-communism courses, units on moral and spiritual values, etc.) but a complete reorientation of the schools, the kind of reorientation that new courses—when they are *well taught*—and the "new kind of attitude" represent. Clearly the schools of 1965 cannot be expected to teach the same morality as the churches of 1865, or train craft apprentices in the same fashion as the journeymen of another age. "Sure American values are important," said Anthony Petrillo, the social studies supervisor for the Jeffco Schools. "But there's a different way to approach them. The parents around here all were bored with their American history courses. They hated them." The difference lies not merely in finding material that will be relevant to a particular group of children, in adjusting the data to fit the cultural and social situation of the local population, but also in using that situation to develop modes of thought applicable to any set of conditions, to make motion and change the central propositions of thought. Education, as the tool of a democratic society, is inextricably associated with the search for the good society, and the variety of choices, the infinite possibilities with which democratic society and education are concerned, are themselves elements which bring ethical content and significance to these institutions. There are great risks in each; democracy and education are both dangerous social experiments (and it would be easy to find someone to argue that neither has ever been tried), and it is only by an act of faith that we have been willing to indulge either of them. Democracy, after all, can choose stupidity as well as wisdom, suicide as well as survival, and oppression as well as freedom; and the kind of education that rejects absolutes in favor of quest and experimentation may yet produce amoral, anxious, and unheroic technicians. But that risk has always been part of the bargain. Where there is no choice there is no moral dilemma and, therefore, no chance for any significant act, moral or otherwise. Jefferson County appears to be willing to take that chance. There is no way of knowing whether it will pay off, or even of recognizing success when it comes. As in other democratic institutions, success lies in the quest itself.

8

The Open School

"WHEN ONE CONSIDERS . . . the education of a nation's young,"
said Whitehead in "The Aims of Education," "the broken lives,
the defeated hopes, the national failures, which result from the
frivolous inertia with which it is treated, it is difficult to restrain
within oneself a savage rage. In the conditions of modern life the
rule is absolute, the race which does not value trained intelligence is doomed. Not all your heroism, not all your social charm,
not all your wit, not all your victories on land or at sea, can move
back the finger of fate. Today we maintain ourselves. Tomorrow
science will have moved forward yet one more step, and there
will be no appeal from the judgment which will then be pro-
nounced on the uneducated."

The statement was made to the Mathematical Association
of England in the year 1916—it deserves to be repeated, even in
America a half century later.

Our schools have come a long way in recent years, and a long
way indeed since 1916. There are new courses and techniques,
special programs for the gifted and the underprivileged, better
pay for teachers and, in general, a greater understanding and
concern for education. And yet many schools are still inadequate,
not because their buildings are ancient and their teachers underpaid, or because they have not adopted all the new gimmicks on
the market (which, in some places, have merely been added to
the old program, like mushrooms in a dull sauce) but because so
many schools are committed to the wrong enterprise at the wrong
time. "Education," to quote Whitehead again, "is the acquisition
of the art of the utilization of knowledge." It is not the random
distribution of inert ideas, the regurgitation of prepackaged facts,
or the formal exchange of clichés between teacher and student.

Many schools are still storage bins, twelve-year warehouses for the young where, ideally, very little is supposed to happen, and where all events are subject to intensive control. Organized from the outside in, they were created on the basis of buildings, budgets, administrative efficiency, pupil headcounts, accounting procedures and rigid structures. Variety, flexibility and originality are intolerable because they make administration difficult, they ruin normal accounting and scheduling systems, and they make the citizens suspicious. Thus the textbook and the syllabus become the academic analogs of fenders, or tail-lights and spray paint on the assembly line: they are added to the kids as they move through on the curricular belt. It is easy to teach "facts" not only because the culture is fact-ridden, but because it is easy to test for learning when "facts" are to be regurgitated. So far we have no machines for evaluating good prose, originality, or the elegance and effectiveness of a student's power to reason. Even the teachers of some of the prestigious suburban advanced placement courses are sometimes afraid to experiment; their object is to prepare students for the College Board advanced placement examination. They are not there to teach them how to think.

Too many schools, too many teachers, too many communities are fearful of the one thing that education is supposed to achieve: the capacity to think. Thinking students ask nasty questions. Thinkers get too big for their britches. They want to change things. If you challenge students too much they may turn around and challenge you. Ask them real questions and they start discussing things that the teacher or the community doesn't like to discuss: why Negroes are treated badly, why adults aren't a little more honest about sex and morals, why the local politicians are corrupt. In the Bible belt the idea that God created the universe in six days is not a discussable issue, and all the ideas and prejudices rooted in rural South fundamentalism and racial segregation remain almost as untouchable now as they have ever been. J. Evetts Haley, one of the leaders of the right-wing Texans for America, issued a manifesto a few years ago proclaiming that "the stressing of both sides of a controversy only confuses the young and encourages them to make snap judgments based on insufficient evidence. Until they are old enough to understand both sides of a question, they should be taught only the American side."

But the inadequacies are rooted not only in local or regional prejudices—in Catholic strictures against sex education in Chicago, in fundamentalist Protestant opposition to the teaching of evolution, or in Alabama redneck resistance to honest discussions of integration, civil rights and human dignity—but also in outgrown and irrelevant notions about the nature of education and the purposes of schools. Because it was—and is—a creature of the community, the public school was traditionally oriented to the small world at hand, drew its ideas and values from that world, and prepared children for life as the community lived it, not for success in, and mastery of a larger, rapidly changing world beyond its borders. Grandpa survived without the new math—just as he survived without many other things—but when his schools failed him, he always had the farm, the shop and the frontier to fill the gaps. But the school of hard knocks is closed and the dehydrated textbook wisdom of the past is inadequate to the problems of the future. The children of Appalachia can only be successful in the accustomed existence of relief, unemployment and despair because they are not being trained for anything else; the graduates of some of the smaller schools in the rural Midwest have trouble in Chicago because their major orientation is to the technology and morality of the farm rather than the city; and even the modern schools of suburbia sometimes find it difficult to present viable choices to students who are not qualified for admission to prestige colleges and the professions to which they lead. No educational system, no institution can still afford dependence on a single voice of wisdom, or reliance on a particular style of life and thought. Chicago's failure to bring its schools into closer relationship with the community—the reluctance to listen to local elements, Negro and white—is as damaging as the isolated nepotism of Perry County, Kentucky; and the single-minded acceptance of the college standard in some suburbs is, in its own way, almost as crippling as the obsession with agrarian fundamentalism in parts of the rural South and Midwest.

It is easy to train people for life as they already know it, easy to teach them to use today's machines, or to make them repeat the data of a narrowly defined body of information. But that is no longer the function of education—if, indeed, it ever was. The schools must train people to make choices, must equip them to live in a number of worlds, must prepare them to educate themselves. There are schools—as in Newton, in Jefferson County, and in some other places—where teachers and administrators have a sense not only of their own community but also of the opportunities and the demands that the larger world presents. They understand the possibilities and are trying to realize them. But in many communities the experience and intelligence of the larger world are still struggling to be heard, and the schools are still governed by the formulations of the past.

II

What are the possibilities?

They lie, first of all, in a recognition that the moral, political and social certainties of our rural days have passed, and that the contemporary world demands new techniques and new attitudes. This does not mean that children should no longer be taught not to steal or cheat, but it does mean that success in producing social order and controlling the effects of an impersonal technology depends on training far more sophisticated than the catechism according to *Poor Richard's Almanac*. To tell a child in the slums of New York or Chicago that honesty is the best policy is to preach something that, in his experience, is patent nonsense. He has been cheated and exploited all his life, and any person who tells him otherwise must be either a fool or a liar. The only genuine morality and honesty is to try to teach him acceptable means of social control, to demonstrate that an understanding of civil rights and legal procedure is likely to be more fruitful than reliance on violence. The frustration of rural southerners with "outside agitators" rests on convictions of moral rectitude; children are being murdered by men who are defending moral standards.

There was a time in America when there was little disagreement on what was right and wrong. Schools could operate according to the premises of a "nondenominational" morality, which meant Protestant morality. Children said nondenominational prayers, sang nondenominational hymns and recited nondenominational and nationalistic maxims. But in a pluralistic society those prayers and hymns, and those values, must be reduced to the lowest common denominator. Since the school is often the only place in which a community must express its *collective* sense of things, must try to articulate its beliefs and values, the teaching and preaching of values becomes pap. Where everyone holds—and often exercises—a veto power over topics of local controversy the school is usually the last place where the really important issues are discussed. The more passionately a belief is held, the more important it becomes, the less likely the chance that it will get a free hearing at school. At the same time the sentimental temptation to inculcate a set of moralistic and nationalistic constants persists, although they become more diluted and less relevant each year. The simple maxims of an agrarian society are meaningless and sometimes dangerous in a complex technological world. The universe demands challenge as much as obedience, toleration as much as rectitude.

The central fact of the modern world is change: every day science and scholarship add pieces to the collection of human knowledge. Few of them can be mentioned in a twelve-year period of public education, even if the schools were considerably more efficient than they now are. And yet the shibboleth of "coverage" persists. Coverage of what? Why coverage, sir, of whatever it is I've been teaching for the past twenty years. George Washington and the campaigns of the American Revolution; what a yellow dog contract is all about; why the albatross got hung around that sailor's neck; how you can remember the one by Beethoven by singing "It's the Fifth, It's the Fifth" when the right passage is played in the second movement.

The possibilities lie in the teaching of processes—in trying to get students to *do* physics or history, not talk about them, to achieve their own conclusions, not merely memorize those of others. Good teachers have always attempted to do this, even before the new courses came along, but they now have materials that have never been available before. If they are taught correctly the new courses in mathematics, physics, biology, and other fields *demand* independent investigation, the formulation of generalizations by well-defined inductive and deductive methods, the testing of hypotheses and the evaluation of conclusions. They are aimed toward generating a sense of what a discipline is, of what one can do with it, and what its limitations are. They lie in a self-consciousness about thought. Any discipline, after all, is a human construct, not something that lies *out there* as an objective kind of reality waiting to be discovered.

The rationale for such education lies in teaching students to learn for themselves, to assimilate and organize data, to evaluate opinions and impressions and propaganda. It rests not on teaching life adjustment, but on propagating techniques of control, of stimulating curiosity, and on developing effective means of making choices. It is devoted not so much to preparation for this or that vocation or a certain kind of college or the enjoyment of the good life in a California suburb, but to the development of attitudes and skills which are necessary for all of them. To a certain extent almost all secondary education is still organized around vocational assumptions, and students are forced to choose at the age of thirteen or fourteen, and sometimes earlier, whether they are going to follow a college track or a "general" track (leading, often, to no particular goal) or a vocational track. Thus, as adolescents they already have to close doors behind them, have already been selected in or selected out. It is a harsh choice to impose on people of their age. And it is probably unnecessary. The greatest danger is not that kids will lose time, but that they will lose their humanity.

Critics of American society have often noted the dichotomy between our respect for education and our streak of anti-intellectualism. Democratic attitudes, frontier independence and the practical concerns of everyday life made us impatient with authority, and especially with what we came to regard as the presumptions of an effete intellectuality. A simple education in school taught you all you had to know.

In recent years that dichotomy has begun to disappear. There is more respect for intellectual achievement because its fruits, especially in science and technology, are now becoming apparent to most Americans. Nevertheless, we still tend to identify intellectuality with *knowing a lot* and we are, therefore, trying to achieve it—have been trying to achieve it for years—through an education oriented toward the distribution of data. In a sense we have begun to accept the worst of what we traditionally rejected and to ignore the best of what we had. The man we have always respected is not the one crammed with a lot of information but the one who could solve problems, who was able to find out what he needed to know and use it for the improvement of himself and his society. One of the challenges for education is to adapt that healthy frontier attitude and its techniques to the demands of modern understanding, to teach people how to think, and how to use the intellectual tools that our culture has produced in such abundance.

The greatest drawback of American education—considering the tenets of the American faith—is in its failure to be the great social switching yard that people like Jefferson, Lester Frank Ward and John Dewey hoped it would become. The schools helped Americanize immigrants and trained generations of American boys and girls into the most competent industrial labor force on earth. But as they function now, they are unable to surmount the social and economic handicaps of a majority of their students. For the most part the academic tracks pass each other by and only a minority of students from poor backgrounds are able to change to the programs for the able, and to prepare for higher education and the more skilled professions. The chances that a white boy or girl will attend college, for example, are several times as great as those of a Negro, a situation most of us still consider somehow unalterable. The schools still operate on that assumption, partly because teachers and administrators are not exempt from common attitudes, partly because of the paralysis of the old conception of democratic education (which was blind to cultural differences) and partly because most academic specialization has been oriented to the students' future rather than their past. Except for special problems like mental retardation, teacher training and recruitment have been directed almost solely toward particular levels (e.g. elementary, kindergarten, secondary) and toward particular subjects. Only recently have some teachers' colleges and school systems begun to consider the task of training personnel for slum schools, for first-grade classes of children with cultural disadvantages and for all the special tasks that various kinds of deprivation and various backgrounds require. The object of these specialties is not to run a perpetual holding operation for deprived children, to maintain a twelve-year track for the unmotivated, the hostile and the unsuccessful, but to bring all children into the mainstream. The school, which has always been passionate about selecting children according to where they are going—or where the school would like them to go —is going to have to pay intelligent attention to where they *came from* and, before planning their lives for them, is going to have to bring them into a position of genuine academic and social equality. If school integration means anything, this is it.

III

What the community wants it generally gets. Good teaching and outstanding schools are, with rare exceptions, no accident; dull classrooms are maintained by apathy and local demand. The community makes its choices through the money it pays, the teachers and administrators it selects, and through the ideas and attitudes to which it responds and which it decides to encourage. And yet concern for education is—and must be—regional and national as well. Miseducation is a highly mobile commodity: children who are not educated have a habit of showing up as social burdens a thousand miles from where the damage was done. Poor education is permanent. This is what gives meaning to federal aid and, even more emphatically, to the broader consequences of civil rights. Only when the Negroes of Alabama— and of South Chicago—can make themselves heard at the meetings of the school board, when the mountaineers of Appalachia understand the difference between good education and bad, only when there is real concern with the minds of children—and not with all the paralyzing problems that surround the school—can genuine education take place in the classroom. All the demonstration projects, all the special programs in the world, will make little difference if the basic program is weak.

The *big* school system finally involves all of us. It is affected by social and economic forces, by political pressures, by the ethnic composition of cities and suburbs, by the patterns of population change—by *what we are* and what we do. Because some of the factors of this system are so overwhelming, the schools cannot ignore the problems of the surrounding community—the conditions of family life, housing and neighborhood planning—just as they can't afford to isolate themselves from outside ideas, techniques and suggestions, no matter what the source. They must become open, flexible agencies ready to teach children of three as well as adults of thirty, hospitable to all comers, ready to expand the school day, and the school year, ready to enlarge the scope of their social functions.

But even if the schools are prepared to become vast new social agencies, and even if they do this effectively, they will not provide panaceas for all social evils. Education may be able to prepare people for jobs, but it cannot create them; the schools may be able to overcome the effects of deprivation, but they cannot clear slums or develop successful public housing projects. The schools are part of a large social and political system, a circle of success or failure, and the only way they can be made ultimately successful is to break the circle not in one but in many places. Effective education depends not only on funds, but also on jobs, health, housing and on public concern, and while increased federal aid will help, it will not foster the local interest the schools require. Well-heeled apathy is not far above destitute disregard.

We can expect a great deal from education, but we must expect at least as much of ourselves.

Index